JONATHAN SWIFT AND THE VESTED WORD

Jonathan Swift

AND THE VESTED WORD

DEBORAH BAKER WYRICK

THE UNIVERSITY OF NORTH CAROLINA PRESS
CHAPEL HILL & LONDON

©1988 The University of North Carolina Press
All rights reserved

Library of Congress Cataloging-in-Publication Data
Wyrick, Deborah Baker.
  Jonathan Swift and the vested word / by Deborah Baker Wyrick.
    p. cm.
  Bibliography: p.
  Includes index.
  ISBN 978-0-8078-5716-8
  1. Swift, Jonathan, 1667–1745—Knowledge—Language and languages.
2. Language and languages in literature. I. Title.
PR3728.L33W96   1988   87-24632
828'.509—dc19   CIP

The paper in this book meets the guidelines
for permanence and durability of the Committee
on Production Guidelines for Book Longevity
of the Council on Library Resources.

Frontispiece from *A Tale of a Tub, with Other Early Works, 1696–1707*, by Jonathan Swift, edited by Herbert Davis (Oxford: Basil Blackwell, 1957).

to my mother and father

and to my grandparents

CONTENTS

Acknowledgments ix

Texts and Abbreviations xi

Preface xiii

Chapter 1. Investigations:
Swift and Theories of Language 1

    Tangible Substance 3
    The Idea of a Mouse-Trap 9
    According to Mine Intentions 15
    The Deepest Designs 20

Chapter 2. Investitures:
Swift and Verbal Authority 30

    Furnishing Out an Exact Dress 33
    Fixing Our Language for Ever 40
    Proper Words in Proper Places 46
    To Travel Thro' This Vast World of Writings 54

Chapter 3. Divestitures:
Swift and Wordplay 63

    The Anagrammatick Method 65
    Letters in Death's Alphabet 69
    The Girl at Bartholomew-Fair 74
    A Sort of Jabber 80
    Ourrichar Gangridge 85

Chapter 4. Vested Interests:
Swift and the Textual Self 93

   Th'Idea from an Empty Name 95
   Indulging Our Reflections 102
   J.S.D.S.P.D. Hospes Ignotus 108
   Heaps of Never-Dying Works 113
   The Cure Prescribed 119

Chapter 5. Transvestitures:
Swift and the Parallel Sign 128

   My Cloths Very Ill Made 132
   The Lexicon of Female Fopperies 141
   The Best Irish Wool 149
   I Wonder Where You Stole 'Em 158

Chapter 6. Investments:
Swift and the Tragedy of Language 167

   What Will It Import? 170
   I Boldly Pronounced Yahoo 176
   Wisdom Crieth in the Streets 184

Postscript 189

Notes 197

Select Bibliography 223

Index 237

ACKNOWLEDGMENTS

WITHOUT THE combination of encouragement and challenge offered by Wallace Jackson, this study could not have been written. His sensitive and penetrating responses to my work have been invaluable, and to him I owe a deep debt of gratitude. I have benefited immeasurably from Robert Gleckner's careful readings; his attention to style, logic, and critical direction represents a generous contribution of time and talent for which I am most grateful. I wish to thank Oliver Ferguson for sharing with me his broad knowledge of Swift and for demanding standards of historical and critical accuracy I may not have demanded for myself. At a later stage in my writing, Leigh DeNeef's advice, G. Douglas Atkins's helpful comments, and Carole Fabricant's intriguing questions about theory, practice, and argument were perceptive stimulants to revision. I appreciate this help very much.

The English Department of North Carolina State University has provided me with motivation and opportunity to undertake this project. For valuable discussions, assistance, and support of all kinds, I thank Larry Champion, John Bassett, Tony Harrison, Jack Durant, and Barbara Baines. The friendship and scholarship of all my colleagues have created an atmosphere in which work is truly a joy. My students, too, have contributed to this atmosphere; their doubts and discoveries as they tackle Swift's writings help keep Swift fresh and exciting. I am also grateful to Dean Edith Sylla and my university's Humanities and Social Sciences Research Committee for providing financial assistance toward publication of this book.

Working with the University of North Carolina Press has been a pleasure because of Sandra Eisdorfer's encouraging professionalism and Martha Rappaport's careful copyediting.

My special gratitude goes to my daughter Laura, who prefers Tennyson to Swift but who never lets shadows sicken sunlight; to Sam, who has valiantly tried to counter Swiftian impulse with Johnsonian spirit; to

Mom, Dad, Alison, Michael, and little Michael for their support and love; to Linda, a friend in need, in deed, indeed; to Eleanor, Al, Mary, Wally, Ginny, Frances, and Gladys; and to my inspiring great-aunts Laura, Ruth, Florence, and Ellen. Finally, I wish to thank Mr. Smith and Mr. Tanaka, whose profound and spirited dialogues reopened for me the mysteries and sweetness at the heart of language.

TEXTS AND ABBREVIATIONS

Full publication information can be found in the Select Bibliography.

Battel *The Battel of the Books* in *A Tale of a Tub*, edited by A. C. Guthkelch and D. Nichol Smith. References are to page.

Corr. *The Correspondence of Jonathan Swift*, edited by Harold Williams. References are to volume and page.

GT *Gulliver's Travels*. Vol. 9 of *The Prose Works of Jonathan Swift*, edited by Herbert Davis. References are to book, chapter, and page.

JS *Journal to Stella*, edited by Harold Williams. References are to volume and page.

MO *The Mechanical Operation of the Spirit* in *A Tale of a Tub*, edited by A. C. Guthkelch and D. Nichol Smith. References are to page.

PW *The Prose Works of Jonathan Swift*, edited by Herbert Davis. References are to volume and page.

SPW *Swift's Poetical Works*, edited by Herbert Davis. References are to page, and where applicable, line.

Tale *A Tale of a Tub*, edited by A. C. Guthkelch and D. Nichol Smith. References are to section (numbered or titled) and page.

PREFACE

SWIFT ENJOYED writing prefaces. Along with the dedications, apologies, booksellers' notices, and advertisements that frequently adorn his works, prefaces gave him the opportunity to parody self-promotional writing practices and to discuss the nature of the writing endeavor. He realized that although traditionally "the Principal Duty of a Preface" is to force "Imagination to make the *Tour* of [the author's] Invention" ("The Preface," *Tale*, 42), its actual function is to stake out textual territory. It does this by de-facing the works of others, sullying their claims upon the subject in order to eject them from the literary space one wishes to occupy. In response to the common practice of complaining about the proliferation of "*Scriblers*" and "*Would-be-wit[s]*," Swift inserted a comic parable in the middle of "The Preface" to *A Tale of a Tub*:

> *A Mountebank in* Leiscester-Fields, *had drawn a huge Assembly about him. Among the rest, a fat unweildy Fellow, half stifled in the Press, would be every fit crying out, Lord! what a filthy Crowd is here? Pray, good People, give way a little . . . At last, a* Weaver *that stood next to him could hold no longer: A Plague confound you* (said he) *for an over-grown Sloven; and who (in the Devil's Name) I wonder, helps to make up the Crowd half so much as yourself? . . . Is not the Place as free for us as for you? Bring your own Guts to a reasonable Compass (and be d—n'd) and then I'll engage we shall have room enough for us all.* ["The Preface," *Tale*, 46]

Like the "fat unweildy Fellow," contemporary criticism also makes space-clearing gestures; today, books and articles frequently begin by pointing out previous errors of interpretation and areas of neglect, offering themselves as remedies for these blots and gaps in literary scholarship. I choose instead to side with Swift's churlish Weaver: there is room enough for us all.

This capaciousness is particularly true in the case of Swift scholarship. Many splendid studies of Swift have appeared in the twentieth century, approaching his work from a variety of angles. I have learned a great deal from biographies and psychoanalytic discussions, from analyses of seventeenth- and eighteenth-century history and thought, from critiques of style and imagery, from source studies and genre studies, from thematic explorations and deconstructive readings. Although I hope to synthesize, add to, and expand upon it, I in no way wish or expect to supplant the work that has preceded and enabled my own. On the contrary, the crowded field of interpretation is, in a sense, my subject. Its noisy bustle is engendered by Swift's intense and unusual attention to problems of language and meaning, and its continued expansion in turn invigorates Swift's work. The space I claim, therefore, is within the already shared space of critical discourse, discourse defined by the structured text, which in turn is controlled by Swift's verbal strategies and by the demands and desires he invests in writing.

Although Swift examined, tested, and satirized contemporary beliefs about words and meanings, he did not have a cohesive theory of language (or of signification, or of interpretation) because he never tried to establish a position outside of language from which to scrutinize linguistic operations.[1] He did have fears about and goals for language, however, that shaped his narrative and argumentative tactics. Two maxims from his "Thoughts on Various Subjects" and four lines from an early ode illustrate his range of expectations and trepidations about the written word:

> When I am reading a Book, whether wise or silly, it seemeth to me to be alive and talking to me. [*PW* 4:253]

> A Copy of Verses kept in the Cabinet . . . is like a Virgin much sought after and admired; but when printed and published, is like a common Whore, whom any body may purchase for half a Crown. [*PW* 4:249]

> > Nature's fair Table-book our tender Souls
> > We scrawl all o'er with odd and empty Rules
> > . . . .
> > For Learning's mighty Treasures look
> > In that deep Grave a Book.
> > ["Ode to Sir William Temple,"
> > *SPW* 19.32–33, 35–36]

These passages evidence a sense of language as embodiment, as transcription of authorial presence into writing. This textual body can live and communicate through time in a way that the physical body cannot. Thus writing is privileged over speech by the simple fact that it covers inevitable absence with a graphic simulacrum of presence. Yet the covering, as Swift's second aphorism implies, also uncovers the vulnerability of writing: accessibility invites abuse. Swift's awareness of the potential for arbitrary assignments of meaning, for interpretations that assault and usurp original intentions and significations, motivates his multigeneric attempts to make his own language protect itself, even as it solicits the dangerous engagements necessary to sustain its life. Keeping one's words sealed from outside interference entombs them, but publication in "that deep Grave a Book" sentences them to a different sort of death. The tender soul decomposes, leaving skeletal scrawls; Lockean epistemology translates into writing, the only legible trace of existence.

Swift's avoidance of theoretical rigidity and his attention to investing himself in language have shaped my own critical pluralism and my focus on his awareness of the risks and rewards of writing. This study is, I hope, informed by modern Continental and American literary theory without being bound to any single school of criticism. I have found such works to be stimulating in their own right and tantalizingly applicable to Swiftian texts. Their applicability stems, I believe, from Swift's interest in and exploration of what are now thought of as phenomenological, structuralist, poststructuralist, and new-historicist concerns: how a life in language comes into being, how semiotic systems determine meaning, how texts open up their own systems to other texts and to multiple interpretations, how written words enter into dialogues with time and culture. Swift's skeptical fascination with textual power is evident in his earliest writings as well as his late ones, in nonfiction as well as in fiction, in poetry as well as in prose. Although throughout his career he continued to ask the same questions of language and invest his work with the same urgencies, the textual answers to these questions and the returns on his verbal investments changed as his life changed. The problematic nature of language and writing remained a constant, but its use and effects took on new, even tragic, implications.

Swift's continuously ambivalent wish to be known through his writing yet not be violated by reading, his disguisings and dressings and undrapings of himself through language, have made my study also deal with questions of intentionality and authorial function. I thus do not pursue the end recommended by Roland Barthes, for instance, to "amputate" the individual subject, the originating intent, from literature.[2] Neither do I accept the ideal of critics like E. D. Hirsch who, by locating the authorizing will outside of and prior to language, situate meaning in the somehow objectively recoverable subjective act.[3] My conception of Swift's textual investments to an extent resembles J. Hillis Miller's view of the self as a linguistic construction, as perhaps a trope of selfhood.[4] But Swift would insist on the self as a concrete point of departure, not only as a rarefied effect of rhetoricity. He was also too aware of the hazards facing written words, and further, of the insufficiencies and fallibilities of language itself to trust a text in which the lines of filiation had been completely severed.

"I'll come again tonight in a fine clean sheet of paper," Swift wrote to Esther Johnson after breaking off a letter he had begun in the morning (letter 12, Dec. 1710–Jan. 1710/11, *JS* 1:154). The need to wrap oneself and one's thoughts in writing betrays its own impossibility. An inked sheet of paper is no longer clean, no longer immaculate: writing is defilement. Further, the graphic act engenders additional danger. As the inscribed page is sent to friends or to printers, it begins a journey of estrangement, subject to use and abuse. Swift confronted these issues, and the larger linguistic problems of which they are a part, by means of an enabling metaphor that allowed him to spin elaborate strategies that would protectively clothe and seductively disclose verbal significance as well as authorial desire. This is the trope of the vested word, the textile text that unfolds and enfolds from *A Tale of a Tub* to the late Irish political tracts. It is no accident, then, that the crabby defender of writing in Swift's preface is a weaver. For weavers—and drapiers, and tailors, and spiders—are all writers; and the text as product and process is encompassed by the concept of clothing.

Readers have long noticed the prominence of clothes in Swift's works. Kathleen Williams remarks that the "signification was an old one among Christian moralists, who inferred from Genesis that the urge to clothe ourselves is an urge to cover our nakedness both of body and mind, and a direct consequence of the Fall."[5] Martin Price gives clothes a less pejorative interpretation: "Clothes in general show man's acceptance in the natural order, neither beast nor angel, and man's particular dress signifies his rational acceptance of his proper place in a social order."[6] These two representative views suggest that Swift's vestmental metaphor functions as a rather simple badge of identity, signaling man's natural, cultural, or religious status. Swift often used clothes in this manner, and certainly Biblical fig leaves serve as undergarments for the testamental coats, noisome frocks, and Yahoo-skin suits that adorn his works. Genesis, however, provides a complementary sign of man's peccability: Babel, the confusion of communication, the radical imperfection of human language. Swift's metaphor sews these signs together into a complex semiotics at once didactic and self-reflexive. Clothes are not fallen nakedness, and writing is not fallen speech. They are uniquely human correctives for uniquely human errors, flawed and fragile fabrications that celebrate as well as condemn.

I take, then, my own organizing metaphor from Swift. In trying to justify my title and structuring figure, I am again following the example of *A Tale of a Tub*; its preface starts with a story explaining the diversionary merits of tubs in whaling and in writing. If I were to mirror Swift's precedent more closely, I would now submit a list of matters that should have been treated, that have been treated in texts that have mysteriously disappeared, or that will be treated in the future. And if I were to do that, I would admit that this study does not adequately attend to Swift's marvelous and enduring humor, his beautifully honed verbal comedy that is, after all, the reason most of us read his works in the first place. Instead, I will heed Swift's ironic reminder that voguish prefaces tend "to be *large* in proportion as the subsequent Volume is *small*" ("The Preface," *Tale*, 54) and, in hopes that the following discussion is of reasonable compass, begin it at once.

JONATHAN SWIFT AND
THE VESTED WORD

1 / INVESTIGATIONS
Swift and Theories of Language

SAMUEL JOHNSON, after applying to Swift the stylistic criteria of simplicity and purity that Swift himself had recommended as standards of good writing (*Proposal for Correcting . . . the English Tongue, PW* 4:15; *The Tatler* #230, *PW* 2:117), makes the following judgment: "This easy and safe conveyance of meaning it was Swift's desire to attain, and for having attained it he deserves praise, though perhaps not the highest praise."[1] Johnson was able to ignore Swift's complex treatments of verbal meanings by dismissing *A Tale of a Tub* as an anomaly and by sweeping Swift's lifelong verbal playfulness under the general heading of peculiarity. Today, few readers would be brave enough to attach the terms "easy" and "safe" to any author's conveyance of meaning. But in connection with Swift, the terms are particularly inaccurate. His works show intense, informed, and skeptical confrontations with problems of verbal significance. Swift investigates not easy words and safe methods but difficulties of meaning and risks of writing.

One passage from *A Tale of a Tub*—a book that is not an extracanonical anomaly but a concentrated precursor of themes and techniques in Swift's later works—exemplifies the vulnerability, plasticity, and ultimate opacity of meaning. Near the end of "A Digression Concerning Madness," the Tale-writer describes "a *Taylor* run mad with pride" in a manner that totally disfigures the meaning of the image:

> This considerable Student is adorned with many other Qualities, upon which, at present, I shall not farther enlarge. - - - - - - - - - - - - - - - - - * *Heark in your Ear* - I am strangely mistaken, if all his Address, his Motions, and his Airs, would not then be very Natural, and in their proper Element. [*Tale* 9.179]

The Tale-writer's contradictory concealments keep his words from being "considerable" and suppress them into considerations hidden from the reader. He refuses to discuss the tailor's adornments, but he follows this denial with an ellipsis that denies the denial. The silence is broken by a summons to the reader, part intimate whisper and part underscored annunciation; the promise of fulfillment is betrayed by more dashes, and the author denies this denial by implying that the words supplanted by ellipses make the mysterious meaning of the tailor's attributes natural and proper. From this snarl of renounced and concealed meanings the text retreats to a footnote, traditionally an authoritative anchor for floating significances. But rather than mending the textual ruptures, the new and unnamed interpreter supplements the unraveling process of de-authorization; he affirms the existence of meaning while denying the possibility of ascertaining it: "*I cannot conjecture what the Author means here, or how this Chasm could be filled, tho' it is capable of more than one Interpretation*" (*Tale* 9:179). This fragmented dialogue of denials leaves the problem of meaning open, and the reader is stranded in the silent spaces in the text. In its visual reification of the chasm of verbal significance, the passage emblematizes Swift's attention to and ambivalence about the relationship between words and meaning, between author and text, between text and interpreter. Swift's writing demonstrates a continuing engagement with these relationships, an engagement that can be followed by analyzing his investigations of various theories of language.

Swift's investigations are not themselves theoretical. They are, instead, enacted through his prose fictions, poems, pamphlets, and personal writings. Neither are they programmatic. Swift appears to try on and cast off different concepts of language throughout his work, responding to the exigencies of his texts and of historical contexts rather than constructing his text as a test of any particular linguistic idea. Nevertheless, it may be helpful to have a framework to guide inquiry into Swift's fluid examinations of language. To this end, I have used William P. Alston's classification of language theories[2] and have added a final one to cover some conjectures about language omitted in Alston's schema, conjectures raised by Swift's work and echoed by the problematics of contemporary criticism, conjectures that exert a constant pressure on Swift's writing.

In the referential theory, words mean the things to which they refer, and their purpose is to name and therefore to make ordered sense out of the real world. In the ideational theory, words mean the idea in the author's mind that they try to convey, and their purpose is clear communication of these ideas. In the behavioral theory, words mean the desire of the author and the response of the audience, and their purpose is to precipitate action in a particular language situation. In the textocentric theory, words mean whatever the text allows them to mean, and their purpose is to control significatory and interpretive potential by either holding it open or forcing it to a close. Swift, I believe, alternately and sometimes simultaneously embraces and rejects the first three views of language because of the ambivalent claims of the fourth. He does not arrive at a synthesis, and his contradictions, retreats, and denials create a kind of negative dynamic that flows from and returns to the text itself. Each negation generates a new investigation or a reinvestigation from another linguistic or textual angle, investigations that keep centering upon the phenomenon of the word, the topography of meaning, the risks of writing, and the threats of interpretation.

Although the four categories enumerated above are to some extent a universalist model of language possibilities, they derive particular force from theoretical debates and historical problems of Swift's own time. In eighteenth-century England, loss of faith in verbal absolutism grew from seventeenth-century revolutions: political, religious, and epistemological. These historical forces shaped Swift's conservative and institutional attitudes about language, yet their very existence covertly sanctioned his liberal and idiosyncratic uses of language, particularly in works written while he lived in England and was situated within the perimeter of governmental power. After Swift returned to Ireland and became involved with more reactionary politics, his attitudes about language were shaped less by the past than by the revolutionary potential of the present and the future. These matters, and the personal investments they entailed, will be the subject of the second half of this book. The first half will attempt to demonstrate the uneasy textual bargains Swift makes and breaks throughout his career as he negotiates between desire for linguistic authority and desire for verbal freedom, desires that emanate from Swift's beliefs and fears about textocentric power.

TANGIBLE SUBSTANCE

Swift disputed the referential view of language, that ultimately there exists a one-to-one correspondence between a word and a thing named. In part, the *res et verba* controversy, as A. C. Howell has shown,[3] grew from a misreading of Cicero's distinction between words designating things and words used metaphorically. Perhaps following the stricter admonition of Quintilian and certainly reacting against euphuism and baroque literary ornament, many seventeenth-century writers on style condemned those who studied words and not matter.[4] Thomas Hobbes, for instance, not only decried metaphorical writing and philosophical jargon, but he also based his theory of words and reasoning on proper naming of things: speech consists "of names or appellations, and their connexion . . . truth consisteth in the right ordering of names in our affirmations."[5]

The referential theory was most notably articulated by Thomas Sprat in his introduction to the *History of the Royal Society*: language should "return back to primitive purity, and shortness, when men deliver'd so many things, almost in an equal number of words."[6] Swift parodies such object-ive language, as well as its host society, in book 3 of *Gulliver's Travels*:

> The other [project] was a Scheme for entirely abolishing all Words whatsoever; And this was urged as a great Advantage in Point of Health as well as Brevity. . . since Words are only Names for *Things*, it would be more convenient for all Men to carry about them, such *Things* as were necessary to express the particular Business they are to discourse on . . . many of the most Learned and Wise adhere to the new Scheme of expressing themselves by *Things*. [*GT* 3.5.185]

Along with the marvelous literalization that transforms Sprat and likeminded society members into Lagadan academicians weighted down with sacks of reified word substitutes and the specific satire of universal language schemes[7] is a darker linguistic parody. The "new scheme" in Lagado makes its adherents captives of their own words, bearing the burden of discourse (all complaints of spirit dismissed because the a-verbal method is good exercise for the body). This scheme leaves no room for imaginative or rational operations of the mind since words are strictly limited to communication about preordained "particular business."[8] Not only words would be abolished, but human communication—the ability to act and react verbally—as well. No problems of meaning or interpretation would exist because meaning would be reduced to pointing, to tautological signification. "Words name things" has become "things name things."

Another way Swift mocks the referential theory of language is by changing the functions of the equation: "words name things" shifts to "words are things." The Tale-writer maintains that "Words . . . are also Bodies of much Weight and Gravity, as it is manifest from those deep

Impressions they make"; therefore, they should be dropped by orators from above into the open mouths of the audience, so that "every one carries home *a Share*" (*Tale* 1.60–61). By literalizing the Lockean concept of sensible "Impressions" and by implying that the word-thing is infinitely divisible and therefore without tangible integrity, Swift smuggles alternate theories of language into the *Tale*'s humorous referential manifesto. Similarly, books should be judged by their physical properties (as when rival literary fraternities challenge the Grub Street Brotherhood "to a Comparison of Books, both as to *Weight* and *Number*" [*Tale* 1.64]) or by their crop-value according to seasonal growing conditions ("The Conclusion," *Tale*, 206–7). Such satiric tactics may reflect the tendency of seventeenth-century linguists to treat words as physical entities. Grammarians and etymologists agreed that a word's referential meaning is constructed from its material parts, from its letters and sounds.[9]

The word as (potentially edible) thing receives more complex treatment in section 6 of *A Tale of A Tub*. The Tale-writer, certain that readers will subscribe to a companion work because they have "already had such a taste" of his talents, states:

> *Zeal* . . . is, perhaps, the most significant Word that hath been ever yet produced in any Language; As, I think, I have fully proved in my excellent *Analytical* Discourse upon that Subject; wherein I have deduced a *Histori-theo-physilogical* Account of *Zeal*, shewing how it first proceeded from a *Notion* into a *Word*, and from thence in a hot Summer, ripned into a *tangible Substance*. [*Tale* 6.137]

This passage attacks philosophies of language and meaning in two ways. First, it parodies the referential theory by mimicking its underlying pattern of Biblical generation: God's intention → the word → the material world. "Ripned" suggests fruit, and perhaps Swift hints at the tempting word-apple, particularly attractive to the Enthusiasts whose zeal allows them to invest God's notions and words with their own self-authorized meanings, or to any putative exegetes who wish to imitate Ezekiel or St. John the Divine by eating the word to gain verbal inspiration (Ezek. 3:1–3; Rev. 10:9–11). But the word ripens in the hot summer, a circumstance implying both fruition and putrification, a spontaneous generation from corruption, like maggots gestating in moldy cheese (see *Tale* 1.66). The process of producing an exotic and unsavory outgrowth oddly mutated from its origins demonstrates the nature of the thing itself. Second, the passage inverts and perverts Locke's ideational theory of language; in the Swiftian reduction, the final product of language is not communication of an idea but reconstitution of a material thing, the sensory evidence of which, according to Locke, would give rise to the "Notion" in the first place. The tangible "sub-stance" is, literally, Lockean "under-standing." Again, meaning—even in the case of this "most significant Word"—is revealed to be either arbitrary (the self-generated interpretations of the Enthusiasts) or tautological (it means its physical self). Its demonstrated significance lies only in its ability to produce more words: a three-volume text heralded by a ten-syllable adjective. "*Histori-theo-physilogical,*" of course, parodically imitates "learned" compounds, but its italics, sheer length, and almost unlimited range of meanings and authorizations make it more a tangible textual object than a comprehensible verbal unit. It is a universal word that in its infinity of meanings means nothing.

Throughout the *Tale*, Swift uses verbal materiality to puncture inflated claims for verbal significance. Thus the Tale-writer in his role as secretary to the Universe relays an arcane recipe for concocting "an universal System in a small portable Volume, of all Things that are to be Known, or Believed, or Imagined, or Practised in Life" (*Tale* 5.125). The nostrum treats books like lead, forcing them through elaborate alchemical rites until their essences are distilled in an author's head into the universal literary gold of "*an infinite Number of Abstracts, Summaries, Compendiums . . . and the like, all disposed into great Order, and reducible upon Paper*" (*Tale* 5.127). The parody of occultism also reverts in a roundabout way to another aspect of the referential theory of language.

In Christian tradition, the idea of the creative Logos lies behind belief in interpenetration of words and things, what Michel Foucault has called "the peculiar existence and ancient solidity of language as a thing inscribed in the fabric of the world."[10] The Book of Nature trope was pre-Enlightenment Europe's most common metaphor of the referential theory of language; reading the legenda stamped on the world's face would uncover God's original text. Sciences from alchemy to zoology were concerned with proper naming: knowing the name meant controlling the thing. The same belief underpinned much religious esoterism and pseudoreligious occultism. Swift's dislike of "dark authors" is well known,[11] as indicated by his swipes at Thomas Vaughan, Henry Moore, Jakob Böhme, Paracelsus, and other assorted mystics in the *Tale*, as well as by his annihilation of the contemporary astrologer Partridge in *The Bickerstaff Papers* and the Merlinic prophecy poems. Beneath Swift's criticism of turgid style or irrational credulity lies a distrust of "magical" treatment of language: that the secret word is an instrument of force over the physical universe, which is just an array of materializations of hidden language. Meaning is displaced into things, and the meaning of meaning is reduced to the wielding of power.

The referential theory of language thus incorporates theories of meaning. The scientific writing and speech espoused by the Royal Society bound meaning to the things of the world, words pointing unambiguously to physical facts capable of empirical verification. This "seventeenth-century linguistic atomism"[12] predicts the logical atomism of philosophers like Bertrand Russell, who believes that "words all have meaning, in the simple sense that they are symbols that stand for some*thing* other than themselves."[13] The older, theologico-mystical branch of the referential theory implies that meaning is encoded in things. Deciphering the secret signatures in the world confers knowledge and power. The branches intersect in the works of a man like John Wilkins, an influential seventeenth-century linguistic theoretician and member of the Royal Society; he translated the arcane referentialism motivating schemes to recreate the universal language of Adam into a "scientific" proposal for a new, universal character to substitute for the lost original tongue. To Wilkins, meaning remains a function of naming, and the right word leads to the truth of things: "[W]e should, by learning the Character and the Names of Things, be instructed likewise in their Natures."[14]

Swift's various attacks on the concept of words as merely names of things demonstrate his disagreement with the ideas about meaning as well as the descriptions of language functions contained in the referential theory. For instance, in *An Argument Against Abolishing Christianity*, he responds to the hypothesis that removing Christianity from England would remove political factionalism:

> But, will any Man say, that if the Words *Whoring, Drinking, Cheating, Lying, Stealing*, were, by Act of Parliament, ejected out of the English Tongue and Dictionaries; we should all awake next Morning chaste and temperate, honest and just, and Lovers of Truth . . . Or if the Physicians would forbid us to pronounce the Words *Pox, Gout, Rheumatism*, and *Stone*; would that Expedient serve like so many Talismans to destroy the Diseases themselves? Are *Party* and *Faction* rooted in Mens Hearts no deeper than Phrases borrowed from

Religion . . . Are *Envy, Pride, Avarice* and *Ambition*, such ill Nomenclators, that they cannot furnish Appellations for their Owners? [*PW* 2:32]

Naming is extrinsic, not instrinsic, to things. Envy by any other name would stab as sharply. Nonetheless, this satirical treatise and its presumably straight-faced companion, *A Project for the Advancement of Religion, and the Reformation of Manners*, rest on the belief that even merely nominal Christianity is preferable to no Christianity at all. In the absence of the spirit, the letter can have some regulatory value. Similarly, Swift's calls for standardization of vocabulary and verbal form in *A Proposal for Correcting . . . the English Tongue* and *The Tatler* #230 build upon a concept of words as certain influential types of things. They are not signs or marks of tangible substances, but substantial entities that can generate their own sequences of effects, linguistically and phenomenally.

Swift, then, does not adhere to the standard forms of the referential theory of language. Throughout his works, his inventive experiments upon verbal forms and significances show that the issue of meaning was not to him a simple matter, capable of resolution by series of one-to-one, word-to-thing correspondences. It is easy, however, to confuse his clear and sturdy style—its dependence upon nouns and verbs rather than adjectives and adverbs, its tendency to define abstractions with concrete exempla, its avoidance of elaborate rhetorical figures, and its habitual literalization of metaphor[15]—with the sort of linguistic scientificism recommended by the Royal Society, a fact-oriented approach to writing that locates meaning outside of language.[16] Yet these very techniques tend also to reclaim significatory origins, as extratextual referents are displaced by inter- and intratextual necessities. Literalization, for instance, draws attention to the word itself; the textual negation of multiple meanings affirms their existence by showing that layers of metaphor cannot be safely peeled apart. Figurative truth is neither reducible to a sensory thing nor the sum of facts about things.

Many critics have termed Swift's treatment of figures "incarnational": literalization is the word-made-flesh, the clothing absorbed by the body.[17] The religious trope of the incarnate word stands behind the referential theory of language because it proposes a fundamental unity of, even an interchangeability between, word and world. If primal unity is recoverable in the religious or scientific word, meaning can be atemporal. Although Swift's religious writings evidence no quarrel with Christian incarnational doctrine, they do suggest antipathy to an incarnational theory of language. Swift does not wish to understand God's mysteries. His explanations of the "dark or mystical" meanings of the first chapter of St. John ("In the Beginning was the Word . . .") and of the gift of tongues are merely confessions of ignorance and humility before Divine inscrutability; concerning the Trinity, he states that "what that Union, or what that Distinction is, all Mankind are equally ignorant, and must continue so . . . it is folly not only to doubt Mysteries but also to endeavor to explain a Mystery which God intended to keep secret from us" ("Sermon on The Trinity," *PW* 9:161, 167–68). Swift's skepticism about the history of holy texts and church teaching shows not a trust in transcendent logocentrism but a "deteriorationalist" view of language as a concomitant of man's ongoing fall, subject to chance and decay. As he writes in "A Sermon upon the Excellency of Christianity" when discussing the corruptions and controversies marking the progress of Christianity, "if this be the present language and practise among us Christians, no wonder that Christianity doth not still produce the same effects as it did at first, when it was received and embraced in its utmost purity and perfection" (*PW* 9:250). Time corrupts language, and verbal meaning cannot be saved through attachment to the things of the world or reincorporation with the originating word. Swift's incarnated words—his literalized metaphors, his puns, his neologisms, even his attention to the significatory potential of typography[18]—seem to operate in a different way. They do not redeem the verbal through the physical but deem the verbal as physical, by making the word into a separate order of thing. This variety of verbal incarnation, though, provides no stable solution to the problem of significance. Instead, it invites new attacks upon the text, ones that will be explored at the end of this chapter and, indeed, throughout this study.

Referential incarnationalism situates meaning in the outside world; Swiftian incarnationalism places meaning on the written page. Between these two points, however, is the author, and it is the author's relationship with verbal meaning that Swift explores in his investigations of the ideational and behavioral theories of language.

THE IDEA OF A MOUSE-TRAP

The flaws Swift uncovered in the standard forms of the referential theory seem to be offered plausible redress in the ideational theory of language.

John Locke, the first major British exponent of this philosophy, sets forth his theory in book 3 of *An Essay Concerning Human Understanding*. He explains that man's thoughts are "invisible and hidden from others, nor can of themselves be made to appear"; since "communication" is necessary to "the comfort and advantage of society," articulate sounds are used as "external sensible signs" of a man's internal ideas. Words come to be employed by men as signs of their ideas "not by any natural connexion that there is between particular articulate sounds and certain ideas ... but by a voluntary imposition, whereby such a word is made arbitrarily the mark of such an idea. The use, then, of words, is to be sensible marks of ideas; and the ideas they stand for are their proper and immediate signification."[19] Words do not signify things but ideas; the purpose of language is clear communication of one person's ideas to another; linguistic structure imitates not the taxonomy of the natural world but the epistemological process of the human mind.

In a general way, Swift probably agreed with Locke. As he lambastes corrupted and affected style in *The Tatler* #230, he mentions that "Words are the Cloathing of our Thoughts" (*PW* 2:176). The section from *An Argument Against Abolishing Christianity* quoted above expressly denies a necessary "natural connexion ... between particular articulate sounds and certain ideas." Many modern scholars, in fact, believe that some of Swift's work deliberately ratifies Lockean theory. Frederik N. Smith, for example, claims that *A Tale of a Tub* is Swift's personal philosophy of language, based largely on Locke.[20] Rosalie Colie would ally Swift linguistically with Locke against Stillingfleet,[21] and Frederick Keener believes that *Gulliver's Travels* is a fictionalization of Locke's *An Essay Concerning Human Understanding*, Gulliver exemplifying the epistemological progress of mind from *tabula rasa* to *tabula plena*.[22] Yet other critics detect anti-Lockean elements in Swift's writings. Although Denis Donoghue thinks Swift's mind was "notably in tune" with Locke's, he opposes Locke's view of language to what he perceives to be Swift's resolutely referential, thing-oriented one.[23] W. B. Carnochan reads *Gulliver's Travels* as a satire of Locke's *Essay*, designed in part to prove the dangerous frailty inherent in depending upon nominal essences, rather than upon underlying absolutes, for knowledge.[24] R. J. Dircks goes farther, suggesting that book 4 is expressly anti-Lockean, the dispassionate Houyhnhnms being Lockean reasonable creatures in extremis.[25]

My discussion of Swift and the referential theory disclosed both agreements and disagreements with, or at least parodies of, Locke. Swift seems to accept the notion that words communicate ideas and that they should do so clearly and rationally; he also, however, takes issue with Locke's explanation of the nature of ideas, with his presuppositions about the adequacy of words to carry rational discourse, and with the assumption that rational discourse is obtainable and always desirable. Overall, Swift's work manifests a deep-seated ambivalence towards Locke's theory of language.

Locke begins his *Essay* with a chapter arguing against the existence of innate ideas and principles. He maintains that all ideas are manufactured by sensory experience and mental operations, like reason, reflection, or willful absurdity; this argument rests on the demonstration that the idea of God is not innate. Swift specifically opposes these "dangerous Tenets" in his "Remarks upon Tindall's *Rights of the Christian Church*," although he concedes that otherwise the *Essay* is useful (*PW* 2:97). But innate ideas can be quite a sticking point. Locke probably dismantled innate ideas because of their centrality in the Adamic theories of naming he was trying to supersede by his own work on words.[26] But Swift's training and profession treat innate ideas as matters of faith, not as abstract and limited components in linguistic theory. There is no evidence that Swift did not adhere to the concept that man's mind contains at least an innate disposition to believe in God's existence, to be governed by morality (even if it be operable only in terms of self-interest), and to attempt, through reason, to reach truth.[27] Swift's concepts about innate ideas are transcribed most accurately in his sermons, pieces delivered in public without parodic intent or protective personae.

In the sermons, Swift often refers to innate ideas as the universal dictates of Nature: "Nature directs every one of us, and God permits us, to consult our own private Good" ("Doing Good: A Sermon," *PW* 9:232); "Every one indeed is naturally inclined to have an ill Opinion of an Informer" ("On False Witness," *PW* 9:180). Nature seems to dwell within man as Conscience, an innate faculty that overrides and arbitrates our ideas. "The Word *Conscience* properly signifies," Swift explains in another sermon, "that Knowledge which a Man hath within himself of his own Thoughts and Actions ... And therefore God hath placed Conscience in us to be our Director only in those Actions which Scripture and Reason plainly tell us to be good or evil" ("On the Testimony of Conscience," *PW* 9:150). But since conscience works "only" in "plainly" judgeable situations, God has provided man with another absolute—revealed Christian wisdom brought down from above through the gospel.

Swift contrasts faith in Divine revelation with philosophical disputes; his recapitulation of St. Paul's advice to Timothy in his "A Sermon upon the Excellency of Christianity" applies not only to Platonists and Epicureans but also to Deists and Free-Thinkers: "[T]he janglings of those vain philosophers, which they would pass upon the world for science ... did encrease ungodliness, vain babblings being otherways expounded vanities, or empty sounds; that is, tedious disputes about words, which the philosophers were always so full of" (*PW* 9:242). Without innate principles like Nature, conscience, or the revealed word as checks and guides, philosophic discourse becomes meaningless, its empty words conveying only the pride of those who mistake a hoard of hollow rinds for a storehouse of the fruits of knowledge.

Thus Swift's most sustained criticism of Locke, occurring in the unfinished "Remarks upon Tindall's *Rights of the Christian Church*," focuses on vacuous philosophic style, on words as empty abstractions unregulated by innate ideas or by concrete referents. Locke in the form of his surrogate, Tindall, is being damned by his own words; the philosopher's dislike of metaphoric, imaginative writing[28] results not in a vigorous plain style but in a flaccid mass of generalizations that betrays the solipsistic mentalism of the theory. Commenting upon Tindall's statement that "[i]t will be necessary to show what is contained in the Idea of Government," Swift writes:

> Now, it is to be understood, that this refined Way of Speaking was introduced by Mr. Locke: After whom the Author limpeth as fast as he was able. All the former Philosophers in the World, from the Age of Socrates to ours, would have ignorantly put the Question, *Quid est Imperium?* But now it seemeth we must vary our Phrase; and since our modern Improvement of Human Understanding, instead of desiring a Philosopher to describe or define a Mouse-trap, or tell me what it is; I must gravely ask, what is contained in the Idea of a Mouse-trap? But then to observe how deeply this new way of putting Questions to a Man's Self, maketh him enter into the Nature of Things, his present Business is to shew us, what is contained in the Idea of Government. [*PW* 2:80]

Swift then quotes Tindall's abstract and repetitious definition and translates "this refined Jargon into the Old Style" of concrete and vivid prose; he next explains how governmental sanctions must transcend natural consequences by comparing them to hanging a horse thief and, eventually, to using a mouse-trap (*PW* 2:81). As Swift maneuvers the facetious mouse-trap question into an informative analogy, he demonstrates how the things of everyday experience not only generate but also interpret and verify ideas. If questions are put "to a Man's Self," idea addressing idea, a man remains isolated from "the Nature of Things." He also remains trapped in his own mind, unable to communicate his thoughts to others. Immediately after offering a specimen of Tindall's writing, Swift declares: "And, indeed, what a Light breaketh out upon us all, as soon as we have read these Words! How thoroughly are we instructed in the whole Nature of Government? What mighty Truths are here discovered; and how clearly conveyed to our Understandings?" (*PW* 2:80). This ironic encomium to the current philosophical style implies that its failed words do not muffle meaning as much as expose its absence.

Swift did not consider style to be detachable from content, or from self-revelation. His marginal comments in books such as Gilbert Burnet's *History of his own Times* show awareness of repetition, ambiguous pronouns, cant phrases, clichés, and other infelicities as well as disagreement with Burnet's reasoning and judgment (*PW* 5:266–94). Swift also believes that Burnet's inelegant words accurately transcribe his corrupted thoughts and that they reflect personal history: "All these phrases used by the vulgar, shew him to have kept mean or illiterate company in his youth" (*PW* 5:184, see also *PW* 4:182; in contrast, Swift thinks that Sir William Temple's graceful and incisive style mirrors his good breeding). When examining whether Tindall wrote *The Rights of the Christian Church* himself, Swift remarks that if the book were a group project, it shows "that Free-Thinking is a most confined and limited talent . . . the whole Discourse seemeth to be a motley, inconsistent Composition . . . a Bundle of incoherent Maxims and Assertions, that frequently destroy one another" (*PW* 2:68). Having fixed authorship upon one man, Swift maintains that Tindall's circle of thought is kept narrow by his "Talent of rattling out Phrases, which seem to have Sense, but have none at all: The usual Fate of those who are ignorant of the Force and Compass of Words, without which it is impossible for a Man to write either pertinently or intelligibly" (*PW* 2:78). Tindall's attempts to disguise his naturally "harsh," "ungrateful" [*sic?*], "mean," and "trivial" style indicate a particularly "gross Defect in Propriety or Meaning" (*PW* 2:78). The inherently flawed thought is conveyed naturally in corrupted style; verbal cosmetics, like the paint and plumpers used by Swift's decaying nymphs, only render substantial ugliness more bizarre.

Force and compass—effectiveness and breadth of meaning: these are qualities of good writing that Swift believes Lockeans ignore. Ricardo Quintana has made an obvious but often overlooked point, that Locke's hostility to imaginative writing would necessarily provoke Swift's ire.[29] Lockean linguistics defines effectiveness as clear communication; the locus of meaning rests in the idea behind the word. This realm of pure thought is threatened by the necessary evils of words, so words should be as denotatively fixed and circumscribed as possible. To Locke, the most complex task a word can perform is to "knot" ideas together;[30] the word-knot is both extrinsic and functional. In contrast, Swift's ornamental shoulder knots (*Tale* 2.84) extrude upon the word, yet the word can be unknotted to reveal the K-N-O-T, or the C-N-O-T as the case may be, in a parodic inversion of the Lockean arbitrary naming process. Even as Swift in the *Tale* lampoons extracting random, multiple, unauthorized meanings from a word, he exploits the possibility of doing so, displaying the un-Lockean joy of the artificer in knotting and unknotting the strands of language.

Neither would Swift be satisfied with Locke's situating of meaning and narrow view of verbal effectiveness. Swift—like Isaac Bickerstaff, like the Drapier, like Gulliver in Houyhnhnmland—wished his writing to be affective. Transcribing one's ideas as clearly as possible is not always the most effective manner in which to convey authorial intention or to elicit audience response, and the meaning of words seems to adhere not merely to preverbal ideas but also to the dynamics of verbal circuitry, dynamics that can involve connotative and metaphoric potential as well as ironic and parodic strategies. Furthermore, Lockean words can fail as messengers of emotion. The Houyhnhnms, for instance, are perfect Lockean linguists: Gulliver's master believes "[t]hat the Use of Speech was to make us understand one another, and to receive Information of Facts; now if any one *said the Thing which was not*, these Ends were defeated" (*GT* 4.4.240). Gulliver also sounds like a frustrated Lockean as he takes "Pains of many Circumlocutions to give my Master a right Idea of what I spoke; for their Language doth not abound in Variety of Words, because their Wants and Passions are fewer than among us" (*GT* 4.4.242).

Here Swift, I believe, reveals what he considers the fallacy of Lockean ideationalist theory. It works only when, first, the idea in the speaker or writer's head is matched by a similar idea in the hearer or reader's head and, second, when these ideas are not interfered with by emotions. As the Houyhnhnm master explains, "*Reason* . . . strikes you with immediate conviction ... where it is not mingled, obscured, or discoloured by Passion and Interest" (*GT* 4.8.267). Emotions clog, complicate, and enrich language; the only way Gulliver can finally communicate his unequine ideas is to use the indirect resources of language to move the Houyhnhnms's imagination and emotion: "I had made Use of many Circumlocutions ... I was forced to define and describe by putting of Cases, and making Suppositions. After which, like one whose Imagination was struck with something never seen or heard of before, he would lift up his Eyes with Amazement and Indignation" (*GT* 4.4.244). Gulliver has gotten through, but in so doing, he releases new linguistic forces that contain traps and inadequacies of their own.

ACCORDING TO MINE INTENTIONS

Gulliver's affective appeals to his Houyhnhnm master's emotions indicate a behavioralist approach to language. Behavioral linguists, like Lockean linguists, believe communication to be language's purpose, but they extend meaningful communication to include the conveyance and stimulation of feeling. Not so much a distinct theory of language as a set of assumptions implicit in Western criticism since its beginnings, behavioralism is rooted in classical rhetoric, the art of inciting passion as well as reason in the service of persuasion. Aristotle, for example, defines rhetoric in behavioral terms; the speaker or author's intentional evincing of his personality (*ethos*) helps enable his persuasive words to raise audience emotions (*pathos*) and move them to action. Poetry provides a special case of affective discourse. Plato negatively (and perhaps ironically) ratifies poetry's affectiveness by barring poets from his Republic, whereas Roman writers resanction the emotional power of poetry. Imaginative authors, according to Horace, should inform or delight or combine both aims, and theorists like Longinus emphasize the satisfactions to be found in language's emotional significance. Renaissance humanists, drawing upon classical tradition and patristic belief in the redemptive worth of exegesis, value the ability of words to inspire and instruct mankind.[31] Swift never abandons the behavioral goal of serving public good through kneading together "a *Layer* of *Utile* and a *Layer* of *Dulce*" (*Tale* 5.124), although the resulting mixture's sweetness often surrenders to the acidity of unaccomplished moral purpose. "My chief end," writes Swift to Pope, "is to vex the world rather then divert it" (29 Sept. 1725, *Corr.* 3:102).

A general commitment to behavioralism motivates all sorts of seventeenth- and eighteenth-century oratory and publications, from sermons to political tracts—genres Swift both practiced and ridiculed. Behavioralist assumptions also continue to flow through theoretical writings about literature. Dryden, speaking as Neander in *An Essay of Dramatic Poesy*, criticized French playwrights for their coldness and inability to express or elicit passion. Pope, in *An Essay on Criticism*, stressed the importance of authorial intent: accurate reading requires attunement to the writer's spirit and purpose, an ideal Swift had examined skeptically in *A Tale of a Tub* when the Tale-writer suggests that a reader must put "himself into the Circumstances and Postures of Life, that the Writer was in" ("The Preface," *Tale*, 44), which in this case would involve lying in a garret bed, hungry, sick, and penniless. Among Swift's contemporaries, it was Addison who most directly considered the behavioral psychology of language, positing in "The Pleasures of the Imagination," *The Spectator* #416, that the force and energy of words can stimulate readers' imaginations, thereby also engendering a variety of responses.[32] Augustan behavioralism anticipates more codified modern behavioral theories of language and their location of verbal meaning in "the situation in which the speaker utters it and the response that it calls forth in the hearer."[33]

Behavioral considerations, then, are historically intertwined with literary theory and criticism, and Swift's work shows an engagement with behavioralism similar in its ambivalences to his engagements with referential and ideational theories of language. Swift can seem to agree with two distinct and perhaps contradictory tenets of behavioral linguistics: first, that meaning is a function of use and that language is meaningful according to the action that results from it; second, that meaning is to be found in the speaker's intentions or in the hearer's reactions. Yet Swift is equally aware of the communicatory dangers of linguistic behavioralism and of the difficulty of integrating the written word into such a theory of meaning.

The Houyhnhnm master responds to Gulliver's emotional manipulations in much the same way as does the King of Brobdingnag. Emotion begets emotion: the rulers' comprehension of Gulliver's alien and (to them) irrational meanings leads to disgust, contempt, and a menacing show of force. After the reasonable and practical Brobdingnagian king hears Gulliver's panegyric to gunpowder, he is "struck with Horror" and commands Gulliver to keep silent upon pain of death (*GT* 2.7.134–35). In Houyhnhnmland, the threat of irrationality posed by Gulliver leads to resuming debate about whether to exterminate all Yahoos because of "the violent Hatred the *Houyhnhnms* as well as all other Animals, bore them" and the fear that they once again would "over-run and infest the whole Nation" (*GT* 4.9.271). Gulliver's master, in a maneuver of mercy resembling the Lilliputian king's commutation of Gulliver's sentence of execution to blinding, counterproposes that Yahoos be castrated and Gulliver, before he can lead the Yahoos in rebellion, be cast out to sea. Swift demonstrates that communication of passion and sentiment works, but that it works dangerously, as in the communication of disease.

Swift's awareness of emotional contagion that can destroy the host body, be it verbal or human, underlies the satire of Enthusiastic preaching in *A Tale of a Tub* and *The Mechanical Operation of the Spirit*. The latter work maintains that "in the Language of the Spirit, *Cant* and *Droning* supply the Place of *Sense* and *Reason*" by "adapting the Voice, to whatever Words the Spirit delivers, that each may strike the Ears of the Audience, with its most significant Cadence" (*MO*, 278–79). The significance of words resides in their sound, and such decomposed words are used only to stimulate emotional response. "Thus it is frequent for a single *Vowel* to draw Sighs from a Multitude; and for a whole Assembly of Saints to sob to the Musick of one Solitary *Liquid*" (*MO*, 279). This emotional communication threatens health: "[T]he *Spirit* is apt to feed on the *Flesh*" (*MO*, 280). In the case of the Banbury Saint, this "disease" ravaged his entire body before syphilitically destroying his nose, enabling him to communicate through the affective mode of snuffling. Again, Swift does not deny the capability of words to carry and to stimulate feeling, their meaning discernible in their behavioral situation. Instead, he questions the propriety of such an emotional investment in words and warns of its consequences. A similar affirmation through warning occurs in *A Letter to a Young Gentleman*: preachers who appeal to the passions "would find one Part of their Congregation out of Countenance, and the other asleep" (*PW* 9:69). To avoid producing anger or boredom, or to avoid inviting ridicule, they should "beware of letting the pathetick Part swallow up the rational" argument of their sermons (*PW* 9:70). Yet Swift precedes his condemnation of emotional cant with approving references to classical oratory. Cicero's impassioned appeals to the Roman citizenry, as well as Demosthenes' reasoned arguments in Athens, were always designed to result in immediate action. Therefore, "it was often found of absolute Necessity to enflame, or cool the Passions of the Audience" (*PW* 9:69).

Swift did believe verbal significance could be assigned and assessed according to situational conditions and actions. "I write Pamphlets," he complains to Pope, "and when they are finished . . . I cast them into the fire, partly out of dislike, and chiefly because I know they will signify nothing" (15 Jan. 1730/31, *Corr.* 3:434). Swift implies that his words signify nothing because they will produce no response, raise no emotions, provoke no actions. He wrote this letter a few months after publication of *A Modest Proposal*, that titanic testimony to the uselessness of reasoned words to affect minds and hearts and actions. The most reasonable ideas, minus a "sincere Attempt to put them in Practice," shrivel into "vain, idle, visionary Thoughts," of no significance to anyone (*A Modest Proposal, PW* 12:117). The bitterness of *A Modest Proposal* is sharpened by Swift's knowledge that words did not have to be useless. In the *Drapier's Letters*, he had marshaled his words into galvanizing forces; their meaning would be measured by the significant action that ratified and fulfilled their cautionary and exhortatory message. *The Conduct of the Allies* and *The Bickerstaff Papers* also evidence the triumph of word as deed, of meaning as result, but overemphasizing Swift's early successes in changing behavior reduces him to a (largely ineffectual) polemical pamphleteer.[34]

In a broad sense, as a satirist Swift is necessarily committed to a behavioral theory of language. His subject matter is man's behavior, and his words attempt to change it, or at least to confront badly behaving man with his own absurdities and cruelties in order to shake him out of complacency. From a narrower viewpoint of behavioral linguistic activism, however, Swift's satire programs its own failure or its own self-destruction. Premised upon man's resistance to change, his neglect or abuse of reason, his capacity for delusion and sin, it assumes its own futility. If it succeeds in changing behavior, it renders itself unnecessary and therefore meaningless.[35] That the significance of satire cannot be tied to its results is ironically underscored by Gulliver's peevish letter to his Cousin Sympson. Gulliver bewails the bad judgment that permitted him to publish his book:

> Pray bring to your Mind how often I desired you to consider, when you insisted on the Motive of *publick Good*; that the *Yahoos* were a species of Animals utterly incapable of Amendment by Precepts or Examples: And so it hath proved; for instead of seeing a full Stop put to all Abuses and Corruptions, at least in this little Island, as I had Reason to expect: Behold, after above Six Months Warning, I cannot

learn that my Book hath produced one single Effect according to mine Intentions. ["Letter to Sympson," *GT*, 6]

Gulliver, his intentions untranslated into corrective actions, might put himself out to pasture, but Swift does not. He writes and rails until he dies.

The issue of intention is central to behavioral linguistic theory. The speaker-subject, by filling the silent void that is his signifying intention with speech, is the bearer of meaning; the incarnated verbal meaning, "being" endorsed and disclosed by language, mediates between speaker-subject and hearer-object.[36] Meaning is intentionality, but Swift suspects that intentions can corrupt meaning. Self-interest and expediency can taint an entire text or a single word. Swift believes Milton's treatise on divorce to be invalidated by its author's desire to leave his wife ("Remarks upon Tindall's *Rights of the Christian Church*," *PW* 2:68); the words *Whig* and *Tory* have swiveled in significance according to the intentions of the interest groups they label (*The Examiner* #43, *PW* 3:162–67), as has "the wonderful Significancy of the Word *Persecution*," which may mean inability to assemble for worship, the imposition of the Sacramental Test, a lady's cruelty to her lover, or "every Thing that will not leave it in Men's Power to persecute others" (*A Letter Concerning the Sacramental Test*, *PW* 2:122). The obvious problem Swift addresses is the instability of meaning based on intent. Words could have as many meanings as there are speakers or authors, yet behavioral theory demands that the intended meaning be properly received and enacted in order to realize significance.

If, for example, Gulliver's intentions are neither understood nor acted upon, does one conclude that his words have no meaning? If they are interpreted or acted upon in ways contrary to his intentions, are they stripped of meaning, or clothed in some kind of antimeaning? Swift shows himself highly conscious of the treacherous space words attempt to span between intention and interpretation—particularly when they are exiled from the speaking situation, with its clarifying reinforcements of gesture, expression, and tone of voice that, as Gulliver found out in his initial conversation with the Lilliputians, can communicate feelings and physical needs perfectly well, even if each party understands "not one Syllable" of the other's speech (*GT* 1.1.23).

This is the problem motivating the story of the coats in *A Tale of a Tub*: the problem of how and by whom or what an investiture—the word as the clothing of thought, or feeling, or intention—is given meaning. Sections 2 and 4 of the *Tale* conflate the way of the world, the way of clothes, and the way of the written word; thus the allegory can be read as a paradigm of how Swift explores, if not answers, the question of verbal meaning. As textile, text, and testament (thing, word, and will), the coat is subjected to ceaseless shreddings and encrustations according to how the authorizing document is mangled by reader desire. Fringe can mean broomstick; *K* can mean *C*. One man's bread can mean another man's mutton, but what is the nature of the sacrifice implied by the transubstantiation of communion bread into pascal lamb? Perhaps it is the sacrifice of the word to rapacious interpretation, to a linguistic behavioralism gone mad with power: as Peter thunders to his hungry brothers who "*do not comprehend*" his reading of the meal, which looks to them like a mere loaf of bread, "*eat your Vittles and leave off your Impertinence . . . it is true, good, natural Mutton . . . and G—, confound you both eternally, if you offer to believe otherwise*" (*Tale* 4.117–18).

A meaning (interpretation) subsequent to and different from an original meaning (intent) can be force-fed, but that does not make it true or good or natural. As Martin's decision to leave some closely worked embroidery in his coat indicates, even in contrast with Peter's commitment to textual defacements and Jack's zeal for textual destruction, original meaning cannot be completely uncovered through hermeneutic discoverings and recoverings. Once it is uttered, it is lost. The allegory of the coats argues that the properties of truth, goodness, and naturalness do not apply unequivocally to meanings.[37] As soon as the word is separated from thing or thought or feeling or intent, it is no longer bound to ontological absolutes. Its open capacity to mean now includes the capacity for deceit, the capacity for evil, and the capacity for artifice; it has magnified its own polysemic possibilities.

THE DEEPEST DESIGNS

If there is truth behind the text, it is never safe. "Laws penned with the utmost Care and Exactness, and in the vulgar Language, are often perverted to wrong Meanings; then why should we wonder that the Bible is so?" asks Swift in "Thoughts on Various Subjects" (*PW* 4:248). No author can guarantee "correct" interpretation of his written words because they are stranded in print, autonomous. Separated in space and time from the referential thing, the original thought, the authorial intent, and the behavioral situation, printed texts are vulnerable to as many interpretations as there are readers. A priori meaning cannot be recaptured; a posteriori meanings cannot be reconciled. The center of meaning, therefore, collapses upon the word itself, fecund and unpredictable; verbal meaning can be safeguarded only by the network of words on a page, by intertextural authorizations. These concepts of words and meanings, examined repeatedly throughout Swift's work, call for a fourth type of language theory, one I will term *textocentric*. As is the case with his treatments of other language theories, Swift approaches textocentrism with ambivalence; he affirms that words can work this way while questioning the sufficiency or desirability of their doing so. It is this dissatisfaction with and distrust of the autonomous word that, even more than an almost three-hundred-year time gap, differentiates Swift's textocentrism from the modern poststructural and deconstructionist theories that it in many ways resembles. Although Swift frequently follows liberal textocentric impulses such as exploiting the freedoms and risks of polysemy or inviting multiple interpretations, he also frequently engages in conservative textocentric strategies that bind meaning to the written page, that protect the word against extratextual invasion, and that trap interpretation into recognizing its own error.

In his discussion of Swift's "Tory Anarchy," Edward Said maintains that Swift's texts embody the "dramatic encounter between the anarchy of resistance to the written page and the abiding tory order of the page."[38] Although my adjectives "liberal" and "conservative" also necessarily implicate Swift's linguistic attitudes in a larger ideological field, both are meant to apply to pressures enacted within the text. Liberal textocentrism is neither Tory anarchism, Whiggism, nor Irish patriotism; it is the thrust toward freedom of signification that can have both politically liberal and politically conservative consequences. Neither is conservative textocentrism merely adherence to institutionalized Tory order; in its attempt to bind signification to the text, it too can further various political agenda. The early *A Tale of a Tub*, for instance, uses liberal textocentric tactics to serve conservative political strategy. Conversely, the later *Drapier's Letters* employ conservative textocentric tactics to accomplish politically liberal aims. In both works, a strong persona with strong ideological allegiances seemingly controls the text. Yet the Tale-writer and the Drapier are products of textocentrism. They are not masks but purely verbal presences whose writerly authority is made possible by Swift's removal of himself from his text.

The behavioralist theory of language ties meaning to presence, a self-projection into words. Like ideationalist theory, it assumes the priority of speech over writing: written words are a dress of a dress or, perhaps, the clothing for the body (sounds) housing the spirit (thought or intent or "being"). In contrast, textocentrism ties meaning to absence, a withdrawal of self from words. It also, at least in the modern garb of deconstructionism as posited by Jacques Derrida, questions the priority of speech over writing, the concept of writing as the "outside" of language.[39] Derrida believes instead that writing covers itself and that it creates a different sort of meaning from spoken language: a deferred but open potentiality of meaning.

In a way, absence and the suspension of significatory closure justify fictional license. When Sir Philip Sidney states that a poet "nothing affirms, and therefore never lieth,"[40] he implies that imaginative writing is an independent system with its own rules, that it is privileged discourse absolving its author from responsibility to extratextual truths, that artifice is different from nature. Celebration of this license can lead to what Mikhail Bahktin has called "carnivalesque" texts such as Erasmus's *Moriae Encomium*, Rabelais's *Gargantua and Pantagruel*, and Swift's *A Tale of a Tub*.[41] The license of textual autonomy manifests itself in wordplay, in anagrams, in codes, and in puns—puns in particular embodying the anarchic power of language to contradict its own meanings yet to disclose truths peculiar to texts. Swift recognized textocentric autonomy and often exploited it; instances include the deliberately open and multi-egressed structure of *A Tale of a Tub*, the paronomastic dynamics behind satiric literalization, the fabricated languages in *Gulliver's Travels*, the reliance upon pseudonyms and anonymous authorships. Yet textocentric autonomy also makes Swift uneasy. He is loathe to release any author (except, possibly, himself) from responsibility for his writings. His case for censoring subversive writings rests on awareness of the dangerous difference between thoughts and texts: to publish, to utter, is to make real and exterior the hidden interior and unleash a force that may escape an author's control. "If such thinkers keep their thoughts within their own breast, they can be of no consequence, further than to themselves," Swift maintains. "If they publish them to the world, they ought to be answerable for the effects their thoughts produce on others" ("Some Thoughts on Free-Thinking," *PW* 4:49). Here Swift employs the behavioralist theory to counter the threat implicit in textocentrism, a threat that can also menace him personally. This fear, articulated in Plato's *Phaedrus* and recently reinvestigated by Derrida,[42] involves the ability of orphaned texts to rebel against the absent progenitor, to usurp his authority and abscond with meaning. Swift wants both the protection of absence and the effective control of presence. He wants his targets to know when they're bit; he may wish to disguise authorship, but he does not wish his works attributed to someone else; even as he constructs polysemic texts, he wants to be read properly. The absolutist desire for true, good, and natural meanings conflicts with the liberal textocentric desire for infinitely open significance.

Swift's "Apology" to *A Tale of a Tub*, added in the 1710 edition, shows his recognition of multiple interpretation and his displeasure with having his own words wrenched about. He asks that his "*Faults may not be multiply'd by the ignorant, the unnatural, and uncharitable Applications of those who have neither Candor to suppose good Meanings, nor Palate to distinguish true Ones*" ("Apology," *Tale*, 4–5). Again, the triad of naturalness, goodness, and truth is applied to meanings, but the fact that Swift thinks "*the Author's Intentions*" had been twisted or overlooked indicates the copresence of forced, bad, and false meanings. Such disputatious meanings occur because any text can be perverted to mean anything:

> *There are three or four other Passages which prejudiced or ignorant Readers have drawn by great Force to hint at ill Meanings . . . the Author solemnly protests that he is entirely Innocent, and never had it once in his Thoughts that any thing he said would in the least be capable of such Interpretations, which he will engage to deduce full as fairly from the most innocent Book in the World.* ["The Apology," *Tale*, 8]

One should probably suspect Swift of protesting his innocence too much, particularly when he subsequently defends himself against those who, on the trail of anti-Trinitarianism, "*have endeavour'd to squeeze out a dangerous Meaning that was never thought on*" ("The Apology," *Tale*, 8) from his allegoric use of the "Number Three"; he explains that he had written about four machines but that the custodians of his manuscript had cut out the last one. Nevertheless, the *Tale* itself gives ample evidence that there is no such thing as an innocent book. Its original sin exists in both active and passive forms: a text is either strong enough to overthrow extratextual meanings or so weak that it invites mayhem on its own body of meaning.

Beneath the parable of the coats lies one truth of the textual body; naked and passive words solicit corruption. Peter's dissection of his father's will to find authorization for affixing shoulder-knots to the coats epitomizes the defenselessness of the word against onslaughts of interpretation. By chopping sentences into individual words, words into individual syllables, and syllables into individual letters, Peter can finally force his own will upon the written will, making it yield the meaning he was determined to find, even if he must brand as bastard and banish a "modern illegitimate Letter" in order to supplant it with a cooperative pretender to the throne of significance. The act encodes a primal aggressiveness, familial[43] and historical: vanquishing the father (authorial intent), violating the mother (tongue), and calumniating and exiling rebellious adversaries (the illegitimate letter). The resulting *"Jure Paterno"* (*Tale* 2: 84) authorizing shoulder-knots is not the Father's law but the usurping son's.

Peter's version of the received text and perversion of the received textile form a reductio of strong reading,[44] a demonstration of how interpretation penetrates and defiles the seductively passive word. Similarly, in the quest to authorize "Gold Lace," Peter invades the *"altum silentium"* of the text, filling the "scriptory" gap with *"Nuncupatory"* matter, obeying the surrogate licensing of Aristotle's *"de Interpretatione*, which has the Faculty of Teaching its Readers to find out a Meaning in every Thing but it self" (*Tale* 2.85). The desire for "Satin Lining" leads Peter to tack self-authorizing codicils to the unresisting text, and the wish for "Silver-Fringe" demands suppression of the text's latent metaphorical activism: *"Fringe*, does also signifie a *Broom-stick*, and doubtless ought to have the same Interpretation in this Paragraph" (*Tale* 2.88). Metaphor is stretched to absurdity, broken in two, then frozen. Peter's final solution is to lock away the text in a prisonhouse of unintelligible language so that "perpetually altering" fashions could be followed with no regard for the body they are designed to clothe. Interpretations have conquered the text completely and can accumulate in "infinite Number" (*Tale* 2.90).

Interpretive aggression also occurs in *Gulliver's Travels*. Gulliver's "improvements" on a Lagadan language project not only ridicule violent interpretation; they also indict texts that allow words to remain passive, inarticulate forms—objects defined by their structural components, their letters or their grammatical categories. The nationals of Tribnia, Gulliver explains, scoop out significance from words and stuff them with arbitrary meanings. The written letters and papers of suspected traitors are seized and

> are delivered to a Set of Artists very dextrous in finding out the mysterious Meanings of Words, Syllables and Letters. For Instance, they can decypher a Close-stool to signify a Privy-Council; a flock of Geese, a Senate; a lame Dog, an Invader . . .
> When this Method fails, they have two other more effectual; which the Learned among them call Acrosticks and Anagrams. *First*, they can decypher all initial Letters into political Meanings: Thus, *N*, shall signify a Plot; *B*, a Regiment of Horse; *L*, a Fleet at Sea. Or, secondly, by transposing the Letters of the Alphabet, in any suspected Paper, they can lay open the deepest Designs of a discontented Party. [*GT* 3.6.191]

To decipher (from the Arabic *sifr*, empty or zero, taken into Latin as *cifra*) is to replenish the meaningless sign with meaning. Yet these dextrous code artists reverse the process. Their literal legerdemain closes the word to comprehensible communication and de-signs the captive texts rather than "lay[ing] open the deepest Designs of a discontented Party." In actuality, their subject is dis-contented, a hollow form deprived of any significance whatsoever. Swift's allusions to the methods used to convict his friends Bishop Atterbury and Lord Bolingbroke of political plots add another layer to this passage's linguistic satire. Swift himself is employing an analogical code that hides an intended meaning beneath an outer verbal covering.

This sort of complicitous authorial tactic makes words participants in their own active textocentric sin against meaning. Particularly in *A Tale of a Tub*, Swift has deliberately constructed a jumbled and ruptured text that prohibits the possibility of its own significatory closure. On one hand, such a construction is admonitory: modern authors who exile themselves from the authority of literary history will find their works displaced not only from the continuity of tradition but also from originating idea and intent. Infinite significatory potential is, perhaps, the same as no significance at all. On the other hand, risking loss is part of playing games, and none of Swift's most sustained works is as structurally and verbally playful as *A Tale of a Tub*. Textocentric license allows words to be moveable pieces in the game of the text. The text does not transmit meaning from the real world or speaking voices or Being or action; as play surface (or game board, or linguistic roulette wheel) upon which the problematics of reading are encountered,[45] it permits and commits meaning.

For example, section 10 of the *Tale* contains a modest proposal to generate infinite interpretation of itself:

> [E]very Prince in *Christendom* will take seven of the *deepest Scholars* in his Dominions, and shut them up close for *seven years, in seven* Chambers, with a Command to write *seven* ample Commentaries on this comprehensive Discourse. I shall venture to affirm, that whatever Difference may be found in their several Conjectures, they will be all, without the least Distortion, manifestly deduceable from the Text. [*Tale* 10.185]

Swift makes fun of writers with dark and deep designs as well as of the commentators and critics who feed on them; "without the least Distortion" translates through litotes into "with the most Distortion." Concurrently, he suggests that enduring meaning resides in and is authorized by the text: Prince → Dedication to Prince Posterity → princeps → prints. Furthermore, he creates a series of significations through the physical presence of words. The alliterative chains, reinforced by italicization and by capitalization of nouns, have a purely verbal generative power of their own. On an expanding textual field (X times seven times seven) *Christendom*'s Chambers Command Commentaries, Conjectures; *deepest* Dominions' Discourse → Difference, Distortion. The positive significatory values of textual interpretations, "comprehensive" and "deduceable," are demoted to nonitalicized, lowercase adjective forms, trailing the primary alliterative sequences. The text thus explains and enacts its own fall—the difference of the written word, the distortion to which it is susceptible—by embedding its own meaning in the look and shape of words. Yet Swift punctures textocentric potential two paragraphs later by using logomathesis to ridicule arbitrary transformations of verbal materiality into secret meanings: "I have couched a very profound Mystery in the Number of *O*'s multiply'd by *Seven*, and divided by *Nine*" (*Tale* 10.186–87), advises the Tale-writer. *O* or zero multiplied and divided by anything is still zero, and the author's deep designs are again de-signed into nothing, into empty ciphers.

The Tale-writer's desire for fame in this life also discloses Swift's ambivalent stance between indulging in textocentric play and fearing its consequences. Commissioning interpretation immediately would allow the living writer to cheat death and taste immortality, since fame usually feeds and flowers upon a dead corpus.[46] He can escape the deathly traps of hermeneutic closure through textocentric tropes that, once set in motion, will operate independently, ad infinitum. The Tale-writer begins this process by asking "whether [Fame] conceives, her Trumpet sounds best and farthest, when she stands on a *Tomb*" (*Tale* 10.185–86), pairing two meanings of "conceive" (to form an idea of; to become pregnant, to conceive on a tomb, to make life out of death). Two sentences later, the gestated pun bursts into a new life of meaning about meaning:

> *Scholiastick* Midwifry hath deliver'd them [dark Authors] of Meanings, that the Authors themselves, perhaps, never conceived, and yet may very justly be allowed the Lawful Parents of them: The Words of such Writers being like Seed, which, however scattered at random, when they light upon a fruitful Ground, will multiply far beyond either the Hopes or Imagination of the Sower. [*Tale* 10.186]

The passage presents interesting contrasts. The semic seeds are either enfertilizing essence or onanistic spillage; the word-heirs are either legitimate or bastard offspring; the author-parent desires either seminal authority or deliverance from responsibility of authorship; the multiplying text is either a means of self-transcendence through an unforeclosed series of meanings or a betrayal of "Hopes or Imagination," intents and thoughts. The Edenic fruitful ground may be the innocent text or the field of interpretation, but the fall of words is implicit, the "Sower" implies a reaper, and reaping—be it textocentric oblivion as the ultimate zero point towards which infinite signification heads or the severing blows of extrinsically imposed ill or false or artificial meanings—kills the word. Reaping is reading, and Swift can check the fall of the hermeneutic scythe by textocentric undercutting. Undercutting, however, endangers the text from within. A textocentric approach makes the problem of meaning itself a metaphor for the gains and losses of authorship.

Early works such as *A Tale of a Tub* celebrate the risks of writing more overtly than works produced after some of these risks have become actualized. Nevertheless, a relatively late piece demonstrates Swift's continuing investigation of a textocentric view of language. *On Poetry: A Rapsody* (1733) ironically recommends textocentric method. Material elements of a written text authorize meaning, or meaning is left to the vagaries of interpretation:

> In modern Wit all printed Trash, is
> Set off with num'rous Breaks——and Dashes—
>   To Statesmen wou'd you give a Wipe,
> You print it in *Italick Type*.
> When Letters are in vulgar Shapes,
> 'Tis ten to one the Wit escapes;
> But when in *Capitals* exprest,
> The dullest Reader smoaks a Jest:
> Or else perhaps he may invent
> A better than the Poet meant,
> As learned Commentators view
> In *Homer* more than *Homer* knew.
>   [*On Poetry: A Rapsody*, SPW 569–83.93–104]

This self-enacting passage is comic, but it is surrounded by the overtones of tragic loss implicit in textocentrism. Swift constructs a chain of bastardization and renunciation. A poet is the most illegitimate and abandoned of bastard offspring, in a worse state than a "Bastard of a Pedlar *Scot*," or a "Spawn of Bridewell" or a Gypsy orphan; being "blasted with poetick Fire" is being branded and blighted with a physical legacy of sin (lines 33–42), and "*Court, City, Country* want you not" (line 47). Poetry inherits the patrimony of illegitimate exile: "The Product of your Toil and Sweating; / A Bastard of your own begetting" (lines 115–16), it must be disowned by its creator, cast into the world nameless and unacknowledged. A poet must relinquish "fond paternal Pride" and keep silent (lines 123–30). The situation worsens: the poet progressively prostitutes himself, enters a cannibal chain of poetic competition, denies his Grubstreet origins, and dives into the gulf of Hell.

Concurrently, the poem's structure degenerates, ellipses increasingly fissuring its final lines, until it breaks itself off with the mocking textocentrist promise of meaning yet to be fulfilled: *Caetera desiderantur*. This poem, as an allegory of the self-authorizing text, demonstrates the dangers of desire deferred through de-authorization. Like the passage from *A Tale of a Tub* with which this chapter began, *On Poetry: A Rapsody* creates openings for meaning at once tempting and trapping, a thin tissue of potential significations stretched across the void.

Swift's exploration of textocentric issues highlights a question also motivating his affirmations and denials of the referential, ideational, and behavioral theories of language: how are verbal meanings authorized? His ambivalent and skeptical investigations examine the phenomenon of the word, map the shifting centers of meaning, and weigh the risks of writing and reading; in so doing, they indicate the need to invest words with some sort of stabilizing authority. Without such investitures, the text would collapse under its chaotic burden of significatory contradictions and indeterminations and fall into its own chasm of silence.

2 / INVESTITURES
Swift and Verbal Authority

"How inconsistent is Man with himself," observed Swift in "Thoughts on Various Subjects" (*PW* 4:245). Swift is not exempt from his own apothegm, and nowhere is his inconsistency more apparent than in matters of language theory and language practice. Swift's explicit writings about language champion conservatism: he lauds a simple and proper style; he calls for censorship of subversive publications; he proposes that the formal elements of language be fixed through institutionalization. His use of language, however, is frequently innovative, often directly contrary to his conservative pronouncements. Particularly when he follows the liberal textocentric impulse, he allows himself to play with complicated linguistic games, puns, and codes, to construct allusive fantasies open to charges of being irreligious, and to concoct neologisms or decompose linguistic form into idiosyncratic verbal signs. This apparent contradiction between theory and use can be clarified through the Saussurian distinction between *langue*, the common and in a sense institutionalized verbal fund of any language, and *parole*, the individual speaker or writer's appropriation and manipulation of language.[1] In a general way, Swift's conservatism calls for preserving *langue* so it can provide strong and firm authorization for the licenses of *parole*. The means by which Swift gives authority to his texts are the subject of this chapter.

The investiture of texts with verbal authority is not a simple transference of power from the common language warehouse to individual language constructions. Human authorship is an act of authorization, both of originating, generating verbal meaning and of giving, relinquishing meaning to the text. To the sometimes conflicting authorizations of the language institution and of the individual writer must be added the authorization of the text itself.

Swift frequently reiterates the cliché that books are like children, and the parallel extends to matters of authority, of responsibility, and of the power of determination. Is a child or a text a gift of God, a product of society, a creation of parents, or an independent being? Through which of these frames should actions and values be judged? The questions include the issue of origins, but origins as a function of distance and time: the farther biological or textual offspring are removed from formative parental control and the longer they exist, the more responsible they are for their own deeds and their own determination of meaning, either by choice or by default, yet the more vulnerable they are to exterior expectations and judgments. In a sense, writing itself can counter time with space, can turn movements and moments into monuments. But monumentality has its own danger: the potential of destroying verbal vitality by entombing *parole* in a well-fortified mausoleum of institutionalized *langue*. To circumvent this dead end, Swift seeks textual permanence and stability through various systematics of propriety and placement.

Propriety involves both ownership and decorum; as bounded verbal property, it becomes contingent upon authorized placement. Placement implies a spatial aesthetic that invests the text with authorization over its own meaning and subjugates the reader to a preexisting textual order. Spatiality, rooted doubly in Judeo-Christian and in Hellenic tradition, grounds Western thought about literature. It requires that a reader distance himself from the text and regard it holistically to determine its origins and its ends. As map (flat, self-contained referential space) or icon (included images interpretable internally), the text formally repudiates the temporal experience of reading; it appropriates and encloses meaning by making it contingent upon folding forward propulsions (narrative sequence, logical argument, character revelation, jokes) back upon themselves.[2] Swift partakes of this general tradition of literary spatiality, but he also makes specific textual gestures to counter specific threats of impropriety, displacement, and unauthorized interpretation.

In *A Tale of a Tub*, Swift approaches the tangled problem of authorization via the book's root metaphor. Investiture is the trope of creation. In the fiction, cosmic dressing determines the shape and order of the world according to the vestmental theology surrounding the tailor-god. Behind the fiction, the trope determines the text: pregrounding the allegory of the coats, equating textiles with texts, and setting up form and placement as requirements for responsible authorization, requirements that the Tale-writer blithely jettisons.

Nevertheless, the metaphorical frame is only vaguely parodic. Swift literalizes the structure of medieval cosmology into a charming display of enclosing garments:

[Worshippers] held the Universe to be a large Suit of *Cloaths*, which *invests* every Thing: That the Earth is *invested* by the Air; The Air is *invested* by the Stars; and the Stars are *invested* by the *Primum Mobile*. [*Tale* 2.77–78]

This image of serially supportive investiture reflects the orthodoxy of Swift's sermons, the assertion, for example, that "God hath contrived all the Works of Nature to be useful, and in some manner a Support to each other, by which the whole Frame of the World under his Providence is preserved and kept up" ("On Mutual Subjection," *PW* 2:143). In the *Tale*, the consequences of the suit-of-clothes literalization weave fantasy more than satire: the sea a waistcoat of water-tabby, the Beech-tree a beau topped with a stylish wig, the ornaments of language the embroidery, laces, and furbelows adorning plain material. The concept of man as microcoat belongs in part to the gentle grotesquerie with which Swift depicts investiture, although, as will be discussed below, even here man disrupts the ordered donning of dress, prefiguring the more explicit disfigurements Peter and Jack will perform on the coats and on their father's authorizing word.

Swift's lyrical tableau of investiture lacks satiric bite because Swift believed in the process of ordered transmission of authority.[3] In *The Sentiments of a Church-of-England Man*, for instance, he praises England's mix of legislative power and hereditary monarchy for its ability to rule fairly and without interruption. He praises episcopacy for the same reason: it is "fittest, of all others for preserving Order and Purity" (*PW* 2:5). Since "All government is from God, who is the God of order," whereas disorder is "of the Devil, who is the author of confusion" ("Doing Good: A Sermon," *PW* 9:238), the metaphor of investiture serves the concept of authoritative order particularly well because it is drawn from religious practice. In the Anglican church, investiture occurs when a cleric assumes a new office in the institutional structure. The ceremony marks both the conferral of authority by the church hierarchy, a conferral itself authorized by religious tradition and ultimately by God and his divine word, and the acceptance of an increased level of authority by the clergyman. As the word *investiture* attests, the ceremony's visible focal point is the giving and the wearing of special clothing symbolizing the power of office: for instance, the bishop's surplice or the cathedral dean's cope. Investiture is both a putting in and a putting on; the vestments, as outward signs of inward power, are badges of distinction, of privileged authority and proper placement within a preexisting order. In Swift's time, clerical clothing also signaled adherence to a definite politico-religious conservatism. Swift points out that the "wicked Puritans" first attacked "Surplices and other habits" before they went on to greater destructiveness, abolishing the "whole order" of church government and then overturning civil government as well, erecting in place of these venerable structures "a Babel" ("Upon the Martyrdom of King Charles I," *PW* 9:225–26).

Swift's synecdoche spreads in many directions: Babel—a usurping structure, a confusion of tongues, the de-authorized text, the disobedient word, linguistic corruption and verbal meaninglessness as punishment for the violation of order. According to his sermon, the road to Babel starts with undressing or improper dressing, with ignoring or perverting the act of investiture. The pre-text for this sequence is the awesome series of transgressions and retributions in the first eleven chapters of Genesis; disobedience, dereliction of duty, wickedness, and presumption bring consequences symbolized by clothes, by chaos, and by confounded language. Swift may have believed that both clothes and words are ultimately "accidentals" in the Lockean sense of being supplementary rather than "necessary" attributes of man (*PW* 11:280), but man's fall has bonded these accidents into the very texture of man's existence. Investiture can manage these necessary accidentals in a proper and orderly fashion so that chaos will not come again.

FURNISHING OUT AN EXACT DRESS

At the end of *A Tale of a Tub*, section 1, the Tale-writer explains that since books are "the Children of the brain," he has christened his treatise on Grub-street arcana with a variety of titles (*Tale* 1.71). Nevertheless, the marginal note reveals that *"The Title Page in the Original was so torn, that it was not possible to recover several Titles which the Author here speaks of"*; furthermore, the Tale-writer has been unable to follow Dryden's authority and provide his book with "a Multiplicity of *God-fathers*" (*Tale* 1.71–72). Thus the book is unsponsored, defaced, severed from its origins, and subsequently abandoned by the Tale-writer as he turns to the allegory of the coats. The nameless, orphaned text, then, is not merely a satiric digression upon literary sycophancy and mystification. It also emblematically introduces a complex of considerations underlying the microcoat trope and the vestmental tale: the "Untwisting or Unwinding" of the filial filaments (*Tale* 1.67), the issue and tissue of verbal authority.

Section 2 of the *Tale* begins with a family scene, a ceremony of investiture. A nameless father calls his three nameless sons to his deathbed so he can bequeath to them a coat (the institution of Christianity that covers, identifies, and protects its members) authorized and interpreted by the testamentary written word. Text and textile perform supplementary investitures of meaning; each informs the other, the coat giving outer form to the word, the word giving information necessary to preserve the coat. Thus the flexibility of the coats, which "*will grow in the same proportion with your Bodies . . . so as to be always fit*" (*Tale* 2.73), implies a reciprocal flexibility of the words. This flexible "fit" paradoxically reinforces conformity to the invested filial body and to the authorizing paternal will; it also relies on the observance of "very good Order" (*Tale* 2.74). Death having displaced originating will into words and having removed authorizing presence from written presentation, the word-made-text moves from mythological synchroneity ("Once upon a Time, there was a Man who had Three Sons," *Tale* 2.73) to historical time, where it is misinterpreted and maimed by its less spiritual brothers. The filial word is torn asunder, and the usurping brothers become increasingly estranged from paternal authority, from each other, and from the text in which they have their fictional being.

The quick rush of time teaches estrangement by trivializing human actions and depreciating human language through what Roland Barthes has called "the asyndeton of behavioral statements":[4] the brothers "Writ, and Raillyed, and Rhymed, and Sung, and Said, and Said Nothing; They Drank, and Fought, and Whor'd, and Slept, and Swore, and took Snuff . . . They talk'd of the Drawing-Room and never came there, Dined with Lords they never saw; Whisper'd a Duchess, and spoke never a Word" (*Tale* 2.74–75). Their decision that they have reached "the proper Age" (*Tale* 2.74) to cut asyndetically through the real world is mirrored not only by their hacking away at the words of the will and the multiple, self-authorized surgeries on their coats but also by the Tale-writer's morsellation of their story to the point at which the scattered fragments cannot be reconstituted. He admits that they "have now slid out of my Memory, are lost beyond all Hopes of Recovery. . . [in] an Accident past remedy" (*Tale* 11.205). Wounds are undressable, loss is permanent, and investitures of power turn to, in Jack's words, the destructive desire to "*Strip, Tear, Pull, Rent, Flay off all*" (*Tale* 6.139).

Swift's allegory of the coats in *A Tale of a Tub* discloses a radical pessimism about the effective transmission and maintenance of authorized order through words and institutions, a pessimism that by default ratifies a textocentric theory of meaning. Since the *Tale*'s "clothes theology" presents a system of significance severed from its origin and subject to successive interpretive assaults and appropriations, the only site for meaning with any chance for permanence is an orderly fit of words, vested in a self-authorizing, guardian text. But this precarious textocentric condition is hardly a cause for celebration, of artistic license or of human free will, because it is a consequence of man's violation of divine order, a paltry imitation of this order, and an invitation to repeated reenactments of sins against authorized meaning.

In terms of the allegory, the dead father is God, yet Swift seems to be not so much anticipating Nietzsche as reaffirming a belief in the unknowability of the *deus absconditus*. Swift thinks that it is presumptuous to try to understand Divine mystery and to think that God interferes in daily life. Man lives estranged from originating authority, connected by textual threads that to Swift are the only link to God's will yet are almost hopelessly crossed and twisted by human transmission.[5] All men are in the position of Adam, who finds himself adrift in a feral and lawless universe after being ejected from his privileged filial position. Swift's short analysis of the creation and the history it engendered, for example, is marked by ruptured and rapacious order. An inscrutable arche and its remarkably uncommunicative written testament have allowed "the perverseness, the avarice, the tyranny, the pride, the treachery, or inhumanity" of mankind to authorize a frightening, Hobbesian world:[6]

> The text mentioneth nothing of his Maker's intending [Adam] for, except to rule over the beasts of the field and the birds of the air ... However, before his fall, the beasts were his most obedient subjects, when he governed by absolute power. After his eating the forbidden fruit, the course of nature was changed, the animals began to reject his government ... The Scripture mentioneth no particular acts of royalty in *Adam* over his posterity ... or of any monarch until after the flood; whereof the first was *Nimrod*, the mighty hunter who, as Milton expresseth it, made men, and not beasts, his prey ... men degenerate every day. ["Further Thoughts on Religion," *PW* 9:264]

Degeneration is woven into generation. The issue of the creative act contains an inner corruption operating individually and institutionally, as both people and human history deteriorate.[7] So do written words; texts can remain recalcitrantly silent about their maker's intentions, as does the book of Genesis, or can yield to destructive and contradictory interpretations, as does the father's testament in the *Tale*.

The centrality of corruption in Swift's thinking cannot be overestimated. A consequence of original sin, the belief in which contributes to the harsh moral realism invigorating Swift's ironic and polemic works,[8] corruption is a core truth of the Swiftian world. He repeatedly exhibits its formative and deformative force in religion, history, politics, and literature. For example, the early odes show how "northern" barbarians are poised to invade civilizations made soft and vulnerable by internal deterioration; *Sentiments of a Church-of-England Man* details the erosion of respect for Church and State authority; *Gulliver's Travels* indicates that the ancient Lilliputian utopia has rotted into petty factionalism and presents Gulliver, as he concludes his Glubbdubdribbian necromancy by summoning up a historical cross section of Englishmen, lamenting the increased pace of corruption, made visible by exterior signs: "[I]t gave me melancholy Reflections to observe how much the Race of human Kind was degenerate among us, within these Hundred Years past. How the Pox ... had altered every Lineament of an *English* Countenance; shortened the Size of Bodies, unbraced the Nerves, relaxed the Sinews and Muscles, introduced a sallow Complexion, and rendered the Flesh loose and *rancid*" (*GT* 3.8.173). The corrupted body is not just a microcosm of the body political; neither is it an isolated exemplar of the fragmented corpus of the institutionalized church nor of social or racial degeneration over time. Rather, these larger bodies are tropes for the individual human body, the locus for and origin of corruption, the Ur-text from which can be read the signs that mark all corruptions on all bodies. These signs—shrunkenness, flaccidity, and foulness—are the inheritance of sexuality.

Whatever his psychological peculiarities may have been, Swift obviously writes within a tradition of Christian homiletics when he connects sin and decay with sexuality. Like St. Paul and St. Augustine, William Langland and John Skelton, Swift presents the fissured body as proof of internal corruption. What distinguishes Swift from this tradition is his emphasis on corruption as indwelling, inexorable process. In this sense, the Yahoos, often identified as Christian emblems of sin,[9] are anomalous; they are fully realized filthy beasts, perfect in their lewdness and violent emotions, and their nakedness is no more revelatory than that of the Houyhnhnms, similarly complete but clean beasts, perfect in their restraint and reason. More typical of Swift's iconography of corruption are the Struldbruggs, *transi inter vivos* who die every day, eternally,[10] or on a less fanciful level, the assortment of stinking and decaying women inhabiting the scatological poems. In privies, dressing rooms, and marriage beds, these Caelias and Chloes and Corinnas are caught *en deshabille*, and their undressing exposes the unrelentingly repetitive processes of evacuation, disease, and aging. Not even Esther Johnson can escape the physical furrowings of time (see "Stella's Birth-day, 1721," *SPW*, 213–14), but Swift's cloacal nymphs do not have the modesty to cover their nastiness or to protect themselves from a peeping Strephon or Cassinus or Jonathan. Love turns to disgust, the carnal pulls down the spiritual, when the outward forms of order and decency are ignored, perverted, or destroyed. The sexual urge that motivates exposure finds rank fruition in the pox or in repressed coprophilia, in children born, as Augustine said, *inter foeces et urinas*, or in "mortal Ink and Paper of this Generation" that end up as disposable scraps interpreted into new meanings and uses in "a *Jakes*" or "a *Bawdy-house*" ("The Epistle Dedicatory," *Tale*, 32, 36). "Books, like Men their Authors," explains the Tale-writer, "have no more than one Way of coming into the World, but there are ten thousand to go out of it, and return no more" ("The Epistle Dedicatory," *Tale*, 36). We return to the uncovered, orphaned text, stripped into waste paper, vulnerable to the outrages of the world yet complicitous, through its very essence, in its own degradation.

To Swift, stable outward forms defend against the all-pervasive erosion caused by internal corruption. Corruption cannot be stopped, nor should it be, since it is the world's rightful legacy. But it can be slowed, limited, contained, even beneficially disguised. Thus Swift's authoritarianism (his support of constitutional monarchy, of episcopacy, of the Sacramental Test, of plutocratic economics, of nominal Christianity if the alternative is unbridled nonbelief, of censorship, of an Academy to fix the English language) is part of a larger philosophical formalism. Fashioned in part from a seventeenth-century context that distrusts extremism and social or intellectual unrest, Swift's formalism also is based on a grimly uncompromising assessment of the body and the products of the body. He believes that God allowed passion to prevail over reason so that, first, the species can be propagated; and second, man would not despise life "and wish it at an end, or that it never had a beginning," as he reasonably should do ("Thoughts on Religion," *PW* 9:263). This logic, finding sexuality an evasion of death that itself issues from sexual transgression, clearly includes all bodily issue in the cycle of corruption. As the body turns its insides out—its undigested food, its unwritten words, its unborn children—it betrays its origin, and its end.

Hence investiture also serves as a somatocentric trope. Dressing confers power over the body, at least in the sense of accepting God's authority; humans do not live in innocence, and nakedness is shameful.[11] Clothes, like discrete languages, are badges of human sin; as such they are more accurate indices of man's condition than bare skin. In a way they do conceal corruption, but they also display it—in a manner that does not solicit further transgression. The notorious outside/inside dilemma in *A Tale of a Tub*[12] implodes: men are known by their clothes, so "*Suits of Cloathes*, are in Reality . . . Men" (*Tale* 2.78); man was "compounded of two *Dresses*, the *Natural* and the *Celestial Suit* . . . the *Soul* was the outward, and the *Body* the inward *Cloathing*" (*Tale* 2.79). The Tale-writer may be amazed that a flayed woman and a stripped, dissected Beau reveal "unsuspected Faults" (*Tale* 9.173), but Swift is not. One can prefer the outside to the inside on aesthetic grounds, but not on ontological ones.

Nevertheless, authoritatively invested outsides can regulate unauthorized proliferation of insides, and the authority that Swift overtly invokes is usually institutional. This reasoning sanctions the Brobdingnagian legal code, laws being unable to "exceed in Words the Number of Letters in their Alphabet; which consists only of two and twenty," thereby preserving themselves from multiple interpretations and legal commentaries, the latter practice discouraged further by being named a capital crime (*GT* 2.6.111). It also sanctions *A Project for the Advancement of Religion and the Reformation of Manners*. In view of "universal and deep-rooted Corruptions," having a ruler exercise lawful authority to make "Piety and Virtue become the Fashion of the Age" (*PW* 2:47) can be a remedy. Outward form can re-form inward chaos, and disguise can shift into regulatory clothing. "Hypocrisy is much more eligible than open Infidelity and Vice," Swift maintains. "It wears the Livery of Religion, it acknowledges her Authority. . . . Nay, a long continued Disguise is too great a Constraint upon human Nature . . . Men would leave off their Vices out of mere Weariness . . . it is often with Religion as it is with Love; which, by much Dissembling, at last grows real" (*PW* 2:57). Again, clothing is a metaphor of invested outer form that can coerce the rebellious inside into harmonious congruity, annihilating deception and dichotomy.

Human beings, however, resist the constraints of outer form, of institutionally authorized dress and propriety and linguistic stability. Swift's myth of investiture in *A Tale of a Tub*, section 2, reveals how man habitually upsets ordered decency. Man-as-microcoat is presented not as putting on physical and mental garments but as taking them off.

As to his Body, there can be no dispute; but examine even the Acquirements of his Mind, you will find them all contribute in their Order, towards furnishing out an exact Dress: To instance no more; Is not Religion a *Cloak*, Honesty a *Pair of Shoes*, worn out in the Dirt, Self-Love a *Surtout*, Vanity a *Shirt*, and Conscience a *Pair of Breeches*, which, tho' a Cover for Lewdness as well as Nastiness, is easily slipt down for the Service of both. [*Tale* 2.78]

This sequence of undressing lists items in the order in which most men take off their clothes: outerwear, shoes, surtout (or suit jacket or cassock), shirt, pants. Without the outer covering, corruptive inner forces can be exteriorized, escaping the ordering of investiture to breed and contaminate and usurp.

The urge to undress, sandwiched in the overview of the vestmental religion, activates the three brothers' specific undressings of the authoritative word and the improper dressings of the form-giving coat. Wishing to authorize fashionable shoulder-knots, for instance, the brothers strip words from sentences, detach syllables from words, separate letters from syllables, and expel any troublesome letters like the "modern illegitimate Letter K" (*Tale* 2.84) from the family textual group. These primary violations of verbal integrity perhaps explain Swift's insistence upon proper verbal form, his dislike of abbreviations and unorthodox spellings (e.g., *A Proposal for Correcting ... the English Tongue, PW* 4:11; *The Tatler* #230, *PW* 2:175–77); once the outer form of a word is attacked, the inner meaning lies bare, vulnerable to perversions, to appropriations, and to the generation of illegitimate issue. Like the abandoned book at the beginning of the *Tale*, naked texts and their unprotected meanings are orphaned from originating authority, and the textile filaments of literary relationships among authors, texts, and readers, are wounded and unwound. In the main allegory of *A Tale of a Tub*, the father's will is replaced and forgotten; the text is disfigured and banished; the brothers usurp the *jure paterno* and ultimately fall into unresolvable internecine warfare.

Intertwined and mutually cancelling authorities contribute to Swift's conservative textocentrism, one valuing not open textual play but closed textual guardianship. By acting *in loco parentis*, the written word performs its own usurpations of generating authority and generated meanings. Therefore, after the brothers demolish the authority of the word as written, they are able to substitute alternate authorities: the word as spoken, the word as added, the word as troped, the word as altered, the word as hidden. In the *Tale*, these unreliable authorities criticize theological and exegetical practices of the Roman Catholic church such as recourse to oral tradition and to the Apocrypha, but the point extends to writing in general.[13] For Swift, written form is not necessarily limited to serving as an expendable and subsequent outside for a spoken or about-to-be spoken word. Instead, Swift inverts traditional logocentrism:[14] the outside becomes essential and prior to the inside; the durability of written language precedes, transcends, and authorizes spoken expression. Such is the import of the parenthetical comment in *A Proposal for Correcting . . . the English Tongue*; after asserting that people should not spell as they speak, Swift explains, "It would be just as wise as to shape our Bodies to our Cloathes and not our Cloaths to our bodyes" (*PW* 4:11).[15] Inscription is the authorized, invested body of language.

FIXING OUR LANGUAGE FOR EVER

Swift's best-known solution to the problem of investing language with proper authority is *A Proposal for Correcting, Improving, and Ascertaining the English Tongue*, a pamphlet endowed with the rare personal authority of his own signature. The main premise is simple and straightforward: since linguistic change opens space for linguistic corruption, institutional defense against change can close or at least slow the process of decay. Swift states that

> our Language is extremely imperfect; that its daily Improvements are by no Means in Proportion to its daily Corruptions; that the Pretenders to polish and refine it, have chiefly multiplied Abuses and Absurdities; and that in many Instances, it offends against every Part of Grammar . . . if it were once refined to a certain Standard, perhaps there might be Ways to fix it for ever, or at least till we are invaded, and made a Conquest by some other State. [*PW* 4:6, 9]

Swift's suggested remedy is the establishment of an authorizing society, modeled on the French Academy, invested with the power to fix the English language—both in the sense of refurbishing or correcting damaged words and usage and in the sense of making language a stable, relatively closed system.[16] Behind the first sense of "fix" lies Swift's irritation at abbreviations, random spellings, cant phrases; behind the second crouches a perceived threat of urgent danger. If the two meanings of "fix" collide, Swift would have the first yield to the second:

> [W]hat I have most at Heart, is ... Fixing our Language for ever ... it is better a Language should not be wholly perfect, than that it should be perpetually changing; and we must give over at one Time or other, or at length infallibly change for the worse ... As the Romans did ... such as we meet in *Tacitus* and other Authors, which ended by Degrees in many Barbarities, even before the *Goths* had invaded Italy. [*PW* 4:14]

Swift's use of political and military metaphors and allusions to describe the dangers of linguistic change is striking. It struck the Whigs, who called the *Proposal* a partisan document, espousing Jacobitism and Tory cronyism;[17] Swift, however, maintained that "tis no Politicks, but a harmless Proposall" (letter 47, 31 May 1712, *JS* 2:555), and he envisioned society membership open to both parties (*Proposal, PW* 4:14; letter to Archbishop King, 29 Mar. 1712, *Corr.* 1:295). Since the format of the *Proposal* is an epistolary appeal to Harley and since Swift actively sought to strengthen his position in the Tory literary establishment, his disclaimers are rather disingenuous. Moreover, his embattled tone is reminiscent of his description of his clerical office as "one appointed by providence for defending a post assigned me, and for gaining over as many enemies as I can" ("Thoughts on Religion," *PW* 9:262); it casts Swift in the role of defender of the established literary faith against upstart wits whose works "have over-run us for some Years past" (*Proposal, PW* 4:12).

The socio-political ramifications of Swift's ideological linguistics surface in a different way in *The Tatler* #230, the precursor to the *Proposal*. In the *Tatler* essay, Swift deals humorously with specific instances of linguistic corruption and suggests a tyrannical power play in which official words would control rebellious ones—a suggestion that, in light of his serious calls for censorship of subversive or irreligious writings (e.g., *The Sentiments of a Church-of-England Man, PW* 2:10), is only partially hyperbolic. The letter-writer tells the *Tatler* editor that such linguistic abuses are ones "you ought to correct: First, by Arguments and fair means; but if those fail, I think you are to make use of your Authority as Censor, and by an annual *Index Expurgatorius*, expunge all Words and Phrases that are offensive to good Sense, and condemn those barbarious Mutilations of Vowels and Syllables" (*The Tatler* #230, *PW* 2:176). The particular opprobrium received by "Mob" (the abbreviation for *mobile vulgus*) and "banter" (a new coinage that Swift had explained as originating with the bullies of White-Friars and moving to the custody of footmen and pedants, cf. "The Apology," *Tale*, 19) stems not merely from the words' unaesthetic form or unauthorized novelty. As Ian Watt has pointed out, their meanings convey the forces that corrupt language and the ordered society of language users; fixed language is threatened by the shifting crowd and their hostile, common words.[18] Again, Swift is the beleaguered guardian of linguistic purity, and the "war" is social and political as well as verbal: "I have done my utmost for some Years past, to stop the Progress of *Mob* and *Banter*, but have been plainly born down by Numbers, and betrayed by those who promised to assist me" (*The Tatler* #230, *PW* 2:176).

Throughout the *Proposal*, the text offers the trope of language as political history drawn from a conservative Tory standpoint: languages like nations endure cycles of corruptions from within and invasions from without; they are subject to "great Revolutions" (*PW* 4:9) by means of pretenders and usurpers, conquerers and barbarian hordes. The imperiled, interlocked hierarchies contaminate each other as well. Unruly and licentious society infects and corrupts language; improper and incorrect language subverts and weakens society. Just as the Puritans' overthrow of England's governmental institutions began with a seemingly innocuous campaign against clerical clothes and ended in the crumbling structures and mumbling tongues of Babel, the corrupters of language who abuse the outer forms of words will bring about a new reign of Babel in which people from different English towns and counties will not be able to understand each other and history itself will atrophy since, with the passage of time, it will become virtually unreadable. Unregulated change, then, leads to disorderly stagnation, to "Mortification" (*PW* 4:18). According to the logic of the *Proposal*, preserving life in language requires entombing language within regulations against change.

This paradox exposes the rigor mortis of this particular attempt to prevent de-authorization of *langue* by history and by individual linguistic abuses of *parole*. Even Swift's rather feeble aside, that "I do not mean that [our Language] should never be enlarged" (*PW* 4:15) because new knowledge must be able to be accommodated, is wedged between references to sepulchered language: first, the example of enduring stylistic simplicity provided by the burial service in the *Book of Common Prayer*; second, a rebuttal of "What *Horace* says of Words going off, and perishing like Leaves, and new ones coming in their Place" through reference to the continued existence of Horace's writings, "his *Monumentum aere pe-*

rennius" (*PW* 4:16). Making monuments, it seems, is what Swift's institutionally and inscriptively authorized language is best suited to do. And language can only perform this function through being written, by trading the authorizations of originating presence and guardianship of meaning for the authorization of enduring visible form. "Words more durable than Brass" can correct "that false Compliment to Princes: That the most lasting Monument . . . is the Hearts of their Subjects" (*PW* 4:17). Without a fixed language, preserving "the Memory of Times and Persons" is "like employing an excellent Statuary to work upon mouldring Stone" (*PW* 4:17–18). With a fixed language, "our best Writings might probably be preserved . . . and the Authors have a chance for Immortality" (*PW* 4:9).

Forty years after Swift wrote the *Proposal*, Samuel Johnson entertained the same perverse dream of interring language to protect it from change. Johnson's *The Plan of An English Dictionary* has as its "great end . . . to fix the English language," its "purity, and . . . meaning," preserving orthography and pronunciation from "corruptions of living speech," guarding against illegitimate words so that the elements of language "might attain the firmness and immutability of the primogenial and constituent particles of matter."[19] Johnson actually tried to carry out his own proposal; in so doing, he discovered that one man's authority, or that of any sanctioning body organized at a specific point in time, cannot counterbalance the disordered vitality of verbal form and significance. He admitted in the 1755 "Preface to the Dictionary" that he had learned that words were imperfect daughters of the earth, that "while our language is yet living, and variable [, many] words are hourly shifting" and their "exuberance of signification" defies fixing or differentiating shades of meaning. Johnson's experience directs him to laugh at his attempt to insulate language "from mutability. . . [to] embalm his language, and secure it from corruption and decay."[20]

Swift did not have to recant because his scheme was never instituted. Yet his works as a whole give ample evidence of his practical repudiation of it or, at least, of his ability to allow liberal textocentric practice to exist within the boundaries of a larger, conservative textocentric program. His writings do exploit the exuberance of signification, and they abound with coinages, abbreviations, fashionable phrases, and strange spellings arrayed for playful as well as for satiric purposes. Moreover, removal to Ireland caused Swift to question some forms of institutional authority; his post-1720 writings evidence this distrust and show a revaluation of liberal linguistic attitudes. Near the end of his career, he praised the "genius" of his early work, *A Tale of a Tub*, that most open-formed, linguistically chaotic composition, and he lampooned fixed linguistic structures in *Polite Conversation*. But two episodes in *Gulliver's Travels*, book 3—the visits to the Struldbruggs and to the Academy of Lagado's language machine—stand as Swift's most specific disavowals of the linguistically conservative ideas behind the *Proposal*.

Swift had suggested in the *Proposal* that the problem of meaning could be solved, or perhaps bypassed, by walling significance within the language institution that, if well fortified against invasion, could protect meaning from the corruption of time and thus guarantee memory. Fixed linguistic structure is the starting point; enduring linguistic memory is the result. The authorizing sequence, however, is altered in the land of the Struldbruggs, and the alteration discloses the essential causative function of memory. Hopelessly senile and devastatingly immortal, the Struldbruggs cannot communicate because their memories atrophy along with their bodies; they cannot talk because they forget words; they cannot read because they forget the beginnings of sentences by the time they reach the ends; and they cannot understand mortals or Struldbruggs of another age, "[t]he Language of this Country being always upon the Flux" (*GT* 3.10.213). Verbal meaning is sealed off from time, entombed in a structure that will never die. Gulliver's visit to the Struldbruggs shows that without the authority of memory, without the ability to think through time and to adapt to the inevitable changes of language, meaning has no meaning and the institution of language collapses.

The image of the Academy of Lagado's language machine reveals another criticism of fixed linguistic structure:

> It was Twenty Foot square, placed in the Middle of the Room. The Superficies was composed of several Bits of Wood, about the Bigness of a Dye, but some larger than others. They were all linked together by slender Wires. These Bits of Wood were covered on every Square with Paper pasted on them; and on these Papers were written all the Words of their Language in their several Moods, Tenses, and Declensions, but without any Order . . . at every Turn the Engine was so contrived, that the Words shifted into new Places, as the square Bits of Wood moved upside down. [*GT* 3.5.184]

The physical site of meaning exhibits a crazed, mechanical fixity. The huge frame occupies the whole laboratory, and its components are linked by an interlocked network of wires. Fixity is reinforced by linguistic completeness: the machine contains the Lagadan language's entire vocabulary, grammatical structure, and traditional syntactic arrangements, "the strictest Computation of the general Proportion there is in Books between the Numbers of Particles, Nouns, and Verbs, and other Parts of Speech" (*GT* 3.5.184). Thus the frame represents language—the given language as the repository of meanings and possibilities against which all language users draw, the authorizing source for "those rich Materials [that can] give the World a compleat Body of all Arts and Sciences" (*GT* 3.5.184). Although in this reductive trope Swift is attacking the institution of *langue* by parodying the notion of fixity, he is also exposing the abuses and illusions of *parole*.

The most obvious point of attack is the substitution of mechanical operation for conscious and conscientious authorization, either by individual intelligence or by traditional knowledge. Even "the most ignorant Person," explains Gulliver, can use the frame to produce writings "without the least Assistance from Genius or Study" (*GT* 3.5.183–84). Such texts join Swift's other products of mechanical operations—the zeal worked up by Enthusiasts, the project to turn Irish babies into cash crops carefully calculated by the Modest Proposer—in a lineup of at best meaningless and at worst pernicious creations. The writings cranked out from the machine are not only nonsense but vicious nonsense. They are violent decompositions, the occasional fragmentary meanings promised by "broken sentences" (*GT* 3.5.184) being the issue of deliberate linguistic corruption, of breaking apart. Their recomposition, despite the dreams of the projector, would consume almost infinite amounts of wasted time and labor. The fragments of meaning are also the children of chance; they ride on wooden blocks "about the Bigness of a Dye." To Swift, chance is a vicious explanation of causality because it denies any sort of authorized order. As he writes in "A Tritical Essay Upon the Faculties of the Mind," embedding in his opening paragraph the standard of order against which the incoherent and unruly patchwork of garbled citations and ideas will be measured satirically, "how can the *Epicureans* Opinion be true, that the Universe was formed by a fortuitous Concourse of Atoms; which I will no more believe, than that the accidental Jumbling of the Letters in the Alphabet, could fall by Chance into a most ingenious and learned Treatise of Philosophy, *Risum teneatis Amici, HOR.*" (*PW* 1:247).

Thus another point of attack is the *parole*-operator's disregard of the order inherent in and necessary to *langue*. The Lagadan language machine is designed on the principles of disorder and displacement. Words, positioned "without any Order," must be "shifted into new Places" and "moved upside down." Throughout Swift's writings, this type of reversal signals his displeasure and despair, his apparently genuine belief that man's natural condition is to be "a topsy-turvy Creature[, h]is Animal Faculties perpetually mounted on his Rational; his Head where his Heels should be, groveling on the earth" (*A Meditation upon a Broom-stick*, PW 1:240). Man as physical being wrenches himself out of his proper place; man as language user, either author or reader, wrenches words out of their proper contexts. And it is the synthetic concept of "proper words in proper places" that Swift uses to address the problem of fitting the order of *parole* to the order of *langue*, the problem of investing texts with authority and of fixing the language without turning it into a Struldbruggian death rattle or a capricious and impersonal Lagadan machine.

PROPER WORDS IN PROPER PLACES

Investiture is placement within an authorized order, outer forms realizing inner significance. Swift's *A Proposal for Correcting . . . the English Tongue* suggests a way to preserve the authorized order of language from without; a deterministic institution could exclude individually expressive usages, presentations, and meanings. It also would prohibit liberal textocentric usurpations. In one sense, the desire for depersonalized institutional authority denudes men's actions and words of moral quality: tyrannical or collective decision supersedes individual responsibility. Such an arrangement is necessary if one believes, with Hobbes, in man's fundamental irrationality and natural brutishness. In another sense, such an argument may be welcome if one believes, with Shaftesbury or the Cambridge Platonists, that a carefully designed social institution can foster man's innate rationality and moral conscience;[21] in this case, institutions would fortify individual responsibility. Swift, particularly in the years before the death of Queen Anne, seems to adhere to both beliefs. For instance, the Hobbesian *An Argument Against the Abolishment of Christianity* discredits the existence of remnants of true faith that, along with feigned faith, the Shaftesburian *A Proposal for the Advancement of Christianity* wishes to foster. Swift does not advocate abdicating self to system completely, unless the system deserves unquestioning obedience, as do the institutions of constitutional monarchy or the churches of England and Ireland.[22] Even in these cases, however, Swift feels obliged to set himself against individual components of the system, as his rancorous disputes with bishops and politicians attest. This is especially true in works written before his resettlement in Ireland; as will be discussed in chapters 5 and 6, Swift's mature involvement in Irish politics shook his trust in institutional authority itself and the systems that embody it.

In considerations of language, Swift also sets self against system in matter and manner. His literary innovations frequently develop through parodic inversion or creative scrambling and therefore actually ratify traditional literary authority, but the authorial quality Swift seems to value most highly in himself is originality. His defensiveness about *A Tale of a Tub* could be extended to cover his total literary output; he asserts that originality is a *"tender Point . . . he has not borrowed one single Hint from any Writer in the World . . . He conceived* [his work] *was never disputed to be an Original, whatever Faults it might have"* ("The Apology," *Tale*, 13). Often, the words themselves were "all his own" (*Verses on the Death*, SPW 506.318), neologisms concocted for play (for self) and for satire (of system). Swift's valorization of verbal originality, therefore, pushes his best-known definition of style—"Proper Words in proper Places" (*A Letter to a Young Gentleman, Lately enter'd into Holy Orders*, PW 9:65)—toward falsehood, error, self-deception, or towards another kind of verbal authoritarianism. Rather than preserving language from without, as advocated in *A Proposal for Correcting . . . the English Tongue*, in *A Letter* Swift advises preserving language from within, by disciplining *parole*. One can invest one's own text with the authority of "propriety" and place one's words in order. Style, then, helps to guarantee meaning; it fits individual language products to institutional language structures.

Swift's bland dictum has received much attention because he rarely addressed himself specifically to style. Some critics have de-emphasized it by pointing out that the letter is concerned largely with pulpit oratory, not with imaginative or polemic writing. Perhaps embarrassed by drawing-room visions of primly crossed *t*'s and syllables sitting neatly in a row, visions not unsupported by Swift's own advocacy of proper written form in *The Tatler* #230, other critics dismiss the comment as a throwaway piece of advice he did not really mean.[23] Swift's continuing engagement with the concepts of verbal propriety and placement suggests, however, that he meant what he wrote; the entire letter glosses his definition and extends it beyond clerical speech. *A Letter to a Young Gentleman* describes a literary formalism designed to counter more disruptive textocentric impulses, and it seriously examines the question of verbal authority. Nevertheless, Swift's own playing with terms complicates and perhaps undermines the formalism they attempt to define.

"Proper Words in proper Places, makes the true Definition of a Stile: But this would require too ample a Disquisition to be now dwelt on" (*PW* 9:65). Swift knows that the maxim's apparent simplicity is misleading. *Proper* can mean "suitable," "correct," "decorous," "supportive," "appropriated," and "one's own"; *places* can mean "physical environments," "specific locations," "relative scalar points," "property," "status," and "employment." Using only these subdefinitions, one can arrive at 216 different readings of Swift's sentence. Swift's disclaimer is also misleading, for he does dwell on, and within, the multiple meanings constructed into his aphorism. In general, he uses both large senses of "proper" ("relating to self" and "decent") and both large senses of "place" ("definable space" and "relative situation"). For instance, he warns against vulgar, mean, or threadbare expressions which "when applied in the Pulpit, appear by a quaint, tense, florid Style, rounded into Periods and Cadencies, commonly without either Propriety or Meaning . . . [they are] indecent . . . and will seldom express your Meaning as well as your own natural Words" (*PW* 9:681). Such words are out of place in context, since they are appropriate to the coffee house but not to the church; they are also out of place in syntax, since tension between intention and presentation creates unnatural style. Their impropriety arises not only from unsuitable context and inappropriate syntax but also from indecency (an absolute judgment) and lack of ownership or natural generation (a relative quality). Meaning is also at double peril. Improper words can be absolutely "without . . . Meaning" or relatively ineffective in expressing authorial intent. They fail according to both the ideational and the behavioral theories of language.

The letter's behavioral presuppositions are bound to the question of order, of authorized placement. Although probably written for the general public rather than for a specific acquaintance,[24] it features a titular advisee who has recently entered Holy Orders, the authorized hierarchy of the Church which, theologically, guards Divine Order on earth and, historically, replaced the disorder of the fragmented Roman Empire.[25] His entrance, however, has been made in a state of disorder; having rushed through his studies retaining only snippets of learning, the ill-prepared clergyman hurries to seek his living wherever he can. Swift's ostensible purpose, then, is to keep or strengthen order within Order. Well-ordered clerical discourse helps its deliverer avoid ridicule and disdain, but more important it combats ignorance, the genesis of moral corruption, political unrest, and "Contempt ... for the whole Order" (*PW* 9:80). An effective style is vital to these tasks, since it is through ordered words that the quaternary message of order (Divine, Ecclesiastical, political, individual) is transmitted. Hard words, for example, are out of place because the audience will not understand them; extravagant emotional appeals are not "of any great Use towards directing Christian Men in the Conduct of their Lives" (*PW* 9:69). Improper placement causes disorder, the disorder issuing not from an absence of order but from a clash of incongruent orders.[26]

Nevertheless, Swift cautions against absolutist behavioral standards of authorial intent. Desire is not meaning; in fact, words can accurately convey desire (the wish to appear learned or worldly, for instance) and in so doing obscure or destroy meaning. The authorizing force thus becomes ideational. "When a Man's Thoughts are clear," Swift explains, "the properest Words will generally offer themselves first; and his own Judgment will direct him in what Order to place them, so as they may be best understood" (*PW* 9:68). However, Swift undercuts his Lockean assumptions by moving placement and order from context to syntax. Personal judgment seems to be relegated to fitting words to an orderly structure which accurately displays their natural significance. Swift's comments thus contain elements of referential theory: words themselves have inherent, atomistic meanings, and a language system (the grammatical and syntactical grid of placement) has determinative, combinatory meaning. Verbal impropriety, then, can be an absolute and impersonal quality of writing. For example, Swift's "Short Remarks on Bishop Burnet's History" imputes to the author a rough style, "full of improprieties" (*PW* 5:183). Checking Swift's marginal comments in Burnet's volume identifies these improprieties as redundancy, repetitiousness, ambiguous pronouns, affected words, choppy sentence rhythms, and unnecessary tense shifts (*PW* 5:266–94). Yet Swift's concern with what Jacques Derrida has called the "metaphysics of the proper"[27] keeps the authorial self as counterforce to predeterminative definitions, usages, or grammatical rules. The self is invested in the text; the text should be proper to the self.

Therefore, an equally undesirable abuse of propriety occurs when an author cedes his text to other writers; words are no longer proper because they belong to someone else. Throughout the *Letter to a Young Gentle-*

man, Swift lauds verbal originality as discourse's authorizing force: one's thoughts should be clothed in one's own words, not in a borrowed fabric appliqued with quotations from other authorities.[28] One reason is that authorities frequently are not authoritative. For religious discourse, the classic philosophers have limited use because of "the Want of Divine Sanction; without which [they] failed in the Point of Authority" (*PW* 9:73), although Swift carefully points out the value of their moral and ethical insights. Similarly, the ancient church fathers should be consulted with caution because they "lived in the Decline of Literature," because they should be revered for their holiness rather than for their "Genius and Learning," and because "many of [their texts] have extreamly suffer'd by spurious additions" (*PW* 9:74). A second reason is that borrowed words eclipse men's "own natural Reason" (*PW* 9:76). Stitching together references from concordances and commonplace books replaces one's proper words with "a manifest incoherent Piece of Patchwork" (*PW* 9:76). Swift treats even Biblical citation as a necessary evil which threatens proper words: "I do not altogether disapprove the Manner of interweaving Texts of Scripture through the Style of your Sermon; wherein, however, I have sometimes observed great Instances of Indiscretion and Impropriety" (*PW* 9:75). As for quotations from other religous authorities, Swift suggests an almost wholesale appropriation: early church fathers can be cited on specific doctrinal points, but "In other Cases, we give you full Power to adopt the Sentence for your own, rather than tell us, *as St. Austin excellently observes*"; inappropriate and unappropriated reference to the words of modern writers should be completely banned, for "to mention [them] by Name, or use the Phrase *of a late excellent Prelate of our Church*, and the like, is altogether intolerable" (*PW* 9:75).

Swift's belief that propriety is a function of ownership, not necessarily an essentialist quality of words themselves, also motivates many of his satires. *Polite Conversation*, for instance, burlesques popular conversation manuals and the folly of learning sophistication by rote;[29] but its strangeness emanates from Swift's techniques of depersonalization,[30] from the disconcerting interchangeability of the speakers and their lines. The dialogues owe their bizarre nature not to their basic inanity[31] or to their apparent endlessness, but to their renegade neutrality: all characters appropriate whatever phrase is handy, with no thought of making words their own. To highlight the mechanical nature of the discourse, Swift lets his persona, Simon Wagstaff, patently misinterpret his own text, declaring that he has made "every Character in the Dialogue, agreeable with itself

... all the persons ... strictly observe a different Manner peculiar to their Characters, which are of different Kinds" (Introduction to *Polite Conversation, PW* 4:114). Yet Wagstaff soon boasts that these individual linguistic manners are, instead, universally applicable—proper to all people at all times:

> Those [expressions] which are proper for Morning Tea, will be equally useful at the same Entertainment in the Afternoon, even in the same Company, only by shifting the several Questions, Answers, and Replies, into different Hands. [*PW* 4:118–19]

Thus the treatise exhibits the same weird fixity as the language machine at Lagado. Everything is contained within the scheme, and linguistic elements need only a shift of place within the fixed frame to become original discourse. Moreover, the rearrangeable elements also possess fixed values that, in turn, stabilize the institution of language. Wagstaff explains, "unto [these polite sayings] we owe the Continuance of our Language for at least an hundred Years ... Because such is the Propriety and Energy of them all, that they never can be changed" (*PW* 4:107). In *Polite Conversation*, proper words in proper places yield nonsense when words are proper to everyone and their proper place paralyzes *langue* and prohibits original *parole*.

A similar nonsense is produced by the scrambled sayings assembled in "A Tritical Essay upon the Faculties of the Mind." Written in 1707, it cheerfully demonstrates stylistic faults Swift would criticize seriously in *A Proposal for Correcting ... the English Tongue* and *A Letter to a Young Gentleman*. The essay, a crazy quilt of quotations sewn with no regard for coherence, shows the consequences of improper appropriation. The author's vows of complete originality intensify his wholesale plagiarism, as does his inability to place his borrowed words in any sort of communicative order. The point of "A Tritical Essay" and of *Polite Conversation* is pointlessness; both satires provide negative confirmations of Swift's beliefs about verbal authority, proprietorship, and placement.

These beliefs are complicated further by the fact that Swift does not always write *in propria persona*; the authorizing voice for many of his texts is a fabricated verbal proprietor. Pseudonymity and anonymity do, in a sense, de-authorize a text; in a practical manner, they distance and protect the actual author from criticism. But they are also modes of authorization. Anonymity can invest the unknown writer with mysterious, unassailable authority; an anonymous political tract, for instance, leaves open the possibility that its author is intimately and importantly connected with the great events and people he describes and judges. Pseudonymity confers a similar but fictive authority: in Swift's writings, personae are fitted to their texts through appropriate style and placement.

The styles in which most of Swift's personae present themselves and their ideas are quite similar. The writings of Gulliver, the Drapier, Simon Wagstaff, even a collaborative persona like Captain Creichton, exhibit stylistic homogeneity: a paucity of modifiers, reliance upon nouns and verbs, seriatim rather than embedded clauses, literalization of metaphor, reification of abstractions, torturing of clichés.[32] Such stylistic consanguinity links persona to persona and subjects them all to the control of their creator, a state of affairs discernible not only to today's readers but to Swift's contemporary audience, which was becoming more and more aware of Swift's disguised identities as his controversial writing career progressed. The overall stylistic intents of these personae are also similar. Gulliver's publisher explains that Gulliver's "Style is very plain and simple ... There is an Air of Truth apparent through the whole" ("The Publisher to the Reader," *GT*, 9); the Drapier in his first letter promises to "tell you the plain Story of the Fact" (*PW* 10:4); Wagstaff's useful conversational science will "avoid the Vexations and Impertinence of Pedants; who affect to talk in a Language not to be understood," and there is "not one single Sentence in the whole collection, for which [Wagstaff] cannot bring most authentic Vouchers" (*PW* 4:104, 114); Captain Creichton's memoirs are "written in a plain unaffected Style" which will "never willfully fail in Point of Truth" (*PW* 5:123). Such declarations and the stylistic presentations which enact them reinforce the obstinately objective yet passionately committed stance the personae take toward the "truth" of their words. They all try to exert the authority of adherence to observed fact; moreover, they have been properly placed in real or fictional situations so they can report what they have seen or heard, even if they misinterpret its significance: Gulliver shipwrecked on foreign shores, the Drapier operating a shop in Dublin's weaving district, Wagstaff ensconced at society tea-tables, Creichton marching through Scottish battlegrounds. Swift distrusts hearsay, as his marginal comments upon various histories indicate,[33] so he invests his personae with the authority of direct participation.

Yet authorized meanings are not automatic properties of real or imagined eyewitness accounts. If the personae are tenants of bounded fictional spaces, Swift remains the landlord, exerting a supplementary, sometimes overriding, control.[34] The rather univocal style imprints Swift as well as the persona in the text. As it does so, it writes intertextual inscriptions about literary meaning and moral truth. When these imprints match, as they do in most of the *Drapier's Letters*, for example, they have the force of double authorization. When they are askew, when the verbal significance read one way by the persona is contradicted by intertextual evidence or by common sense and compassion, a gap opens: the space of irony.

Ironic writing is dangerous property because the author has divested himself of authority over his words and replaced bounded place with open space.[35] Meaning becomes a *tertium quid* held in joint ownership by readers and by the text, and the hold can be so precarious that meaning can be dislodged or disowned altogether. Both poles of propriety can generate dangers. Some readers fail to find any irony at all; those who collapse the space between persona and author in *A Modest Proposal*, for instance, can interpret the work as a serious, outrageous suggestion. The converse of this occurs when readers manufacture an ironic gap that may not exist in order to redeem or replace uncongenial meanings; to interpret the last half of *Verses on the Death* as ironic, for example, could be a deliberate misreading intended to save Swift from unbecoming self-praise.[36] Both types of misreading mishandle the text's tensile strength, making it more or less flexible than it is. Texts can also suffer by creating and occupying spaces that are too mobile, too unbounded. Readers of *A Modest Proposal* who do traverse and interpret its dilating ironic gap often are puzzled when the gap seems to close suddenly, when Swift breaks through the persona and lists his own serious but unheeded projects for helping Ireland.[37] The text appears to abscond with its own interpretive boundary markers, and it can fall into its own gaps. Book 4 of *Gulliver's Travels* occupies similarly treacherous terrain: what are the limits of its ironic space? That a text poses such a question does not indicate a failure of language or of authority, if literary success can be measured by centuries of reader interest and disagreement. Book 4 is situated on the horizon of ironic space, the high-reward, high-risk site where the potentials of meaning are spread to their fullest expanse but also are at the verge of dropping off into nothingness. The perilous de-authorization necessary to irony—its impropriety, its relinquishing of ownership—must be countered by careful spatial management, by the substitution of verbal property for verbal proprietorship. This substitution serves to safeguard not only irony but other literary modes and purposes as well.

TO TRAVEL THRO' THIS VAST WORLD OF WRITINGS

Treating texts as verbal property requires that writing be ordered within spatial territory, and territory is differentiated from infinity or from no-man's-land by limits, boundaries, and lines of demarcation. Some of the limits are physical. A book's cover and binding define its existence in space; individual poems or prose pieces are authorized as discrete units of verbal property by titles and margins. Swift's awareness of the physical boundaries of writing is shown both by his attention to printed format, most notably the bibliosatire shaping *A Tale of a Tub*, and by his frequent conceit of the unauthorized text—the habit of anonymity or pseudonymity often literalized into works that have "lost" their covers or title pages. Within these physical limits, however, operate more complex and problematic limits. Swift designs systematics of placement, theoretical and topographical, to authorize the writer's proper place within and control over the text and to protect its meanings from critical misappropriations.

Swift's views about nonverbal property and placement can illuminate his treatment of textual territory. Swift had a plutocratic belief that wealth, power, and status should stem from real property, from the land and its products. Nevertheless, he inherited no property and his life was a series of migrations between England and Ireland, from country estate to court to rural parish to city cathedral.[38] He thought of himself as a perpetual exile, and his longing for an English bishopric was as much a desire for environmental permanence to compensate for misplaced origins as it was a desire for money and prestige. Ireland was always, to Swift, an improper place. It was not only a "Land of slaves" ("Ireland," *SPW* 332.1) and natural desolation (see "Holyhead. Sept. 25, 1727," *SPW* 331.29–32) but also a land menaced by displacement. The displacers ranged from absentee landlords who displaced themselves yet stripped the land of its resources to the mobs of displaced persons, the "strolling beggars" whose itinerant mendicancy roused Swift's anger. In his sermon, "Causes of the Wretched Condition of Ireland," Swift addresses this specific problem by translating the doctrine of "proper words in proper places" into the realm of social policy. Beggars could be issued badges identifying their place of origin; these badges, easily and unmistakably legible, would authorize charity. Proper meaning would be bound to proper place, and order would be restored by preventing unauthorized movement:

For, if every Parish would take a List of those begging Poor which properly belong to it, and compel each of them to wear a Badge, marked and numbered, so as to be seen and known by all they meet, and confine them to beg within the Limits of their own Parish ... and driving out all Interlopers from other Parishes, we could then make a Computation of their Numbers; and the Strolers from the Country being driven away ... neither would any Beggar, although confined to his own Parish, be hindered from receiving the Charity of the whole Town; because in this Case, those well disposed Persons who walk the Streets, will give their Charity to such whom they think proper Objects ... provided they are ... wearing their Badges of Distinction. [*PW* 9:207–8]

Beggars would be invested into the social order through exterior signs, graphic marks of communication affixed to their clothes. They would wear their words, like Wordsworth's blind beggar in *The Prelude*, book 7, words that would articulate their origin and authorize their destiny. Moreover, the meanings of the words would be predetermined by their textual space; the "well-disposed Persons" could read the book of Dublin and understand the unequivocal significance of its signs. The persistence with which Swift pursued his scheme to give badges to beggars[39] indicates a commitment not only to solving one real social problem but also to realizing its metaphoric goal: the self-articulating text invested with semic safeguards against unauthorized interpretations.

Swift's coercive, boundary-setting vocabulary ("properly belong," "compel," "confine," "within the Limits," "driving out") underscores his design and points back to the tactics of exclusionary and inclusionary verbal space he employed in the fifth edition of *A Tale of a Tub*. Earlier editions had been assaulted by unauthorized interpretations; those that charged the book with abuse of religion were potentially harmful since Swift's authorship was widely suspected. The most influential and hostile criticism came from Swift's literary enemy William Wotton, who, with Richard Bentley's assistance, appended "Observations upon the *Tale of a Tub*" to his published rebuttal of Temple. According to Wotton, in the "irreligious" and "crude" *Tale*, "God and Religion, Truth and Moral Honesty, Learning and Industry are made a May-Game" to show "at the bottom [the author's] contemptible Opinion of every Thing which is called Christianity."[40] Although Swift's usual stance towards contemporary writers was to ignore them so they would not gain parasitical fame,[41] in this case Swift retaliated by appropriating Wotton's words and placing them "at the bottom" of his own text. Wotton is forced into his proper place: subordinate, marginal, unnecessary.[42] To do this, Swift uses spatial juxtaposition to reveal the shallowness of Wotton's commentary and to prove his own charge that criticism is a mirror that "will cast *Reflections* from its own *Superficies*, without any Assistance of *Mercury* [wit] from behind" (*Tale* 3.103). For example, a passage from the *Tale* states that Peter's

> Universal *Pickle* [was] proper for Houses, Gardens, Towns, Men, Women, Children, and Cattle; wherein he could preserve them as Sound as Insects in Amber. [*Tale* 4.109]

Underneath the text dangles Wotton's critical analysis, exposed as nothing more than obvious allegorical identification plus word-for-word repetition:

> *Holy Water,* he calls *an* Universal Pickle *to preserve Houses, Gardens, Towns, Men, Women, Children and Cattle, wherein he could preserve them as Sound as Insects in Amber.* W. Wotton. [*Tale* 4.109]

Spatial placement locks Wotton into the *Tale*, so he cannot threaten it from without, and transforms him into a textual boundary marker. The physical position of the commentary implies that this is the limit of criticism: it can do no more than reflect the text to the text. Furthermore, if Wotton is given the last words on a page, the space for criticism is filled, since no words can follow final words, and the textual territory is safely enclosed.

Swift shuts the gates to interpretive intrusions in a similar way with his own textual notes.[43] Sometimes they form tautological barriers, binding the text on all sides with echoic explanations. For instance, in section 2, the Tale-writer mentions that "the Word *Calendae* hath in **Q.V.C.* been sometimes Writ with a *K*"; the asterisk refers to a marginal note identifying the abbreviation as "**Quibusdam Veteribus Codicibus*," that asterisk refers to a footnote giving the translation as "**Some antient Manuscripts*," and that asterisk refers back to the abbreviation in the text (*Tale* 2.84). While such a strategy almost literally nails interpretation onto the page, it also parodies the entire concept of interpretive commentary. The very idea of an annotated edition implies the existence of single, definitive meanings, of an original text that should be recovered, but writing a burlesque edition does not necessarily imply commitment to open, indeterminate signification. Such a burlesque is a conservative textocentric strategy, investing the page with the signs governing its own play of meaning, be it broad or narrow, and exposing the folly of presumptuous critics who try to usurp the text's authority.[44] This is why, in the staggering litany of animal images Swift applies to critics in section 3 of the *Tale*, the Erasmian Ass predominates; this is why in *The Battel of the Books*, the Ass-headed Goddess Criticism's parents are Ignorance and Pride (*Battel*, 240). Swift's frequent marginal disclaimers of understanding the text (e.g., "*I cannot guess the Author's meaning here*" or "*I cannot well find the Author's meaning here*," *Tale* 11.191–92nn) are of a piece with the more recognizably Scriblerian "learned" notes (e.g., *Tale*, 10.187nn, glossing Irenaeus and Vaughan). If critics do not admit their own ignorance or "*force Interpretation, which the Author never meant*" (*Tale*, 10.186n), usually in a proud display of their own knowledge, they must simply parrot the primary text, as Wotton is maneuvered into doing.

The technique of placing Wotton to reflect the text to itself reinforces textual stability, and stable significance is what is imperiled by critical commentary. In "A Digression Concerning Critics," the Tale-writer explains that the true critic is neither an aesthetician nor a restorer of ancient learning but "*a Discoverer and Collector of Writers' Faults*" (*Tale* 3.95), a malevolent geologist who finds fractures in textual terrain and stuffs them full of deadly explosives. Like strolling beggars, true critics are wandering invaders who upset public order by exacerbating evils that could be limited, even concealed:

> [T]'is easy to Assign the proper Employment of a *True Antient Genuine Critick*; which is, to travel thro' this vast World of Writings: to pursue and hunt those Monstrous Faults bred within them: to drag the lurking Errors like *Cacus* from his Den; to multiply them like *Hydra*'s Heads; and rake them together like *Augea*'s Dung. [*Tale* 3.95]

Their violations of verbal property destabilize the text by sowing disease and death, like the Ass whose flesh is gall and whose bray sparks "*Panick Terror*," like the weed that poisons those who smell it, and like the Serpent whose vomit causes "*Rottenness or Corruption*" (*Tale* 3.99–100). The Tale-writer suggests that this itinerant contagion set its own limits by delivering itself "up to Ratsbane, or Hemp, or from some convenient Altitude" (*Tale* 3.95). Critics usually do not commit suicide on command, however, so Swift selects Wotton as a representative critic and hangs him from the text.

Swift also kills off Wotton in *The Battel of the Books*. The limits of the discourse are unmarked because before the text proper, the Bookseller's advertisement explains that the manuscript's imperfections have erased the battle's outcome, and within the text Jupiter reads the fight's disposition in the book of Fate yet "would communicate the Import to none, but presently shut up the Book" (*Battel*, 239). Therefore, the joined deaths of Wotton and Bentley, the final event in the text, replace the lost resolution. Again, Wotton is situated within Swift's verbal property in order to be silenced. Being consigned to the periphery, in fact, seems to be the proper place for all critics vis à vis the works they criticize. When Gulliver visits Glubbdubdrib, for instance, he "proposed that *Homer* and *Aristotle* might appear at the Head of all their Commentators" (*GT* 3.8.197). Although the commentators "always kept in the most distant Quarters from their Principles in the lower World" because they were ashamed of having misrepresented their meaning, literary necromancy shrinks the distance so that authors can confront critics within a shared textual space even while insuring that critics are rightfully relegated to bordering, not central, positions: "[S]ome Hundreds [of commentators] were forced to attend in the Court and outward Rooms of the Palace" (*GT* 3.8.197). This coercive placement blocks critical mobility, the mobility either to escape authoritative scrutiny or to prowl in search of new texts to savage and to conquer.

As *The Battel of the Books* makes clear, critics sustain themselves through unauthorized and unchecked appropriation of others' verbal property. The Goddess Criticism lives in a den among "the Spoils of numberless Volumes half devoured" and dresses her mother, Pride, "in Scraps of Paper herself had torn" (*Battel*, 240). She literally wears her words and invests herself in the victimized text. Yet Criticism converts all these literary leavings into Spleen to nourish herself and her offspring, including Wotton, thereby appearing as a monstrous transformation of the *Battel*'s self-nourishing spider. Her poisonous bibliophagy indicates that her later protective metamorphosis into a book is not really a metamorphosis at all. She has always been a product of destroyed and destructive writing. The mock metamorphosis, moreover, expresses Criticism's activity in terms of decay and death. The Goddess as "*Octavo* Compass" hulks as a moldering bibliomorphic *memento mori*: "Her Body grew white and arid and split in pieces with Driness," the "Black Juice, or Decoction of Gall and Soot, in Form of Letters" being the sign of putrefaction, and the Spleen, in its original form, fueling the entire destructive process (*Battel*, 242–43). She is the Book of Death, recording her story of corruption and corrosion.

The obvious prototype for Swift's Criticism is Spenser's Error in *The Faerie Queene*, book 1.[45] Swift's manipulations of his model reveal his thoughts about how to appropriate literary predecessors into one's own text as well as his opinions of criticism. In general terms, Spenser's personification embodied theological error, the sin of misinterpreting the Word. Therefore, Swift's use of Spenser's figure invests criticism of criticism with the dignity of a religious cause: texts should be sacred, inviolate. This is a closet investiture, however; Swift never cites his source. He enacts the advice he will later give to the Young Gentleman: to avoid wherever possible mentioning the names of authors from whom you borrow. Renaissance writers seem to give Swift particular problems in this regard. Although he quotes relatively freely from ancient authors like Homer and Aristotle and, with rather less frequency, names modern literary rivals and critical antagonists, Swift rarely acknowledges the writers who appear to have exerted the most influence upon him—Erasmus, More, Rabelais, Cervantes, Sidney, Spenser.[46] Perhaps they are neither ancient enough to give the cachet of classical authority nor modern enough to be threats requiring specific attention. Or perhaps Swift wanted to place himself within their literary territory, one that would not have been as circumscribed to Swift as it is to today's literary historians. To cite means to admit to temporal distance and subsequence; to site, to situate, means to use spatial arrangement for creating contiguous or intersecting verbal properties. And, as opposed to cited material, re-sited material has greater ability to grow independently. Thus Swift can deck Spenser's serpentine Error with the asinine attributes of Erasmus's Dame Folly; he can turn Error's "vomit full of books and papers"[47] into a full-fledged book monster; he can deny Criticism's opponents any permanent victory because, even though they destroy her child Wotton, the Goddess herself has vanished.

Criticism's ability to remove herself from the fray points to another important divergence from the Spenserian model. Error was rooted in her den, afraid to move and face the light of truth; emerging from protective darkness destroyed her. In contrast, Criticism has no compunctions about moving freely in space. Mobility, in fact, is essential to Criticism's destructive work; following Momus's summons, she "flew over infinite Regions, shedding her Influence in due Places" (*Battel*, 242). Criticism is also the enemy of proper placement, the Goddess of Inversion who upsets normative order. She claims to have allowed children to rule parents, coffee house wits to criticize authors, expectant heirs to squander their property; she has "*deposed Wit and Knowledge from their Empire over Poetry, and advanced my self in their stead*" (*Battel*, 241). Patroness of displacement, misappropriation, and impropriety, she is the archetype of the usurping invaders who move through Swift's texts. This vagabond army includes strolling beggars, Gothic barbarians, contaminating prostitutes, rapacious critics, hostile Scots, traders in debased coinage, a bantering mob of fashionable language abusers, enthusiasts driven by perpetually moving vapors—all of whom menace authority and order.

This troop of dangerous wanderers may also include the allegorical Bee from *The Battel of the Books*. Certainly Swift wished to align himself with the Bee, insect avatar of the ancients, rather than with the modern Spider; the Bee's wide-ranging abilities to survey and to sample are central to Neo-Classical aesthetics. Nevertheless, the Spider's ill-tempered characterization of the Bee resembles Swift's descriptions of social and literary ne'er-do-wells and contains hints of covert, unpleasant self-assessment.[48] The Spider argues:

> *What art thou but a Vagabond without House or Home, without Stock or Inheritance; Born to no Possession of your own, but a Pair of Wings, and a Drone-Pipe. Your Livelihood is an universal Plunder upon Nature; a Freebooter over Fields and Gardens; and for the sake of Stealing, will rob a Nettle as readily as a Violet.* [*Battel*, 231]

This accusation harbors a fear of displacement, of disinheritance and exile; it betrays distrust of unbounded literary appropriations. Even Aesop's corrective gloss, that the Bee and the Ancients contain "*Nothing of our own, beyond . . . our Flights and our Language*" (*Battel*, 234), demotes invention and style to a secondary, ornamental level. Swift would not want to claim the Spider's venomous and filthy originality, of course, but his parody of modern writers' pride-filled solipsism does not cancel his partial sympathy with the Spider's actual location relative to the Bee. The verbal property of both insects is expressed in terms of spatial territory and of their positions and mobility within it; Swift's conception and command of verbal space resembles that of the Spider more than that of the Bee.

The Spider dwells in "the highest Corner of a large Window" (*Battel*, 228), on the upper periphery looking down, on the inside looking out. His space in the library is marginal but definitive, the same type of space into which Swift placed Wotton in the *Tale*. Negatively, corners are places of punishment, of being banished from the center. Not only did Swift consider himself as a perpetual outcast, he specifically referred to himself as a denizen of corners; in one unflattering simile, he saw himself "sitting like a toad in a corner of his great house" (letter to Stopford, 26 Nov. 1725, *Corr.* 3:114). Positively, corners provide a certain security as one comes in contact with spatial borders.[49] As legible marks of boundary, corners also authorize space: they define it, enclose it, even shield it. They secure the center, just as Gulliver was protected by the iron corners of his traveling box (*GT* 2.8.141). Various conservative textocentric strategies such as the filling of margins, the vocabulary of limit, and the techniques of appropriation, reinforce the boundaries of discourse to guard against interpretive invasion.

Although the woven text occupies the corner of the library, the Spider is centered within the text proper; no matter how unsavory the text's materials may be, the Spider has authorized them completely and invested himself in them securely. Unlike the Spider's web, a system of fortifications commanded on site by its author (*Battel*, 229), the Bee's literary products of honey and wax are not protectively authorized; after they are synthesized, they leave the Bee's custody. Dangerous mobility also characterizes the literary activity of the "wandring Bee" (*Battel*, 229). He enjoys "*an universal Range*"; he enters the Spider's domain by flying in through "A broken Pane in the Glass" (*Battel*, 229–32). An outsider, the Bee moves freely through space, yet he penetrates the inside and "the Center shook" (*Battel*, 229). In a way, then, he resembles usurping, destructive critics who attack the verbal property of others; one solution to the threat he poses is to trap him within the text. Yet the Spider may also be the captive of his own creation, and he, like the Bee, shares traits with the Goddess Criticism. The Spider's castle is strewn with half-devoured victims, and his self-centeredness recalls Criticism's Laputan-like, in-turned eye. Both insects are ambivalent images, representing the competing claims of mobility and confinement, appropriation and usurpation.

The Bee and the Spider wage a battle for textual territory, a battle that, like the larger one it symbolizes, does not end. The Spider can reconstruct his fabric of defensive tropes;[50] the Bee can return through the broken window and destroy the web again, or be caught in it. Below the insects fight the books, and they struggle over proper placement within the library, the microcosm of "this vast world of writing." Their quarrel over which party gets the best place on Parnassus is intensified by the "strange Confusion of Place among all the *Books* in the Library" (*Battel*, 225). Again, the sins of literary scholarship are sins of displacement expressed in spatial terms. Structural and systematic disorder reflect and project confused meaning, as Swift would declare in *Vanbrug's House*, when he yoked the disconcertingly mobile home to "motley, mingled Style" and to the prideful urge to "Build *Babel* with . . . Tongues confounded" (*SPW* 75–76.109–14, 63, 66). In the *Battel*, Bentley the Librarian "in replacing his *Books* . . . was apt to mistake, and clap *Des-cartes* next to *Aristotle*; Poor *Plato* had got between *Hobbes* and the *Seven Wise Masters*, and *Virgil* was hemm'd in with *Dryden* on one side, and *Withers* on the other" (*Battel*, 226). Behind the specific satire of Bentley's methods and findings lie more general targets of Swift's disapproval: usurpation, disorder, random movement, impropriety. And above the chaos on the library shelves is the Spider, the ambiguous image of conservative textocentrism who wears and weaves webs of words to protect the invested self against unauthorized appropriations of meanings. But Swift does not dwell permanently in safe corners, within networks of protective order and authorization. Just as spiders drop lines from their territory-defining webs, leaving their gossamer garments in order to travel into vast, empty space—twisting, exploring, perhaps building anew—Swift too leaves his texts, trades the supportive safety of investiture for the giddy risks of divestiture, and hazards the recreation of Babel.

3 / DIVESTITURES
Swift and Wordplay

AT THE END of a letter to Swift so jammed with snippets of Latin and references to classical authors that it reads like "A Tritical Essay," Bolingbroke writes: "[Y]ou see I amuse myself *de la bagatelle* as much as you, but here lyes the difference, yr *bagatelle* leads to some thing better, as fiddlers flourish carelessly before they play a fine air, but mine begins, proceeds, and ends in *bagatelle*" (28 July 1721, *Corr.* 2:400). Whether or not Bolingbroke correctly assesses his own efforts, he is perceptive about Swift's. Throughout his life, Swift toyed with liberal textocentric possibilities and amused himself with wordplay of various sorts: puns, anagrams, riddles, mock etymologies, mock-Latin and other macaronic inventions, even mock languages.[1] Swiftian wordplay also "leads to some thing better," or at least to something bigger, since the linguistic strategies in the bagatelles are reorchestrated in larger texts like *A Tale of a Tub* and *Gulliver's Travels*. Swift's verbal fiddling, then, both pleased in itself and provided warm-up exercises for more serious play: wordplay as prelude. Musical preludes often stand alone, introductions to major compositions that were never written; literary preludes can do the same or, as in Wordsworth's *The Prelude*, can themselves become through time and tinkering the major works they were originally meant to predict, to be preliminary to. But the idea of prelude (or bagatelle or wordplay or language game) involves disclaimer and denial of seriousness, of completion. It announces its own divestiture of authority.

If investiture implies putting on, putting in, and assuming proper place, divestiture implies taking off, emptying out, and courting dislocation. An invested text asserts authority over its meaning by direct authorial affiliation, by intertextual networks that weave it into the fabric of literary history, or by conservative textocentric strategies that guard the imperiled word against interpretive aggression. A divested text denies authority over its meaning by authorial abandonment, by mock intertextuality that frays and snaps the filaments linking present writing to past works, or by liberal textocentric strategies that increase the odds of misreading and misinterpretation. The authority challenged by Swift's wordplay is most frequently the authority of the word itself, the Lockean assumption that a well-selected verbal form clothes and discloses a specific, authorized meaning. Swift's language games show that tampering with the container can alter the contained. Whirling words and texts can jumble meanings and interpretations into incoherence, yet stopping the vertiginous motion forces not a fall into significance but a fall into realization of folly, the folly of fixing meaning or of interpreting the uninterpretable. In this way, Swift's wordplay turns into a verbal snare, one designed to catch readers and expose their critical pretensions and illusions. Swift's playful experiments with the body of words show that meaning is relative, that it can be frangible, arbitrary, and subversive. Yet even as he makes these discoveries, Swift maneuvers his language games to create independent textual sanctions, to reassert his own authority, and to counteract the anarchy of significance by covering change and corruption with a cloak of permanence and innocence.

Some of Swift's wordplay begins in the spirit of divestiture and ends in a sort of hyperinvestiture, a swaddling of the bared word in layers of intertextual authorizations. Many neologisms in *A Tale of a Tub*, for instance, are given meaning by the arcane and windy styles they satirize, by their contextual uses, and by their linguistic components. When the Tale-writer explains that Artephius, author of *Dr. Faustus*, "proceeds wholly by *Reincrudation*" (*Tale* 1.68), the significance of the italicized coinage is made clear by its echo of alchemical terms employed by writers like Thomas Vaughan, by the network of alchemical and redefinitional phrases surrounding it ("*via humida*," [alchemical] "Marriage," and "fermenting of the *Male* and *Female Dragon*" all refer to generation through somewhat unclean sexual joining), and by its root (crud/crude → filth/raw, vulgar, base).[2] The meaning of a word such as *Reincrudation* is not indeterminate but overdetermined; the reader must unwrap it, not clothe it in new interpretations. The maneuver of overdetermination also can be extended to the creation of a text so painstakingly constructed that it militates against the linguistic freedom it presumes to reveal, setting the authority of the maker against the deconstructing activity of the thing made. Such a text is replete with terms, with its own idiosyncratic rules, boundaries, limins that become limits; it takes on a solidity so unyielding that a reader cannot move within it. He is free only to turn away, to terminate the game. Textual terminations can be death sentences for interpretations and for words themselves. Swift frequently weaves disease, decay, and dying underneath the surface fabric of his verbal games; his wordplay can "break, or very much entangle the Thread of Discourse" (*Polite Conversation*, PW 4:109) to expose the fatal corruption of language.

Overdetermination accounts to some extent for the repetitiousness that characterizes Swift's wordplay: he is not content to float a joke upon a text; he must anchor it over and over until it threatens to sink. But repetition is also part of another maneuver, the maneuver of regression. The regressive urge is manifested in a certain childishness permeating the play, whether it be the tedious unwillingness to let go of jokes and clever methods or the self-congratulatory and somewhat supercilious obviousness of the jokes themselves. Swift's hyphens and italics cry, "Get it? Get it?" to the reader who "got it" the first time and is tired of it by the fiftieth. Regression is also retreat, retreat from the aggressive verbal violence inherent in wordplay and, in broader terms, retreat from authoritarian demands of adulthood. In particular, the verbal games constituting the "little language" in the *Journal to Stella* seem to signal a search for innocence, for a linguistic house of being that shelters from corruption.

Studying Swift's wordplay emphasizes the remarkable degree to which Swift writes deconstructed texts. His work not only utilizes the methods of modern deconstructionism—puns, anagrams, intertextuality, overdetermination; it also anticipates many of deconstructionism's major premises—the jouissance of the text, the origin of signification in spacing (pause, blank, interval, the nonpresent and nonconscious), the radical difference between the written and the spoken word.[3] But Swift is not our contemporary, and his verbal divestitures are rarely ends in themselves; they disclose unpleasant moral truths about man's use and abuse of language. Moving among punning bagatelles and strategies of vertigo and artificial languages reveals Swift's distrust of and dependence on the word, his oscillation between aggressively trapping readers and regressively masking or circumventing aggression, and his abiding concern with problems of meaning and interpretation.

THE ANAGRAMMATICK METHOD

Swift divests his texts by attacking words' authentic forms and authorized meanings with puns and anagrams. The simplest form of "the Anagrammatick Method" is demonstrated in *Gulliver's Travels*, book 3, chapter 6. Transposition destroys the proper placement of letters within a word or phrase to reveal hidden meanings, turning either nonsense to sense (*Tribnia, Langden* = Britain, England [p. 191]) or the trivial to the significant ("*Our Brother* Tom *hath just got the Piles*," according to Gulliver, can be decoded into "*Resist—a Plot is brought home—The Tour*" [pp. 191–92]).[4] Closely allied with the simple anagram is the anacrostic, which Gulliver interprets as disclosing the secret meaning of letters themselves; naked individual graphs, unprotected by any spatio-temporal sequence, invite interpretive aggression. The anagrammatic method also can include puns, since the alphabetic or aural remains of the host word's formal body may have meanings that disrupt or destroy the host word's common range of significance. For purposes of convenience, then, the term *anagram* can cover a variety of Swiftian assaults upon the written text undertaken to expose the vulnerability of the divested word by ostensibly recovering "the mysterious Meanings of Words, Syllables, and Letters" (*GT* 3.6.191).

In this sense, the Swiftian anagram resembles Julia Kristeva's notion of the "paragram," a concept of anagram expanded to encompass nonrational, nonsymbolic, nonbounded linguistic signifying.[5] It also resembles analogies to anagrammatic practices in esoteric theology. Swift consistently mocks these methodologies (see particularly *Tale* 5.126–28, and 10.187), yet in pointing out the absurdity of arriving at a hermeneutic telos, the hidden but true final meaning, he is also demonstrating truths of interpretation: its instability, its relativity, its open-endedness, its presumption. Harold Bloom makes a similar point in *Kabbalah and Criticism*; he calls the Kabbalistic technique *gematria*, in which Hebrew letters assigned numerical values are subjected to arbitrary arithmetical recombinations, a parody of the "exaltation of language . . . interpretive freedom gone mad, in which any text can be made to mean anything."[6] It is this parodic interpretive madness, flirted with by Saussure in his quest for the names hidden anagrammatically in Saturnian poetry,[7] that infuses Swift's anagrammatic play. Like the Surrealist parlor game *cadavre exquise* in which texts were cut into words, jumbled, and reassembled at random, Swift's wordplay is a game in which silliness and ingenuity push verbal counters around a gameboard of meaning to perform the death, dismemberment, and transfiguration of words.

Underneath the playfulness characterizing Swift's word-play productions like the Tom Ashe papers, the language competitions with Sheridan, and "A Discourse to prove the Antiquity of the English Tongue," runs a current of verbal violence, a violence that radically dislocates linguistic origins. "A Discourse," for instance, is comic wish fulfillment enacted through aggression; it reverses the historical trajectory of linguistic corruption chronicled in *A Proposal for Correcting . . . the English Tongue* by means of anagrammatic autopsies. *A Proposal* had set "the *Latin* Tongue in its Purity," "the Purity of the *Greek* Tongue," and the beautiful simplicity of the Old and New Testaments (*PW* 4:6, 9, 15) against the corrupted English language and had blamed the fall of classical languages upon barbarous invasions. "A Discourse" maintains "that our language, as we now speak it, was originally the same with those of the Jews, the Greeks, and the Romans, however corrupted [these three have been] in succeeding times by a mixture of barbarisms" (*PW* 4:232). To demonstrate this comic premise, bred largely from the Ancients versus Moderns controversy, Swift produces a list of proper names: Homeric heroes, Roman statesman, biblical patriarchs, patronyms dignified by mother tongues. He cuts up these names into English words whose meanings assassinate the characters they denominate. "Diomede," for example, comes from Venus's curse "that he should *die a maid*"; "Caesar . . . ought to be spelt *Seiser*, because he seised not only most of the known world, but even the liberties of his own country" (*PW* 4:233, 237). "Mars . . . when he was angry . . . would cry, 'Kiss *my a—se*' . . . by a common abbreviation, *M'as*; from whence, by leaving out the mark of elision, *Mars*" (*PW* 4:234). Arbitrary meanings strip these great names of respect, and the inversion of linguistic chronology threatens to dislodge them from their historical place. Furthermore, as individual words fall in upon each other, their centers collapsing, their extraliteral traces of integrity being erased, language itself is shown in the process of devolution and its radical instability is revealed.[8]

Obviously, Swift's primary purposes are to show off his wordplay skills, to take passing swipes at contemporary verbal abuses such as abbreviations and lawless orthography, and to mock pompous etymologists (Bentley as philologist is singled out at the beginning of "A Discourse").[9] Swift may also be disputing Locke, who believed that etymology could restore the origins of language and thought.[10] He directs his mockery, therefore, not only at etymological method but at theoretical assumptions that, considering the lesson of Babel as a prohibition against recovering linguistic origins, approach theological presumption. In addition, the gamesmanship and the specific satire demonstrate the difference between written and spoken language: sound divested of written form signifies nothing except furious and spurious invention. By giving free rein to unregulated wordplay, "A Discourse" also discloses the universal linguistic corruption that makes textocentric authorization so precarious, the corruption that festers in all insides when outside coverings are ripped away. Thus Swift's joke upon the maxim *nomen est omen* becomes increasingly ominous, darkly and uneasily so, as it drags along. The English "root words" tend to signify pain and suffering, violence and death, or dirt and excrement. *Ajax* means either "A Jakes" or "Age-aches"; Hector is so called because he "hacked" and "tore" his enemies; Astyanax "had his head cut off, and his body thrown to swine . . . his name . . . preserved entire, *A sty, an ax*"; even the word *dipthong* comes from using a type of slingshot to punish schoolboys who could not spell, since "the master would *dip* his *thongs* (as we now do rods) in p——" (*PW* 4:233, 234, 238). Throughout the entire discourse, then, Swift uses the anagrammatic impulse, syllabic surgery, and homophonic suggestion to pry open words to expose the unpleasantness inside.

"Last Week I saw a Woman *flay'd*," states the Tale-writer, "and you will hardly believe, how much it altered her Person for the worse" (*Tale* 9.173). In "A Discourse," past changes to present, passive observation to active operation. "Now I am flaying words," implies its author, "and look at the ugliness I've uncovered." The anagrammatic autopsy is a joke, divestiture pulled beyond its limits, and the joke turns on itself. Swift ruptures the ancient word, making it split like overripe fruit; but the naked seeds are rotten, corrupted and corruptive. There is no prelapsarian purity, no time when language had not taken a fall and splintered apart. These dismemberments of words strike at historical memory, recorded in etymology and locked in verbal form. The anger that sours the joke is Swift's perpetual anger at the course of corruption traveled by human history, be it individual, linguistic, literary, political, or economic. To re-member is to reconstruct a truth one may not care to confront: the travestied word incarnate, the reassembled verbal corpse, blotched by sin and reeking of mortality.

Dandified words, like the Beau stripped in the *Tale*, have their fancy cloaks snatched away, baring the body and its inescapable embarrassments. After such a rude divestiture of dignity, no other re-covery is possible; the cloak has become a sign of the exposed secret. Thus, the initial dismemberment in "A Discourse" is appropriate:

> *Cloaca*, which [speakers of Latin] interpret a *necessary-house*, is altogether an English word, the last letter *a* being, by the mistake of some scribe, translated from the beginning to the end of the word. In the primitive orthography it is called *a cloac*, which had the same signification; and still continues so at Edinburgh in Scotland; Where a man in a cloac, or cloak, of large circumference and length, carrying a convenient vessel under it, calls out, as he goes through the streets, *Wha has need of me?* Whatever customer calls, the vessel is placed in the corner of the street, the cloac, or a cloak, surrounds and covers him, and thus he is eased with decency and secrecy. [*PW* 4:232]

"Thus he is eased with decency and secrecy." The anagrammatic method hints, and the *s*'s and long *e*'s whisper the secrets the cloak cannot conceal: disease, descent, and secretions. Beginnings become endings; the hollow vessel of the word is filled; etymology is revealed as excremental tautology. The cloacal cloak is the necessary house, all have need, and everything has "the same signification."

LETTERS IN DEATH'S ALPHABET

"To the Earl of Pembroke: The Dying Speech of Tom Ashe" is another example of the morbid cast of Swift's wordplay. This deathbed expression was concocted several years before the notorious punster, Tom Ashe, died in 1719. Unlike *The Bickerstaff Papers*, written to kill at least the reputation of Partridge, "The Dying Speech" seems to have no purpose beyond exploitation of the possibility of a situation, dying, through a particular mode, the pun. Thus, death has been freely chosen as the center from which an unsavory swirl of words not only spins out but into which the associative babble is sucked back. In this bagatelle, divestiture operates through undressing words of their formal coherence, and language dies of exposure. A portion of "The Dying Speech" reads:

> Whatever doctors may *design* by their *medicines*, a man in a *dropsy drops he* not, in spite of Goddard's *drops* . . . I find Death smells the blood of an Englishman: a *fee faintly fum*bled out, will be a weak defence against his *fee-fa-fum.—P.T.* are no letters in Death's *alphabet*; he has not *half a bit* of either: He moves his *sithe*, but will not be

moved by all our *sighs*.—Every thing ought to put us in mind of death: Physicians affirm that our very food breeds it in us, so that in our *dieting*, we may be said to *di eating*.—There is something ominous, not only in the names of diseases, as *di*-arrhoea, *di*-abetes, *di*-sentery, but even in the drugs designed to preserve our lives; as *di*-acodium, *di*-apente, *di*-ascordium. [*PW* 4:264]

Disease, descent, and secretions: the "dropsy" leads inevitably to death. Medicines may be "designed to preserve our lives," but Swift de-signs them. By tearing the seams joining syllable to syllable, he reveals the interior meaning that subverts exterior significance, the secret message of death—"*di*-acodium, *di*-apente, *di*-ascordium"—inscribed in their very names; he shows that they exacerbate corruption, like the food we eat that "breeds [death] in us."

Neither does language offer a defense. The repetitive, incantatory quality of the prose could be interpreted as a sort of homeopathic charm against Death, but Swift reminds us that Death's language is defective. Death operates from the silent spaces in his alphabet where he cannot hear our voice. Or maybe we lure Death from his hiding place in the gaps of language by the hollowness of our empty words. "But, I am going," cries 'Tom Ashe,' "my *wind in* lungs is turning to a *winding* sheet" (*PW* 4:265). The verbal vestment has become a shroud.

One could, perhaps should, object to such a serious reading of a piece intended to be funny. "The Dying Speech," like "A Discourse to prove the Antiquity of the English Tongue," is a joke, a joke framed for friends who enjoyed this sort of verbal acrobatics. Freud has alerted twentieth-century readers to the graver implications of jokes, of course;[11] but it is Swift himself, as ringmaster of his verbal circus, who places his performers in peril. He sets the boundaries of the spaces the puns and anagrams must traverse, widening the gaps in meaning, deepening the ruptures of verbal form. He exposes the fragility of the word's body like a mischievous boy dropping a cat from a rooftop to see if it will land on its feet. That is play, too—play predicated upon risk. The boy transfers the risk to the cat, but a writer cannot transfer the risk to his words without running the risk of being misread. Swift courted this risk throughout his career, yet he also tried to shift liability for misreading to his audience. The textual apparatus enveloping *A Tale of a Tub*, the Scriblerian projects, and the structural puns of *A Modest Proposal* are just a few manifestations of the textocentric risk-games played by a quick-change artist, investing and divesting words of significance, pulling apart words and texts to make their potential gaps actual ones, chancing the disappearance of authorized meanings and the appearance of new ones (or no ones) to fill the void, and hedging his bets so that unauthorized meanings will indict not texts but readers.

Another characteristic of Swift's language games that indicates a certain underlying aggression towards his audience is the tendency to be tedious, the compulsion to keep hammering away at a verbal trick long after it has delivered its charge of humor. Regression, however, often transvests aggression,[12] and pieces like "A Discourse," "The Dying Speech," and the Anglo-Latin trifles evidence a somewhat juvenile and retentive delight in their own cleverness that disregards the limits of tolerance reasonably expected from their readers. In language competitions with Sheridan, for instance, Swift's tiresomely prolonged verbal ingenuity masks aggressive one-upsmanship. His fifteen-part response to Sheridan's eighteen stanzas extolling an Irish spa demonstrates Swift's superiority in light verse; he finds more silly rhymes for "Ballyspellin" than did Sheridan, and he sets up his poem to emphasize internal rhymes hidden in Sheridan's four-line form. But the apparent good humor is buried in relentless, repetitive denigrations of the spa, of its visitors, and of Sheridan, author of "scurvy Lays / And senseless praise":

> Howe'er you bounce,
> I here pronounce
> Your Med'cine is repelling,
> Your Water's mud,
> And sowrs the blood
> When drunk at Ballyspellin
>   Those pocky Drabs
>   To cure their Scabs
> You thither are compelling
> . . . . .
>   Who'er will raise
>   Such Lyes as these
> Deserves a good Cud-gelling
>   ["An Answer to the
>   Ballyspellin Ballad,"
>   *SPW* 358–60.4–5,
>   7–15, 79–81]

Swift seems to be deliberately exhausting and deliberately polluting the available fund of wit connected to the word so that Sheridan has no possible verbal recourse.

In other works, Swift's use of italics and hyphens to make the already obvious joke hit the reader over the head borders on the insulting, even on the hostile. This sort of adolescent self-indulgence seems to be the prime motivation for many of Swift's riddles, particularly those that have privies or posteriors as their subjects, and for the strange companion pieces like *The Wonderful Wonder of Wonders*. The reader solves the riddles almost immediately, but the works keep plodding along until Swift has squeezed every conceivable drop of vitality from a joke that may not have been too funny to begin with. Regressive tedium also threatens better-known works, as happens with the unending series of deadpan predictions in *The Bickerstaff Papers* and the amazingly wearisome collection of clichés and stock exchanges in *Polite Conversation*. In all likelihood, even Swift's friends did not always have the requisite staying power to ride out his jokes. Reading between the lines of *The Memoirs of Martinus Scriblerus*, chapter 13, for example, hints at a friendly dispute between Swift and the other Scriblerians. The chapter centers on the punning of Crambe (from Crambo, a popular rhyming word game enjoyed by Swift) and was probably written by Swift since Crambe's paronomastic method is the same as that in the "Dying Speech" and in Swift's "ass" riddles ("A Letter" and "Probatur Aletur," *SPW*, 638–41). The extant version of the chapter has benefited from a considerable pruning of puns, but still Crambe wallows in a pun-ic delirium brought about by being under the dominion of the "radical word" of the day, which is "led":

> Our Noblemen and Drunkards are pimp-led, Physicians and Pulses fee-led, their Patients and Oranges pil-led, A New married Man and an Ass are bride-led [etc.] . . . And that I may not be tedious— Which thou art (reply'd Martin, stamping with his foot) which thou art, I say, beyond all human toleration—[13]

Perhaps Martin's voice is Pope's or Arbuthnot's or Gay's, trying to prevent the manuscript from being buried in puns. Or perhaps it is Swift's, trying to pull the sting from the charges he knows will be leveled against him and to manipulate the last laugh for his own benefit. Either way, the passage discloses an aggressive-regressive dialectic concerning the appropriation of punning potential, a custody battle for the power to determine and to terminate meaning.

The different varieties of verbal jokes, then, encapsulate in relatively trivial form and with seeming pleasant spirits many verbal forces that Swift unleashes in his more sustained works. Perhaps despite themselves, the jokes disclose attraction for excrement and disease, violence and death, and exhibit the hide-and-seek techniques with which Swift examines the problems of signification, techniques at once sophisticated and childish. "*A* Consultation *of* Four Physicians *upon a* Lord *that was dying*" provides a case in point. In the manner of "The Dying Speech," it couches jokes upon a deathbed. In the manner of "A Discourse," it presents Latin as a mask for English words, but its divestiture operates by taking out, by appearing to empty words of all signifying power. It builds in its gaps, turning typography into a textual topography that conceals meaning. After the patient dies, one doctor says:

[A]bigo ditis hi time, inde editis, forus alto fallas campe ringo fas fastas arato ut offa da iri; fori fera bea tinge veri minute; bimi solido. His lac quis, an das turdis aussi sto ut valet is rea di forus. [*PW* 4:272]

Recomposed, this speech reads:

[A]h by god it is high time, indeed it is, for us all to fall ascampering off as fast as a rat out of a dairy; for I fear a beating every minute; by my soul I do. His lackies, and a sturdy saucy stout valet is ready for us.

Meaning is a function of gaps, the arrangement of space. Swift maneuvers the reader into the position of voyeur, titillated by disembodied forms like the "fallas" and the "turdis." But forced to reconstruct the entire meaning as it passes back and forth in the windows of space, the reader is disappointed: "fallas" translates into *fall as*campering, "turdis" into s*turdy saucy*. Textocentric gaps are interpretive traps, interpretation is exposed as intellectual exhibitionism, and reading falls victim to typographic convention and to the privileging of speech over writing. The joke's on us.

And the joke is of the "heads, I win—tails, you lose" variety. The reader who has been tricked by the homophone "fallas," for example, will ignore the English words that do stand nakedly in the text (e.g., "time," "minute," "his", "valet", "is") as well as the homophonic method that, in general, governs the decoding. The reader who mines the nonsense for Latin roots finds fool's gold; he becomes buried in a pile of irrelevant shadow etymologies that, even disregarding their lack of grammatical interconnection, add a lump sum of nothing to the text's meaning: "ditis" → *dis, ditis* → Pluto, god of death; "time" → *timeo* → to fear; "fallas" → *fallax* → false; "ringo" → *ringor* → to snarl, etc. Finally, the reader who discovers that spaces themselves are shifting loci of meaning and that decoding demands speaking rather than reading faces a tangle of fluctuating aural rules. The final *e*, for instance, is not pronounced in "time" and "minute"; it is pronounced—as ē, as ə, as ĕ—in "inde," "campe," and "tinge." Some reconstituted readings are phonetic ("bimi solido" → by my soul I do), and some are orthographic ("sto ut" → stout). Codification is impossible, and the game can be played only by plunging into the whirl of sounds and silences, abandoning the stability of the letter for the vertiginous spirit of significance. Swift has arranged word games of this type to preclude the possibility of prediction.[14] Diction, the sensible utterance or the sensible reading that are the goals of word games, can occur only in the process of playing. Diction's presence, or its instantaneous sense, arises through the recognition of absence—absence of rules, absence of words (the spaces in the text), absence of equivalence between reading and speaking.

THE GIRL AT BARTHOLOMEW-FAIR

Thus Swift mocks the Lockean position that words clothe ideas. This position contains an implied sequence of dressing: the idea is clothed, given communicative form, by the spoken word that can be clothed, given spatial form, by the written word. "*A Consultation*" breaks apart this sequence and reveals written clothing to be grotesque disguise donned for dissimulation rather than for simulation. Nevertheless, meaning remains a function of dressing: dressing the wounds in the text (the spatial ruptures) so that broken words can heal, rewounding the text in new places and leaving these gaps undressed. Although Swift's awareness of the problems of meaning allows such radical divestitures to be located in the piece, it is the spirit of play that authorizes and informs "*A Consultation*." What sort of play is Swift constructing? Into what sort of game does he lure his readers?

Modern game theory tends to arrange games on a continuum beginning at spontaneous, unregulated (child's) play and ending at calculated, rule-governed (adult) play. Games are categorized broadly as ones of vertigo, of simulation, of chance, and of competition—the latter being the most highly regulated.¹⁵ Dissimulative rather than simulative, illusorily rather than actually random, solitary (unless one considers Swift the master Latinist and word handler as the reader's antagonist) rather than competitive, unruly rather than orderly, "*A* Consultation" seems to belong to the category of vertigo play. Basically, vertigo play means making oneself dizzy: the child who turns himself like a top until he falls down, the world whirling around him, the dancer who spins himself into ecstasy, into a stance outside normal sensory reality.

Roger Callois describes vertigo as "an attempt to momentarily destroy the stability of perception and inflict a kind of voluptuous panic upon an otherwise lucid mind ... Various physical activities .. provoke these sensations, such as the tightrope, falling or being projected into space, rapid rotation, sliding, speeding ... In parallel fashion, there is a vertigo of a moral order, a transport that suddenly seizes the individual. This vertigo is readily linked to the desire for disorder and destruction, a drive which is normally repressed."¹⁶ Vertigo's formal characteristics are rulelessness, self-absorption, and risk of loss. It is "played" with no rules other than the enacted impulse to annihilate rules, particularly those governing "the stability of perception." As a literary game, then, vertigo necessitates a divested, de-authorized text. The reader-player participates without authorial guidelines.¹⁷ The solitary player becomes enmeshed in a paradox: winning the game of vertigo means losing intellectual balance. He must abandon himself to risk by "falling or being projected into space," into the gaps in the text, by "rapid rotation" of words, until meaning adheres only to the letters on the page.

Constructing a text on the principle of vertigo exposes verbal meanings to extraordinary dangers. This is the author's risk, that the gain involved in having the game played will be destroyed by the loss of meanings embedded in the text. Swift pointed to the perils of vertigo when he lambasted "the *Whiggish* Notion of a *Revolution-Principle*" in *The Examiner* #39, May 3, 1711:

> [A]s their Writings and Discourses have taught us to define it, [it] is a Principle perpetually disposing Men to *Revolutions*: this is suitable to the famous saying of a great *Whig, That the more Revolutions the better*, which how odd a Maxim soever in Appearance, I take to be the true *Characteristick* of the Party.
>
> A DOG loves to turn round often; yet after certain *Revolutions*, he lies down to Rest: But Heads, under the Dominion of the Moon, are

for perpetual Changes, and perpetual *Revolutions*: Besides, the *Whigs* owe all their Wealth to *Wars* and *Revolutions*; like the Girl at Bartholomew-Fair, who gets a Penny by turning round a hundred Times, with Swords in her Hands. [*PW* 3:147]

The girl at the fair emblematizes the dangers and small rewards of the Revolution-Principle, of playing the vertigo game. Swift's syntax also underscores this warning. The two meanings of the word *Revolution*, the fulcrum upon which the argument turns, are not expanded figuratively by simile or metaphor; through centripetal compression, they form a pure trope, turning within the word itself. A trope literally is a turn: Swift's habitual technique of literalization[18] plays upon the revolutions meaning can make within the naked word. The centrifugal clarifications of "Revolution" actually blur the argument further. Do the girl at the fair (more analogy than simile) and the self-chasing dog (analogy as bare statement) refer to the Whigs or to the Revolution-Principle, and do the analogies confuse the issue of truth with that of value? The Revolution-Principle is "the true *Characteristick*" of the Whigs, but its payoffs are at best negligible and at worst self-destructive. In addition, the antithetical action of stopping revolutions is performed by a dog. While not following his lunatic head, the animal is nonetheless engaged in the valueless activity of chasing his tail, a meaning found in the analogical ellipsis masking the question of why a dog turns round and round.

The formal principle of vertigo also operates in *Gulliver's Travels* and in *A Tale of a Tub*. Gulliver's four journeys exhibit repetitive circularity and dizzying reversals of large and small, man and animal, safety and peril to mind and body. Gulliver loses his emotional balance as he circulates through his own fiction, ultimately falling into swoons at the sight and smell of fellow humans; his readers lose their interpretive balance too—as the critical history of book 4 attests. The vertigo principle is even more dominant in *A Tale of a Tub*. As a conscious strategy, it blends formlessness and form into a plastic, demonically energetic shape,[19] one designed in part to simulate the operations of literary modernism. The modern Spider, about whom Aesop remarks "*was ever any thing so Modern as the Spider in his Air, his Turns, and his Paradoxes . . . he Spins and Spits wholly from himself*" (*Battel*, 234), is an embodiment of vertigo and an avatar of the Tale-writer. But vertigo encompasses not only the gaps, jumps, and spins in style, voice, matter, and textual presentation but also the dizzy disorientation experienced by most of the *Tale*'s readers.

The Tale-writer seems well aware of the structural and affective qualities of vertigo when he declares his intention to write in circles, "to circumscribe within this Discourse the whole Stock of Matter I have been so many Years providing [so that it] will produce a wonderful Revolution in [the reader's] Notions and Opinions" (*Tale* 10.184). Yet, as mentioned above, employing the vertigo principle as a formal device is a technique of divestiture, a de-authorization, an abdication of control over textual meanings. The Tale-writer knows this too. In his "Epistle Dedicatory to Prince Posterity," he asserts that "what I am going to say is literally true this Minute I am writing: What Revolutions may happen before it shall be ready for your Perusal, I can by no means warrant" (*Tale*, 36).

Vertigo annihilates time, as in the *Tale*, as well as space, as in *Gulliver's Travels*; decades later Laurence Sterne would unite vertiginous time and vertiginous space in his Swiftian novel, *Tristram Shandy*. No other Restoration or eighteenth-century writers, however, use vertigo as a structural principle for satire or consistently exploit its uncomfortable effects on the reader. Pope's *The Rape of the Lock*, for instance, contains improbable journeys, scalar changes, and fantastic creatures,[20] but it is not as disorienting as *Gulliver's Travels*. In the *Rape*, elegant meter and rhyme, prosodic symmetry, mock-epic pattern, and classical allusions help provide textual control. So does the suavely assured narrative voice, reinforced by self-demonstrating mastery of matter and manner. Such control is not exercized by Gulliver, who alternates between confidence and confusion, moral awareness and moral obtuseness, naive desire and cynical judgment. Neither is it exercized by his text, which erects a symmetry in books 1 and 2 only to demolish it in book 3 and complicate it in book 4. In the process, the book's satiric targets shift among contemporary politicians, second-rate travel writers, zealous scientists, endemic corruption, and universal folly, while its style mingles specific formal parodies with general deadpan "truth-telling." Thus when readers try to seize control, they are spun giddily through the text. Swift sweeps his audience into his vertigo game, whereas Pope demonstrates his vertiginous skills on an elevated stage bounded by formal coherence and commanded by an authorial presence that meets no challenge from an articulated persona.

Even Pope's *Dunciad Variorum*, which tries to dislocate meaning through Scriblerian apparatus, does not approach the dizziness of *A Tale of a Tub*. Instead, it presents a solid text and a solid countertext, a complementary and stable double discourse. Two forms of parody, mock-heroic narrative and mock-learned commentary, proceed in conjunction toward a common purpose—exposure of an intellectual world perilously close to collapse. But the *Dunciad* itself does not collapse; it ends with a pleasing sense of finality and a reassuring reference to its own status as a work of art. The *Tale*, however, does collapse. In fact, it is whirling and collapsing from its inception: monologue, narrative, and parody[21] play against each other; allusions, illusions, and delusions interpenetrate; authority is asserted, denied, and ridiculed from every nook and cranny of the page; beginnings are erased, endings are avoided, and the middle becomes the great god muddle. The metafictionality of the *Dunciad* refers to literary products, whereas the metafictionality of the *Tale* refers to literary process, a process that necessarily involves—and revolves—readers.

The essentially stable nature of Pope's satire is, I believe, a result of its polished surface and its pedigreed structure. Pope applies strong linguistic control and coherent imaginative vision upon strong preexisting forms, be they Virgilian epic or Horatian epistle. Similarly, Dryden weaves witty heroic couplets upon classical and biblical frameworks in his verse satires; Butler canters after Cervantes in regulatory four-beat lines; Gay places himself against the expectations of Italian opera or the conventions of pastoral and uses unexpected language to define his opposition to these formal backdrops. Swift's satire is not stable. He often eschews order-giving precursor texts (or he chews them into unrecognizable mush); when he does write satire under the influence of tradition, he usually selects works that are themselves so large and baggy—*The Golden Ass, Moriae Encomium, Gargantua and Pantagruel, The Anatomy of Melancholy*—that they cannot provide a controlling pretext. Swift's personae, who are sometimes three-dimensional characters, sometimes impersonations, sometimes alter egos, sometimes internally contradictory, also keep the reader off balance.[22] And, as my argument throughout this study implies, Swift's problematic view of textuality and the vertiginous language strategies it generates are per se destabilizing.

Using vertigo as a literary tactic, however, does not equal endorsing it as a mode of thought or conduct. Although Callois's subdefinition, "vertigo of a moral order," can be adopted to explain Swift's ambivalent fascination with filth and disorder,[23] when Swift employs vertigo as an overt pattern or image, it carries pejorative implications linked to physical discomfort and moral disapproval. "Deaf, giddy, helpless, left alone" ("On his own deafness," *SPW* 594.1): the man who thus describes his own chronic illness would not seek the pleasures of dizziness.[24] Neither would the man who feared attacks of vertigo and called them "fits" (e.g., letter 13, Jan. 1710/77, *JS* 1:163) embrace the sensory chaos they cause. A fit is not a *furor poeticus*, and Yeats's picture of Swift beating his breast in blind sibylline frenzy in the spiral-filled poem "Blood and the Moon" is surely inaccurate. Swift's dislike of self-induced enthusiasm permeates *A Tale of a Tub* and its coda, *The Mechanical Operation of the Spirit*. The latter work's narrator ironically but clearly condemns spinning oneself loose from sensory and sensible groundlines. Maintaining that "*the Corruption of the Senses is the Generation of the Spirit*," he explains that one can break the senses' hold by diverting, flustering, or trying "to justle them out of their stations" (*MO*, 269–70); one can put oneself in a vertiginous trance by repetitive activities like "the Art of *See-saw* on a Beam, and swinging by Session upon a Cord, in order to raise artificial Extasies" (*MO*, 272).

When Swift refers to vertigo, he frequently focuses on what happens after the artificial ecstasies are produced: the necessary fall. For instance, the head of the bellicose prince in *A Tale of a Tub* contained animating vapors "being in perpetual Circulation" (*Tale* 9.165), but these vapors plummeted to his posteriors and solidified into an anal tumor—a fortunate fall, perhaps, for his war-ravaged subjects but a decidedly unhappy one for their leader. *On Poetry: A Rapsody* displays a voracious chain of biting poets, circling "*ad infinitum*," their mad whirl culminating in infernal descent:

> With Heads to Points the Gulph they enter,
> Linkt perpendicular to the Centre:
> And as their Heels elated rise,
> Their Heads attempt the nether Skies.
> [*SPW* 578–80.340, 401–4]

And the fall can end in a final but unceasing revolution: vertigo as an image of hell. One of Swift's allegorical poems describes how Desire, flying up in pursuit of fortune,

> in Rapture gaz'd a while,
> And saw the treach'rous Goddess smile;
> But, as he climb'd to grasp the Crown,
> She knock't him with the Scepter down.
> He tumbled in the Gulph profound;
> There doom'd to whirl an endless Round.
> ["Desire and Possession,"
> *SPW* 327.45–50]

Images of vertigo, therefore, operate as hyperkinetic versions of the wheel of fortune topos. They represent and predict the disastrous course of presumptuous aspiration, of leaving one's proper place: a pennyworth of ecstasy purchased with exposure to perdition is a poor investment. Vertiginous patterns that work as formal mimeses of pride can serve the same purpose. Their rambunctious vitality energizes the text in a way that counteracts the stern message they embody but simultaneously threatens communicable meaning. The paradoxes inherent in formal vertigo cause Swift to use it cautiously, and sometimes contradictorily. The vertigo principle, however, can dominate a bagatelle like "*A* Consultation" because meaning qua meaning is secondary to game qua game. The issue is not what the doctors say but how, in the absence of cryptogrammatic rules, readers can spin intelligibility, however trivial, out of gibberish. Such word games uncover mistaken or reductive notions of how words in a text clothe meanings and poke playfully but painfully at readers' pride in their powers of interpretation.

A SORT OF JABBER

The "languages" in *Gulliver's Travels* have resisted systematic translation by anyone (except Gulliver) for over 250 years. They represent the vertigo principle *in extremis*: words give off flashes of significance, but the giddy anarchy of their parts cannot be marshaled into stable, intelligible order. Just as a quickly turning pinwheel appears as a solid disk of blurred colors, the words Gulliver learns on his voyages and reports to his readers present themselves as impenetrable, unanalyzable linguistic objects—vertiginous verbal constructions caught and preserved in full whirl, before their fall into meaning. Their unyielding strangeness, however, sets up another fall: the fall of interpretation. In this sense, they contribute to the book-long, and to Swift's lifelong, satiric assault upon man's intellectual pride.

Gulliver, of course, interprets many of these words for his readers. For example, he explains that the names of Lilliputian political parties, *Tramecksan* and *Slamecksan*, come from the distinguishing high and low heels on adherents' shoes (*GT* 1.4.48) and that the Houyhnhnms use the word *Yahoo* as a suffix denoting evil or unpleasant qualities. But Gulliver's self-proclaimed "wonderful facility" in languages, as amazing as any of the creatures he meets on his travels, is suspect. He leaves some words untranslated. For instance, he reports that the first Lilliputian to climb upon his bound body "cryed out in a shrill, but distinct Voice, *Hekinah Degul*," a shout later taken up by the crowd as it watched him throw hogsheads in the air (*GT* 1.1.22–24); one assumes that *Hekinah Degul* means something like "what a wonder," but it could just as well be a phrase meaning "get out of the way" or "all praise to the Emperor." Gulliver states that he later learned what these words signified, but he does not pass on the information to the reader. Gulliver gives other words multiple and inaccurate translations. He says that *Grildrig*, Glumdalclitch's pet name for him, "imports what the *Latins* call *Nanunculus*, the *Italians Homunceletino*, and the *English Mannikin*" (*GT* 2.2.95), but the words *Nanunculus* and *Homunceletino* do not exist. He confers elaborate and mystifying etymologies on still other words:

> The Word, which I interpret the Flying or Floating Island, is in the Original *Laputa*; whereof I could never learn the true Etymology. *Lap* in the old obsolete Language signifieth High, and *Untuh* a Governor; from which they say by corruption was derived *Laputa* from *Lapuntuh*. But I do not approve of this Derivation, which seems to be a little strained. I ventured to offer to the Learned among them a conjecture of my own, that *Laputa* was *quasi Lap outed*; *Lap* signifying properly the dancing of the Sun Beams in the Sea; an *outed* a Wing, which however I shall not obtrude, but submit to the judicious Reader. [*GT* 3.2.161–62]

Through Gulliver, Swift is satirizing his old targets, ponderous philologists like Bentley. But Swift is also undercutting Gulliver's language talents by having Gulliver ignore the Spanish meaning of *Laputa* ("the whore") and forget to heed the process of linguistic corruption that, Swift believed, operates universally and precludes recovery of genuine verbal origins. Gulliver's pretentious and fanciful attempts to force the word into "signifying properly" are as ill-contrived and uncomfortable as the suit of clothes fabricated by the Laputan tailor, described in the paragraph immediately following the discourse on the island's name.

More than the mock-issue of the derivation of Laputa is "submit[ted] to the judicious Reader." If Gulliver, *splendide mendax* in general and facile but unreliable linguist in particular, cannot give an authoritative reading of the languages in *Gulliver's Travels*, who or what can? Readers alerted by the text's attention to translations and etymologies look for clues in the words themselves and in wordplay practices Swift engaged in elsewhere.

Behind this quest lies a basic assumption, that these words do have meanings: meanings apart from Gulliverian translation or Swiftian satire of legitimate travel narratives, meanings buried in letters or sounds, buried so deeply that only a dedicated and skilled verbal excavator can retrieve them. This assumption is not only buttressed by the verbal self-consciousness of *Gulliver's Travels* and by Swift's enduring penchant for word games; it is also lent the authority of precedent by earlier Utopian fiction. Sir Thomas More and Rabelais concocted languages for their works, languages for which one can reconstruct a grammar or puzzle out meanings encoded in a variety of actual languages.[25] It would seem that *Gulliver's Travels*, drawing on this part of the tradition of learned wit, would contain similar linguistic treasures for those who bother to uncover them. Further, the assumption of meaning is built into words. Readers expect that a word printed on the page, even a constellation of syllables as foreign and forbidding as *Glubbdrubdrib*, will signify something. We believe that riddles and mysteries must have solutions, that obscurities can be illuminated.[26] It is with our own hermeneutic impulses, our satisfying experiences of coherent interpretations, our proud urges to know hidden answers, our violent desires to work our wills on stubborn texts, that Swift traps us. In so doing, he sets a *terminus ad quem* for the question of verbal meanings.

The textocentric trap is simple: the bulk of the made-up languages in *Gulliver's Travels* have no secret meaning. They are arbitrary alphabetic nonsense. They have functions—naming people and places that Gulliver encounters and contributing to the book's engagement with language and verbal significance—but they have no literal message. By trying to find such messages, we play into Swift's hands. He baits us by scattering throughout *Gulliver's Travels* artificial but decipherable words like the transparent anagrams *Tribnia* and *Langden* in book 1 and the more Joycean *Lindalino* (a double "lin," or Dublin) in book 3; and he teases with vaguely imitative form like the pompous polysyllables of Lilliputian, the giant consonantal clusters of Brobdingnagian, or the neighing nasals of the Houyhnhnm language. But the more we struggle to pull meaning from the words, the more confusing and recalcitrant they become. The only way to win this particular word game of Swift's is to stop playing, to see the trap and laugh at being caught filling these hollow verbal vessels with personal linguistic fantasies.

To allege that Gulliver's new words have little or no meaning does not require dismissal of the critical articles and parts of articles purporting to decode the imaginary languages. On the contrary, these interpretations form a collocation of exegetical evidence arguing against what, in isolation, each interpretation attempts to affirm. First, the interpretations rarely agree. For instance, the Lilliputians bestow the title *Nardac* upon Gulliver: N. A. Sturm suggests that the word is an anagram for the French *canard*, meaning "duck" or "old, unreliable tale";[27] H. D. Kelling believes it to be a phonetic pun based on the German *narr*, meaning "a fool," and *doch*, meaning "still" or "perpetually."[28] Since Swift often used both these methods of wordplay, it seems as appropriate to accuse Gulliver of being a canard-carrier as it is to call him a perpetual fool. The word *Houyhnhnm* provides another example of conflicting interpretations. Gulliver explains that "the Word *Houyhnhnm*, in their Tongue, signifies a *Horse*; and in its Etymology, the *Perfection of Nature*" (*GT* 4.3.235). Many readers, extending Gulliver's account of the word's simple signification to cover its etymology, see in *Houyhnhnm* a transcription of a horse's whinny. Other interpretations are more complex. Clive T. Probyn maintains that "[t]he closest lexicographical link to *Houyhnhnm* is *homonym*," a word "associated with a logical context of ambiguity and ambivalence."[29] Kelling, in contrast, reverses the word to *mnhnhyuoh*, removes the first two *h*'s, gives the final *h* a germanic *ch* pronunciation, makes the Latin orthographic change from *u* to *v*, and ends up with *mnny*, interpolating letters to raise it to *mannus* (Latin for "superior horse"), and *voc* (Latin *vox*, "voice").[30] Either one must choose among differing interpretations that may appear equally convincing, or one must believe that Swift, like James Joyce, molded his languages deliberately to contain all these meanings, or even to obliterate meaning by stuffing words until they overflow.

The second difficulty is that the languages in *Gulliver's Travels* cannot be made to signify in any demonstrably consistent way. Kelling's study, the most ingenious of the lot, shows the endless series of etymological and word-formative hoops one must jump through in search of meaningful translation. We have seen two examples of his methods; he also pulls derivations from Spanish, Greek, French, and Irish, and he uses anagrams and phonetic translations as well as word reversal and syllabic additions. An only slightly less baroque approach is taken by Paul Odell Clark. Employing a letter substitution code drawn from the *Journal to Stella*, he changes *Borach Mivola*, for instance, to *Volat Cibora* (Latin for "he hurls drinking cups") and *Glumdalclitch* to *Grimdolclutch* (reversed English for "clutch doll grim[ly]").[31] Obviously, Clark's transposition of *l*'s and *r*'s or *o*'s and *a*'s operates only occasionally; his technique also brings many languages into play, and the procedure of reading the "translated" syllables is arbitrary. These examples suggest that wrenching meanings out of all Swift's linguistic fabrications is possible only if one uses every language at one's command and every variety of verbal disguise and disfiguration one can think of. Even so, as Kelling complains, "Swift played his games unfairly, demanding from his reader not only extensive linguistic knowledge but also an acrostic imagination."[32] Such a complaint is predicated upon the belief that the games have rules.

Yet Swift employs literary vertigo to confer a kind of negative authority on rulelessness. In the languages of *Gulliver's Travels*, rulelessness undergoes apotheosis. If words are revolved, reversed, dissected, and reassembled, they may yield snippets of significance in some language or another, but they contain no internal structures of verification. They will not deliver coherent, comprehensible meaning. In one way, these words are products of the Lagadan academy's mechanical writing machine, random and de-authorized assemblages of parts that, according to the law of averages, will occasionally come near to making sense. In another way, these words paradoxically approach what George Steiner calls "the suicidal rhetoric of silence,"[33] the ultimate protest of corrupted language. Swift's made-up words protest by speaking in many fragmented voices, but the voices bury one another like rubble falling from the crumbling tower of Babel.

The tower of Babel symbolized man's pride, his attempt to usurp Divine authority; God's punishment was to break apart human language into mutually unintelligible segments. The lesson of Babel lies behind the amusing look and texture of Swift's nonsense languages: man is imperfect and so is the power of language he vainly thinks separates him from other animals. Man clothes himself in his own illusions, as Gulliver misanthropically suggests to his cousin Sympson, by asserting that European Yahoos "only differ from their Brother Brutes in *Houyhnhnmland*, because they use a Sort of *Jabber*, and do not go naked" ("Letter to Sympson," *GT*, 8). By tricking philologically inclined readers into attempting to decipher the indecipherable, Swift turns them into Bickerstaffs, credulously and incorrectly reading the stars, into Adepti who "transpose certain Letters and Syllables [to] reveal into a full Receit of the *Opus Magnum*" (*Tale* 10.187). Words completely divested of meaning become synecdoches for mysteries intended by Providence to be beyond the reach of man's reason. To Swift, attempting to unravel such mysteries is either an act of presumptuous destruction or a fool's errand. As he argues in the sermon "On the Trinity," "If you explain them, they are Mysteries no longer; if you fail, you have laboured to no purpose" (*PW* 9:159–68; see also *Letter to a Young Gentleman*, *PW* 9:77). Neither linguistic *actes gratuits* nor etymological in-jokes, the nonsense words in *Gulliver's Travels* re-cast wordplay into boundary markers of interpretation.

OURRICHAR GANGRIDGE

If the invented languages in *Gulliver's Travels* mark one linguistic extreme, words as freestanding literal clothing with no body of meaning underneath, then the "little language" of the *Journal to Stella* marks the opposite extreme, words as naked significance, divested of conventionally articulating garments. The attempt to make verbal form so vestigial that meaning can present itself unencumbered, uncorrupted, also discloses a certain sense of regression,[34] a retreat into artificial linguistic simplicity that signals desire for a more radical recreation of innocence.

Basically, the little language is fashioned in two ways: consonant substitution, resulting in a form of baby talk that Swift occasionally augments with deliberately incorrect grammar,[35] and mysterious abbreviations, constituting an emotional code for proper names and, perhaps, for endearments. The baby talk can erupt at any point in a letter, and a barrage of abbreviations usually marks the letter's close. For instance, Swift ends his letter of May, 1712, in this manner:

—Ppt does not say one word of her own little Health. I'm angry almost; but I won't tause see im a dood dollar in odle sings, iss and so im DD too. Gd bless Md & FW & Me, ay & pdfr too, farewell Md Md Md FW FW FW Me

Lele I can say lele it ung oomens iss I tan, well as oo [letter 46, *JS* 2:537–38]

The abbreviations, like so many other modes of Swift's wordplay, seem simultaneously to conceal and reveal meaning. For over two centuries, readers have known that *Ppt* means "poppet," *Md* means "My dear" or "My dears," and so forth,[36] but deciphering has not been absolute. For example, readers are not sure when *FW* means "foolish wenches," when it means "farewell," or when it means both at once. In addition, it is usually assumed that Swift uses abbreviations to disguise his emotions, to avoid an overt presentation of endearments. Yet there is no indication that

Esther Johnson and Rebecca Dingley were in any way puzzled by Swift's alphabetic shorthand. Even the strange word *lele* (interpreted blandly by most readers as "there") appears to have a significance agreed upon by Swift and the ladies, as is evident when Swift maintains that "I can say lele it ung oomens iss I tan, well as oo" (I can say lele yet, young women, yes I can, as well as you). That readers of the *Journal to Stella* may be confused by *FW* or *lele* indicates merely that meaning is being concealed from outsiders, not from those within the initial circle of correspondence. The code may be privileged, but it is not necessarily obfuscatory. Instead, by stripping away conventional linguistic coverings and by bestowing upon private communication a distinct language created to convey emotion, Swift seems to be exposing, not concealing, significant feeling. Through divesting the word of its common form, he invests it with the content of the heart.

But this content is light as well as tenderhearted. Since throughout his public works, as we have seen, Swift rails against abbreviations and unaesthetic consonant clusters,[37] using the devices he otherwise deplores indicates a playful disregard of linguistic authority, even of the authority he himself set up. This sense of freedom from proscription is inherent in the abbreviations and orthographic permutations of the little language. Lightheartedness may also explain the frequent strike-throughs in the *Journal to Stella* manuscripts. Of course, if a later censorial hand, be it Swift's or another editor's, scratched over the endearments and personal asides, the strike-throughs are irrelevant to issues of meaning and language; they would have been made only to tidy up the *Journal* for publication. But if made by Swift as he wrote to Esther Johnson, the linings-out and blots may reveal another dimension of his attempts to loosen the graphic bonds in a written text. They may be, as Émile Pons suggests, part of an elaborate network of metatextual communication, of extraliteral emphasis.[38] This inventive speculation is supported by the appearance of the abbreviations: usually occurring in triplets, they often demonstrate progressive graphological embellishment—the final *MD* in a series of three, for instance, being more densely ornamented with extraneous flourishes of the pen than the first. It is as if Swift, after freeing himself from the constraints of the complete word, is busy demolishing the form of the remaining letters.[39]

The sense of play and the urge for expressive freedom also appear in the "baby talk" portions of the little language. Although translation of the baby talk is not difficult, it is predicated upon commitments to time, to voicing, and to intimacy. For Swift, Esther Johnson, and to some extent Rebecca Dingley, the language is a product of time, of years of playful verbal disguising that produced a mutually comprehensible syntax of sound shifts and lexicon of pet phrases. Its strangeness thus becomes a testimonial to the duration of their friendship. Readers outside Swift's circle of intimacy must make a different pledge to time: they must read large portions of the *Journal* in order to steep themselves in its verbal and emotional atmosphere; they must take the time necessary to learn a new language. Voicing is a more crucial and constant requirement. Swift's deliberately deceptive orthography blocks significance if one reads it silently. Like the mock Latin in "*A Consultation of* Four Physicians," the little language misleads visually: "a dood dollar in odle sings" does not look like "a good girl in other things" because *prima facie* nonsense (*dood, odle*), real English words that must be recomposed into other real English words (*dollar* → "girl"; *sings* → "things"), and real English words that retain their standard forms and significances ("a," "in") are randomly juxtaposed. Reading the little language aloud divests it of orthographic dissemblance and lays bare both its significance and its emotional tone. Murmuring "iss and so im DD too" might make a reader feel somewhat childish, but this childishness is as much the meaning of the words as is their translation into conventional English ("yes, and so is Dingley, too").

One aspect of the childishness inherent in the little language is the quest for a preliterate linguistic Eden, the desire to evade the tyrannous deferral of the written word and to create a compensatory voiced presence.[40] When he is not reporting the day's events, Swift writes as if Esther Johnson were sitting in his room, yet a consciousness of the graphic act constantly challenges the conversational ideal. The paper is both carrier and barrier; "These ugly spots are not tobacco, but this is the last gilt sheet I have of large paper, therefore hold your tongue," he explains to Stella (letter 38, Jan. 1711–12, *JS* 2:455). The illusion of talk contributes to the dramatic immediacy of the *Journal*'s prose,[41] but where do the conversations occur? In part, they take place in Esther Johnson's lodgings, as Rebecca Dingley—per Swift's urgings—reads the letters out loud to her weak-eyed companion or as either lady voices the idiosyncratic code that must be said to be understood, thereby reconstituting Swift's absent voice and the special emotional camaraderie of their private language. In part, they take place in Swift's room. For instance, the end of letter 41, Feb. 1711–12 (*JS* 2:494), states:

> I assure oo it im vely rate now. But zis goes tomorrow, and I must have time to converse with own richar Md. Nite deelest sollahs. [the next day] I am going out; & must carry zis in my Pottick to give it at some generall Posthouse. I will talk further with oo at night.

Again, despite the allusions to talking, Swift shows an equal awareness of the letter as material written object, an awareness that can deflate his conversational fantasy. A passage in letter 35 (Nov. 1711, *JS* 2:425), obviously written in the little language but now accessible only through the interpretations of editors, demonstrates the struggle between talking and writing:

> It goes tomorrow, to nobody's sorrow. You are silly, not I; I'm a poet if I had but, &c.- Who's silly now? rogues and lasses, tinder boxes and buzzards. O Lord, I am in a high vein of silliness; methought I was speaking to dearest little Md face to face. There; so lads, enough for tonight.

Where do the conversations occur? They occur not in Ireland or England but within the boundaries of a large sheet of paper—a finite but mobile space accessible to sender and recipient, a safe meeting ground that blurs the distinction between presence and absence as well as between speech and the written word, an innocent house of being that mediates the urgency of desire.

One way in which Swift's paper conversations mediate is through regression. Childish prattle, or its artificial imitation, indicates presexual communication. The discarnate, reconstituted voice can bear significant emotion (tenderness, playfulness, longing) without being threatened by physicality and its lurking corruptions. The exact nature of Swift's relationship with Esther Johnson remains unknown, but, even if they were secretly married, all evidence points to a physically chaste companionship.[42] The tone of Swift's correspondence with Stella has been interpreted as paternal or pedagogic,[43] and certainly his letters contain fatherly admonitions and schoolmasterly corrections, particularly of her spelling. But father and teacher are adult roles, and the little language is less a grownup talking to a youth than a child talking to another child.

This presexual parity becomes evident when the *Journal to Stella* is contrasted with Swift's writings to and about Esther Vanhomrigh (whom he called "Hessy," "Missessy," and "Vanessa"), the young woman with whom he developed an emotionally charged friendship during the time he was in England busying himself with Tory propaganda and Church politics. Swift's letters to her always adopt the posture of superior (teacher or father figure) to inferior (student or child). They brim with advice as to what to read, how to control spleen, where to exercise; in contrast with advice to Stella on similar matters, they seem less concerned with the advisee's welfare than with her dutifulness in following instructions. Even in more personal passages to Hessy, Swift refers to himself as an adult: "[I]f you cannot guess who is the Writer," he teases, "consult your Pillow, and the first fine Gentleman you dream of is the Man—so adieu" (6 June 1713, *Corr.* 1:367). Swift characteristically closes his letters to Hessy with *adieu*; French, not an invented code or baby talk but a real language used by English adults as a sign of education or sophistication, serves as formal verbal dress to cover feelings. For example, Swift writes, "I can say no more being called away, mais soyez assure que jamais personne du monde a ete aimee honoree estimee adoree par votre amie [sic] que vous" (5 July 1721, *Corr.* 2:392); in another letter he asks, in light of Hessy's frequent complaints about the difficulties of comprehending his meaning, "si vous entendez bien tout cela" (1 June 1722, *Corr.* 2:427), using the language of concealment to disguise inquiry about disclosure.[44] Even pet names, endemic in Swift's correspondence with Stella, undergo a transformation. In the intimate passages to Stella, Swift refers to himself as *pdfr* (an abbreviation probably originating from "poor dear foolish fellow"), thereby putting himself on the same level of address as the *Md* ("my dear[s]"), *FW* ("foolish wench[es]"), and *nauti dollars* ("naughty girls") to whom he writes. In letters to Hessy, Swift refers to himself as *Cad*[enus], an anagram of the Latin form of his official title, *Decanus*, but in an odd way. Cad, the dear friend of Vanessa, has an epistolary existence separate from Swift's. He writes, for example:

> Cad- assures me he continues to esteem and love and value you above all things, and will do to the End of his Life; but at the same time entreats that you would not make your self or him unhappy by Imaginations . . . Cad- hath spoiled you . . . Pray write to me cheerfully without complaints or Expostulations or else Cad- shall know it and punish you- [5 July 1721, *Corr.* 2:393]

Swift has become a go-between for Cad and Vanessa, and Cad in turn protects Swift from the adult demands of Esther Vanhomrigh and is assigned the responsibility for any misreadings or misinterpretations she may have fallen into.

The physical appearance of letters to Esther Vanhomrigh and to Esther Johnson also differs markedly. Swift wrote in a rather small hand, but his letters to Hessy are clear, amply spaced and margined, and relatively undefaced by blots or strike-throughs. In letters to Stella, Swift's writing shrinks to Lilliputian proportions. A typical 6" by 8" side contains 62 lines averaging 29 words each: a total of 1,798 words per page. Margins and interlinear spaces have disappeared, and legibility is obstructed further by frequent deletions and additions.[45] No one can read these pages from a distance of more than a few inches; since Esther Johnson had weak eyes and Rebecca Dingley used spectacles, they must have had to hold the letters right in front of their noses. In contrast, letters to Esther Vanhomrigh can be read comfortably from two feet away. Therefore, the graphic arrangement of the letters signals the degree of intimacy Swift wished to communicate.

In correspondence with Hessy, the verbal strategies in the *Journal to Stella*, and their graphological presentations, have been altered to increase distance and absence. Reasons for such alterations are hinted at by the autobiographical work, *Cadenus and Vanessa*. According to the poem, Vanessa's impassioned metonymy transferred esteem for Swift's writings to love for Swift; while holding his book, Vanessa was shot by Cupid's arrow, so long that "[i]t pierced the feeble Volume thro', / And deep transfixed her Bosom too" (*Cadenus and Vanessa*, *SPW* 114–37.518–19). Despite Swift's attempts to conduct himself with the "innocent Delight" of father and schoolmaster (see lines 548–53), Vanessa conflates book and author (lines 705–6) and "vows to take him at his Word" (line 803). *Cadenus and Vanessa* and all the extant correspondence with Esther Vanhomrigh show Swift attempting to take back his word, to change Vanessa's interpretation of authorization, and to free himself from the claims made upon him through his writings by separating himself from his texts. Hessy complains that Swift's letters to her are cryptic, but the information conveyed by the letters is clear enough. It is the emotional significance that is intentionally masked and distanced in an attempt to siphon it from its containing words. In writings concerning Esther Vanhomrigh, Swift's verbal postures and techniques defend against perceived aggression and form a suit of armor detachable from and protective of the self.

Elements of protection also exist in Swift's correspondence with Stella, yet they react not to Esther Johnson but to the pressures and disappointments Swift encounters in London. Thus the voice of the child soothes the harried adult; in the *Journal to Stella*, Swift frequently seems to comfort himself by weaving with the little language a seamless and permanent cloak of calm and innocence, redress for a patchwork of transitory schemes and rupturing discouragements. He writes in December, 1712:

> I make no figure but at Court, where I affect to turn from a Lord to the meanest of my Acquaintance and I love to go there on Sundays, to see the World. But to say the truth I am growing weary of it. I dislike a million of things in the course of publick Affairs; & if I were to stay here much longr I am sure I shoud ruin my self with endeavoring to mend them. I am every [day?] invited into Schemes of doing this, but I cannot find any that will probably succeed. Tis impossible to save People against their own will; and I have been too much engaged in Patch-work already. Do you understand all this stuff? - No- well zen you are now returnd to Ombre & the Dean, & Christmas, I wish oo a very merry one. & prey don't lose oo money, nor play upon Watt Welch's Game. Nite Sollahs, tis rate, I'll go to seep, I don't seep well, & therefore never dare to drink coffee or Tea after dinner, but I am very seepy in a molning. This is the Effect of Time & Years. Nite deelest Md. [letter 41, *JS* 2:580–81]

Swift writes words on paper to croon himself to sleep, to inscribe his own sweet dreams. The little language is dream language: obedient only to its own rules, pliable to the dreamer's desires, interpretable via emotional codes rather than adult logic. It writes a text of ideal, unthreatened, and unthreatening childhood, perhaps in compensation for Swift's belief that his actual childhood was harsh and loveless.[46] Just as the birthday poems to Stella focus on a permanence transcending physical decay and circumstantial change,[47] the little language also stands against transience and corruption. Swift refers to his closed communication system with Stella in the context of his serious project to fix linguistic meaning, the *Proposal for Correcting . . . the English Tongue*:

> Ld. Treasr has lent the long Lettr I writt him, to Prior, and I can't get Prior to return it; and I want to have it printd, and to make up this Academy for the Improvement of our Language. Fais we nevr shall improve it as much as FW has done. Sall we? No fais, ourrichar Gangridge. [letter 43, March 1711–12, *JS* 2:510]

Even attempts to improve and make permanent the public tongue are subject to chance and change. The private language—its emotional significance fixed yet expressive, its power to counteract time and distance unrivaled, its transfiguration of wordplay joyous yet poignant—is "richar" indeed.

Thus Swift's wordplay has the capacity to make disguise a prelude to revelation, a prelude that can take the place of a revelation never clearly or completely written. Literary divestitures become modes of self-presentation, spelling out emotions and motives in their breaks with textual convention, in their protective regressions, in their traps for interpretation. Textocentric strategies, by abandoning or overdetermining rules for reading in order to isolate the written word, necessarily involve replacement: the text substitutes for the self. Therefore, writing in a way that questions conditions under which words signify, under which words survive, is a most personal sort of speculation. Such speculative investments are risky: they can ruin authorial fortunes, and they can reflect, or deflect, an image one may not wish to behold. But unlike the gypsy girl's swordplay at Bartholomew Fair, Swift's wordplay can secure great rewards. It is this interplay of risk and reward that activates Swift's search for and retreat from the self mirrored in the text.

4 / VESTED INTERESTS
Swift and the Textual Self

THE LANGUAGE GAMES represent one way in which Swift tries to absent himself from his words; he can exploit verbal pressures and then leave his texts to self-destruct, exploding readers' interpretive confidence in the process. Unfortunately, such tactics also threaten Swift's image of himself as a writer, one based not only on linguistic energy but also on authorial pertinence and permanence. The trifles trivialize and torment the trifler; as Swift, longing for his friend's philosophical tranquillity, writes to Bolingbroke: "Nothing has convinced me so much that I am of a little subaltern spirit . . . as to reflect how I am forced into the most trifling amusements, to divert the vexations of former thoughts, and present objects.—Why cannot you lend me a shred of your mantle?" (19 Dec. 1719, *Corr.* 2:334). Swift, of course, was never cloaked in calm, Bolingbroke's or anyone else's. But the anger in this letter, written at a time when Swift was relatively inactive politically and artistically and when he was realizing that he would never hold a high position in England, suggests the necessity of fashioning a mantle of a different sort, one that is woven from textilic texts more substantial and serious than the bagatelles. Characterizing himself as of a "subaltern spirit" implies subordination in the hierarchy of power; since "subaltern" is a term in logic designating a secondary and supporting position, it also implies subordination in the hierarchy of knowledge. Swift's impatience with this sort of diminished reflection perhaps spurred him to reinvest himself in his works. Soon after he wrote this letter to Bolingbroke, he began the great series of political pamphlets and broadsides culminating in *The Drapier's Letters*, turning Irish exile into grounds for literary activism. He also returned to a project neglected since the Scriblerian days;[1] and by 1725, he had completed *Gulliver's Travels*, his most sustained and lasting contribution to epistemology and imaginative fiction.

Swift's desire to write was stimulated by a variety of events. Some were public, like the Wood's halfpence scheme or the movement to repeal the Test Act; some were private, like absence from Stella or railing letters from Sheridan. Coexistent with outside pressures, however, was an inside one. More than most writers of the period, Swift—the man who knew no father, who despised his native country, who was separated for much of his life from his dearest friends, who had neither wife nor children—was compelled to reconceive himself continually through the medium of language. This need to create a composite textual self and thus to create a greater than subaltern spirit lies behind the vitality of Swift's works and the puzzlement of his personality.

Swift most frequently approached textual self-engenderment by means of names. The ambivalent and problematic importance of his own name is indicated by the care with which he protected it through nominal disguise. He draped his pseudonymic substitutes with appropriate names; he exposed his anonymous alter-authors in various states of undress. Through these apparent divestitures of nominal authority, Swift created an intertextual self that sanctioned different works in different genres and that controlled the range of meanings accessible, even vulnerable, to postpublication interpretation. At the same time, Swift was engaged in authorizing himself, in filling the name of Swift with the meanings and accomplishments he wished to be remembered by. These oblique tactics stem in part from the happenstances of Swift's early years and the truculent independence they engendered. Swift's toying with various names and his use of his own texts as mirrors that both reveal and conceal his specular image constitute a search for identity of a peculiar sort. Swift did interpret himself as an exile, an isolato, but these interpretations are compensatory functions for a lack of context, not marks of a rebellious individualism that scorns societal ties. Swift needed to contextualize himself, and he did so through writing.

Swift's desire to be authorized through writing can be detected in the circumstances of his receipt of the Freedom to Dublin in 1730, presented in a gold box. The ceremony had been delayed, in Swift's opinion, because of Lord Allen's maneuvering and the uproar concerning the publication of *A Libel on Dr. Delany*; the delay was also occasioned by Swift's insistence that the box be inscribed with a paean to his patriotism.[2] But when the box was finally presented without an inscription, Swift converted the entire ceremony into a text upon which to inscribe his own version of how and why Dublin citizens should venerate his name and his memory. To engrave his self-justification permanently, he wrote an anonymous account of his speech to the city officials. At the end of this account, he declared that he had wished "that an inscription might have been graven on the box, showing some reason why the citizenry thought fit to do him that honour, which was much out of the common forms to a person in private station" ("The Substance of What was said by the Dean," *PW* 12:148). Swift's flurry of compensatory activity reveals his dependence on writing to authorize the meaning of his name and his work. Without a suitable inscription, the box was merely an object and the appreciation it represented was as hollow as the box itself.

Swift's concerns about how his name is transcribed into and prescribed for history disclose some radical uncertainties about the enabling capacities of language. His vision of postmortem decomposition and disposal of his works in *Verses on the Death* ironically anticipates Wordsworth's lament in *The Prelude*, book 5: texts, as well as bodies and boxes, are terribly frail caskets. As material things, they are subject to decay and destruction; as containers of significance and bearers of vested interests, they are subject to being emptied out, to being consumed and evacuated. Swift's habit of marking his texts with excremental images is one way he protects his words from future indignities. In this manner, the work of evacuation is already performed, conserved and incorporated in the text itself. Furthermore, an excrementalized text wards off intrusive interpretation by making readers see themselves as dabbling in dunghills. But excremental words are more than an allegory of reading. They are also an allegory of writing, writing as a function of fallen language that exhibits its own corruptions lest an author forget the mortality of human products as well as of human beings, yet writing that paradoxically purifies itself. Excrementalization joins Swift's other textocentric tactics in an arsenal of complex, often covert self-authorizations designed to preserve and protect his textually vested interests.

TH'IDEA FROM AN EMPTY NAME

In an age given to protective pen names and anonymous authorships, Swift stands out as a particularly resolute concealer of his proper name. Swift's evasive authorial tactics shielded him from censure and, at times, prosecution while allowing him to write freely in a variety of modes on a variety of subjects. They also allowed him to wait for public reaction before deciding whether to continue dissembling or to acknowledge authorship, at least tacitly.[3] This strategy of withholding formed part of Swift's tongue-in-cheek advice to literary novices in *On Poetry: A Rapsody*;

after the poem is begotten, the poet should be quiet, giving up "fond paternal Pride" to allow the work to be "read without a Name" until critical judgment has been passed (*SPW* 573.127, 129). In addition, these tactics also conformed to the custom of anonymous pamphleteering, nurtured by the real and present dangers of seventeenth-century English politics, and to the ideal image of the gentleman-author, who could indulge his avocation by withholding the patronage of his signature from his own written words. Yet these gestures of concealment also provide oblique means of revelatory identification, identification not necessarily of a received, historical self but of a conceived, textual self. In so doing, they touch on the network of problems surrounding verbal meaning, the power of a text to control the interpretation of its own words.

Sometimes anonymity produced delightful confusion and a rather transparent defense against culpability that allowed true authorship to shine through: Swift wanted readers to think that he wrote a piece without being able to prove it. False discernments of authorship that did not discomfit his targets, however, infuriated Swift. After the anonymous *A Tale of a Tub* was attributed to his cousin Thomas, for example, Swift asked his publisher to help expose "the foolish impertinence" of "that little Parson-cousin" (letter to Benjamin Tooke, 29 June 1710, *Tale*, 349); and in the postscript to the "Apology" of the 5th edition, Swift wrote: "*The Author farther asserts that the whole Work is entirely of one Hand, which every Reader of Judgment will easily discover*" ("Postscript," *Tale*, 20–21). Such claims for authorial control indicate a more complex characteristic of many of Swift's anonymous works. They usually demand to be read as if they harbored a pseudonymic presence who has chosen to remain unnamed. Perhaps this is why commentators cannot resist giving titular or generic names to the "creators" of these works: the Grub Street Hack, the Modern Author, even the Modest Proposer. Thus there is a double covering: anonymity disguising the fictional "real" author disguising Swift. Investiture and divestiture work at cross tensions, allowing Swift to be in and out of the text at the same time. Swift divests himself of authority by creating an authorial character that he invests with an individual shaping voice and set of attitudes, then divests this character of an authorizing proper name so that Swift can reinvest himself in the reopened possibilities of the text.

This strategy permits various effects. For example, the righteously infuriated "Swift" can erupt through the calm calculations of the Modest Proposer because the "me" in a phrase such as "let no Man talk to me of these and the like Expedients" (*A Modest Proposal*, *PW* 12:117) has been left officially vacant; the bothersome anonymous voice embedded in *Verses on the Death* may or may not be impartial, ironic, or self-praising. These crossings of unnamed voices can cause artistic short circuits, in the sense that Swift loses tonal uniformity or the detachment that the very fact of anonymity is often considered to produce. But they do not seem haphazardly unintentional. In part, Swift delighted in the sheer play, in the mystifying trickery that unstable and layered anonymity makes possible. His deliberate chicanery in *A Panegyric on Reverend Dean Swift* (*SPW*, 431–35), ostensibly written by an unnamed Irish Whig masquerading as Delany, is a case in point. Swift went as far as having it published by a Whig printer and publicly complaining about its libelous nature.[4] This poem also weaves intertextual anonymity by incorporating and reinterpreting the anonymous verse satires by Swift against Delany that preceded it; it therefore demonstrates the peculiar elasticity of Swiftian anonymity, one that stretches to encompass the competing ends of authorial exposure and concealment yet can snap back to catch and sting false interpretive certitude.[5] Like Swift's Jove in *The Day of Judgement*, whose inscrutable designs are framed to falsify and damn all interpretations of them, Swiftian anonymity turns pranks to traps. The bite not only hurts, it condemns.

Swift's pseudonyms, however, are different kinds of coverings. On the one hand, they are more complete divestitures than is anonymity. Twentieth-century criticism has shown how pen names evolved into personae, not only masks through which Swift, disguised, can speak, but also characters in their own rights who multiply the levels of satire by concurring and disputing with their creator, fictional authors who nonetheless exercise considerable authority over their works.[6] On the other hand, pseudonyms are divestitures of authority that do not leave texts naked and language exposed to random usurpations. The theory of deictics proposes that linguistic "indicators" or "shifters" such as personal pronouns are empty signs waiting to be seized in order to turn *langue* into *parole*; as Émile Benveniste explains, "language is organized in such a way that it allows each speaker to appropriate the entire language by designating himself as the I."[7] Instead of giving the pronoun the concrete, originating status of his own proper name, Swift uses pseudonymic presences to inhabit the "I." Therefore, he can maintain his absence from the text, can defer responsibility for his words, and can prevent meaning from being tied to—or closed by—the speaking or writing subject. In this way, Swift can circumvent some of the problems, long-term as well as immediate, inherent in the straightforward appropriation of the deictic. Seizing the deictic can actually decenter the proper name, setting it adrift in textual time, at risk of becoming a floating, empty signifier. Swift's chaotic early poem, "Ode to the Athenian Society," outlines this troubling paradox:

> Were I to form a regular *Thought of Fame*,
> Which is perhaps as hard t' imagine right
>   *As to paint Eccho to the Sight*:
> I would not draw th'*Idea* from an empty Name;
>   Because, alas, when we all dye
>   Careless and Ignorant Posterity,
> Although they Praise the Learning and the Wit,
>   And tho' the Title seems to show
> The Name and Man, by whom the Book was writ,
>   Yet how shall they be brought to know
> Whether that very Name was *He, or You, or I*?
>   [*SPW* 13.158–68]

This ode offers no solutions, but it demonstrates the dangers of losing one's name in an effort to preserve it. The solutions come later, as Swift experiments with anonymous and named personae, and as he discovers that he can create concealed versions of the self that will "show / The Name and Man, by whom the Book was writ" better than can an unmediated authorial self. The critical history of one of Swift's rare signed works, *The Proposal for Correcting . . . the English Tongue*, attests to the validity of Swift's query in the "Ode to the Athenian Society"; many readers refused and still refuse to take Swift at his word and believe that Swift did not truly advocate a closed authoritarian language system or, if he did in 1707, that he did so in a transient bout of reactionary pique and that the Swift of this *Proposal* is not the "real" Swift of the anonymous *A Tale of a Tub* or the pseudonymic *Gulliver's Travels*.

Pseudonyms have privileged status among the varieties of nominal disguises because they specifically substitute a new name for an old. Thus, even as they de-authorize or re-authorize texts, they mark a quest for self-authorization. Finding the name entails defining—and knowing—the self. It also permits superscription of a textual family romance upon the preexisting biographical context: author, language, and text replace father, mother, and child. Such a search refashions the Adamic referential theory of language into a hunt for the proper name or, more specifically, a hunt for the specular name.

This idea is based upon Jacques Lacan's theory of the specular image.[8] A mirror shows a unified vision of self, offering a picture of wholeness in contrast to the fragmented body perceivable through unmediated self-scrutiny, imaginable through fears of castration, and translatable into the functional body of language. Recognizing one's specular image marks a child's first awareness of his individuality, but the mutability of the image and its puzzling otherness yet oneness with its beholder make it unstable and vulnerable. Geoffrey Hartman, commenting upon Jacques Derrida's commentary upon the self-baptized Jean Genet, has shifted the Lacanian search for the elusive specular identity into the domain of psycholinguistics. It becomes the search for the specular name—the true, "found name behind the given name," "a name much more genuinely one's own than a signature or proper name." The quest involves "the effacing or defacing of the proper name" and "often leads to the adoption of pseudonyms and nicknames, and even to anonymity."[9] Certainly Swift adopted false names and no-names and divorced himself from his patronym: the questions are whether the new family of names he fathered upon himself are random or carefully bred nominations, how these names refashion the meaning of the name that engendered them, and by what methods they prescribe the play of meanings in the texts attributed to them.

Above all else, Swift's pseudonyms constitute a rather joyous array of task-directing names that affirm the authorial self, and through emanative meaning, the scriptory mission. "Isaac Bickerstaff," for instance, may be the most apt self-baptism ever devised by a satirist: *Isaac* means "he who laughs" in Hebrew and alludes to the suspended sacrificial offering of the father to the Father; *bicker* means to argue, to move back and forth; *staff* signifies the crook of guidance, the rod of chastisement, the penis, the pen, the written sign. As a name specifically designed for a specific task, the exposure and annihilation of the astrologer Partridge, it announces the program of substitution that informs the Bickerstaff papers and predicts the desired response to it. Partridge replaces the victims of his fallacious prophecies, misread signs become modes of punishment for misreaders, and death becomes a laughing matter because it is admonitory, not actual. As a more general specular name, "Isaac Bickerstaff" brilliantly reflects the methods and goals and compulsions of Swift as satirist. It is a name so well-tailored that, once worn, it can be handed down to others. "Bickerstaff" is refashioned, however, in a late pseudonym: Simon Wagstaff, "author" of Swift's *Polite Conversation*. The secondary meaning of *bicker* moves to the front in *wag*, which has its own secondary meaning of *joker*, thereby incorporating the laughing "Isaac." "Simon" (Simon Magus, Simon the Zealot, Simon Peter) confers the illusionary, fanatic authority suitable to this indefatigable compiler of banalities. Yet the Hebrew signification, "that which is to be heard," accommodates satiric desire as well as Wagstaffian material.

Swift's attacks on etymologists and mockeries of significant names in pieces like "A Discourse to prove the Antiquity of the English Tongue" evidence great skill in nominal parsing along with great skepticism of the truth such parsing may reveal. Naming oneself, however, is a different matter. The skill to invest a name with puns and multiple meanings can be employed to mirror a present truth, perhaps to predict a future state, rather than to dig up meanings hidden in the past. The brace of staffs framing Swift's pseudonymic career forms a true name—a proper, a self name that assumes and projects the texts it authorizes and covers the texts in between. However, the playful differences in these two names, as well as the series of names that separates them, indicate Swift's desire to protect onomastic flexibility. The covert task of each specular name is to orchestrate response not just to a particular text but to the composite intertext that creates and preserves the meta-authorial "Swift."

Swift's reluctance to claim a singular specular name, *vide* the passing of Isaac Bickerstaff to Sir Richard Steele, may account for the fate of the name Martinus Scriblerus. This seems to be Swift's name: Swift (Lord Orrery evidently called Swift "Dr. Martin," both birds being members of the swallow family)[10] the Scribbler, the writer. Yet it becomes a corporate name for Swift, Pope, Arbuthnot, Gay, and Parnell, and it finally fragments into individual Scriblerian projects that cast off the Scriblerian name, the name itself lodging in footnotes or recovered by Fielding years later. For Swift, the name may have been too general, too tautological, too undirectional. Other of Swift's pseudonyms are so specific that their use is restricted. For instance, Swift signed his *Preface to the Bishop of Sarum's Introduction* with the name "Gregory Misosarum" (the watchman against [the Bishop of] Sarum), a meaning perfectly consonant with the aim of the tract and perfectly useless for any other undertaking. The usefulness of "Lemuel Gulliver" was limited by the success of *Gulliver's Travels* and the relative fullness of the pseudonymic persona's characterization; Gulliver, identified by the public so closely with his journeys, could not be a credible author for other types of works. The name itself, however, does seem to have been constructed with attention to its shaping resonances. *Gulliver* resembles the word *gullible*, an appropriate description of the voyager's impressionability. *Lemuel*, Hebrew for "belonging to God," was perhaps selected for its similarity to *Samuel*, the given name of one of the seventeenth century's most illustrious travel writers, Samuel Purchas, or perhaps because the prophecy of King Lemuel, lauding the rarity of a virtuous woman (Prov. 31), was a text Swift enjoyed. Swift also may have enjoyed the specular and spectral sedimented words *lemma* (a textual note, a gloss) and *lemures* (night-wandering spirit). In any event, the name designates a (fictional) person who is not Swift. Lemuel Gulliver is an Other, not a double.

"Isaac Bickerstaff" and "Simon Wagstaff" are not attached to identities so resolutely separate from Swift's, though, and they can function as specular names for Swift as writer, just as can more obvious self-namings like "pdfr" and "Cad[enus]." As discussed in chapter 3, these names epitomize Swift's relationships with women. The Latin, the use of title, and perhaps the aural similarity with "Caduceus," the authoritarian staff, make Cadenus exemplify the hierarchy of Swift's relationship with Esther Vanhomrigh; thus the name brings to the surface hidden dynamics, and Swift finally casts off the name, as we have seen, by treating it as a separate consciousness. In contrast, "pdfr" is an unpronounceable quartet of consonants drawn from the intimate little language Swift shared with Esther Johnson, a humble and obscure tetragrammaton that answers the question "Who am I?" with a mumbled acronym for a self-deprecating phrase.

"Who am I?" is answered in a different manner by the pseudonym "M. B. Drapier." The proper name transvests itself in generic identification: the Drapier, the purveyor of clothing, of woven fabrics of words that make the self visible, of the texts that make the microcoatic literary world spin from the skill of the tailor-God. It also hides in its initials. The initials may refer to Marcus Brutus,[11] one of the few historical figures whom Swift regards as a hero (see *GT* 3.7.196); certainly the *Verses on the Death* reveal that if Swift saw himself as heroic at all, his heroism wore the guise of the Drapier. But the initials also suggest reading this name as Swift's revisionary response to the Cartesian cogito. "M. B." is pronounced as "am, be." The syllables conjugate the existential verb and reveal a first-person existential declaration: *texo ergo sum*. To think is not enough; to write is to sew the self into the material, to sow the self in the field of being. The specular name writes the creations and the creator through the metaphor of meaning that Swift employs repeatedly throughout his work. The search for the name, in itself, provides a corollary affirmation: *nomino ergo sum*.

Thus near the end of his life, when illness curtailed his writing, Swift's self-definition loses its context; "I am what I am," Swift explains, according to Thomas Sheridan's account.[12] Such an assertion hollowly echoes Yahvist mystery, replacing the fullness of creative power with tautological emptiness. The texts are gone, the words contract, and the self disappears: "I have been many months the Shadow of the Shadow of the Shadow, of &c&c&c of Dr Sw——." So Swift, with the help of Mrs. Whiteway, wrote to the Earl of Orrery in February, 1737/38 (*Corr.* 5:89). Shadows and abbreviations and dashes no longer signify illusionary losses, as they did in *A Tale of a Tub*; the losses are real and vital, typographic translations of the pain of a decomposing body and a discomposed mind, of the dissolution of the textual self. The "&c of Dr. Sw—" is not "the very name" engraved on the collective memory of "careless . . . Posterity." It is an empty name, and the meaningful idea drawn from it is based instead on inventive and self-definitional fillings and substitutions that Swift performed throughout his career. It was through his divestitures that he invested himself in his texts. His texts are mirrors for his undressings and dressings of the textual self. And they are more than mirrors, because the inscription of the specular name etches the specular image permanently into the glass.

INDULGING OUR REFLECTIONS

A story exists about Swift, in his declining years, facing a mirror and muttering, "poor mad old man."[13] The vignette is poignant because it indicates a divided image: the beholder judges the reflection as if it were an image of a third person. Swift, through age and illness, had returned to the Lacanian premirror stage, the condition of seeing the fragmented body as unrelated to the self. Swift's biographers agree that his last years were marked by extended periods of silence; thus Swift had lost the tool of language that, according to Lacan, allows one to glue together the perceived pieces of identity. If it was difficult for Swift to speak in the 1740s, it was even more difficult for him to write. His writings had formed a succession of mirrors, not only for the follies of mankind but also for a series of self-investitures that revealed and concealed the textual self. By 1743, the ability to write new names on new mirrors was gone, and the paradoxical, precariously held identity that grew from the erasures and rewritings of specular names had stabilized in a permanently broken form. At the end of his life Swift was powerless to invest the mirror's passive illusion of truth with alternate meanings, unable to deface the glass so that reflections would conform to desires. All he could do was to detach himself from the image, leaving it vacant, divesting it of personal identity.

The relationship between mirror image and textual self is the subject of the following specular and spectral riddle poem, first published in Swift's *Miscellaneous Poems* in 1729. As is common in rhymed riddles, it flaunts a naked and empty "I" that seduces the "you" into providing fulfillment:

> By something form'd, I nothing am,
> Yett ev'ry Thing that you can name;
> In no Place have I ever been,
> Yet ev'ry where I may be seen;
> In all Things false, yet always true,
> I'm still the same—but ever new.
> Lifeless, Life's perfect Form I wear,
> Can shew a Nose, Eye, Tongue, or Ear,
> Yet neither Smell, See, Taste, or Hear.
> All Shapes and Features I can boast,
> No Flesh, no Bones, no Blood—no Ghost:
> All Colours, without Paint, put on,
> And change like the *Cameleon*.
> Swiftly I come, and enter there,
> Where not a Chink let's in the Air;
> Like Thought I'm in a Moment gone,
> Nor can I ever be alone;
> All Things on Earth I imitate,
> Faster than Nature can create;
> Sometimes imperial Robes I wear,
> Anon in Beggar's Rags appear;
> A Giant now, and strait an Elf,
> I'm ev'ry one, but ne'er my self;
> Ne'er sad I mourn, ne'er glad rejoice,
> I move my Lips, but want a Voice;

> I ne'er was born, nor e'er can die,
> Then prythee tell me what am I.
>
> [*SPW*, 634–35]

The answer, "reflections in a mirror," is both fulfillment and nonfulfillment. The identity of the signified is just as multiform and potential as the uninhabited "I"; the riddle is a tautological indeterminacy, since mirror reflections can be "ev'ry Thing that you can name." One suspects another of Swift's familiar traps to undermine a reader's interpretational certainty. The assignment of significance becomes problematic because the text continues to challenge the investiture of meaning it has itself invited.

Through the dialectic of soliciting meaning and denying its adequacy, Swift superimposes another solution upon his riddle: the "I" is the textual word, the mysterious and tempting replacement for the human voice that, in the eighteenth century, was inalterably bound to the presence of a living human body. More precisely, the "I" is verbal meaning, the significatory potential of the written sign. The riddle conveys Swift's authorial fear of textual instability through its succession of easy but mutually destructive paradoxes. Its images of hollow investiture show that the body of originating significance has decomposed underneath the textual clothes. In a sense, a published text is dead, as it cannot be changed. It is still (up to whatever time it is read) still (motionless), and its vitality depends upon how it is filled with meaning: "I'm still the same—but ever new." Therefore, the line "Nor can I ever be alone" refers to readers not as unwanted company but as postrequisites for textual existence. The text, like a mirror, is absolutely dependent upon a separate exterior presence for emancipation from the state of being an inert material object. Unlike a mirror, however, a book is not a blank space of infinite imaging capability. It is instead a glass made dark with ink, prescriptions of meaning that may or may not hold their integrity against the onslaughts of interpretation.

Looking in a mirror or another reflecting surface is an obvious trope for the quest for self-knowledge, as clear in the myth of Narcissus as in the theories of Lacan. Likewise, the mirror is an ancient metaphor for the mimetic properties of art.[14] In Plato's *Republic*, Socrates disparages artistic imitation by analogizing its facile derivativeness to "turning a mirror round and round—you would soon enough make the sun and the heavens, and the earth and yourself, and other animals and plants, as in a mirror."[15] Swift's riddle could be read as a gloss on Socrates' simile, but the riddle's personal tone emphasizes Swift's essentially humanist concern with the capabilities of textual mirrors to reflect their makers as well as the outer world. This issue is tucked away in the middle of Socrates' comments, but by the time the trope had passed through the pens of the late medieval moralists who wrote mirrors for mankind to George Puttenham or John Dryden's reading of an author's personality in his style,[16] it had moved to the forefront. Swift frequently refers to this inherited metaphor, and he integrates its emphasis on self-revelation with his own emphasis on man's ability to delude himself. For example, he writes that *"Satyr is a sort of Glass, wherein Beholders do generally discover every body's Face but their Own, which is the chief reason . . . that so very few are offended with it"* ("A Preface of the Author," *Battel*, 215). Since the specular text must alternate revelatory clarity with covering darkness, it can tell us what we want to know but it does not always reflect the truth. When readers can hide behind prescriptions, the text loses its mirror functions. When readers erase prescriptions, the text becomes pure mirror, tautologically irrelevant, as Swift maintains when he disproves the maxim that critics' *"Writings are the Mirrors of Learning"* (*Tale* 3.102) by literalizing it.

Ignoring textual prescriptions can be shatteringly unbearable, as Gulliver's glimpses of his reflection in Houyhnhnmland pools and streams prove to be. Gulliver's vision of himself has no context. The meaning he assigns to his image is arbitrary; since no pre-scribed Yahoo images float on the water, he writes his own fears into his blank reflection. Swift describes this process in "Thoughts on Various Subjects":

> Imaginary Evils soon become real ones, by indulging our Reflections on them; as he who, in a melancholy Fancy, seeth something like a Face on the Wall or the Wainscoat, can, by two or three touches with a leaden Pencil, make it look visible and agreeing with what he fancied. [*PW* 4:251]

Gulliver is victimized by his own reflections because his imagination escapes the constraints of reality. The textual reality he inhabits, however, does give the prescriptions against the blank despair of unmediated imagination; men may look and behave more like Yahoos than like Houyhnhnms, but they do not look identical to, or behave exactly the same as Yahoos. The Yahoos present a possibility, a potential terminus of human corruption.[17] Their fictional being is a prescription—waiting to be filled, or unfilled, or misfilled—against their actual becoming. A similar misinterpretation of a mirror image occurs when Gulliver stares at the double reflection of himself and the Brobdingnagian queen. He feels silly, diminished, inconsequential: "[T]here could nothing be more ridiculous than the Comparison: So that I really began to imagine my self dwindled many Degrees below my usual Size" (*GT* 2.3.107). Gulliver's retrospective choice of the word *imagine*, though, indicates that he has not isolated this particular reflection from its contexts, the reversed context of Lilliput and the framing contexts of England, where all humans are of similar size. The prescriptions of the specular text, then, are necessary mediations for self-discovery.

Gulliver's ability to contextualize his image in the Brobdingnagian mirror by recognizing the dangers of decontextualized imagination indicates a concept of personal identity based on placement within a social network, an epistemology Swift shared with both Locke and Hobbes.[18] As alien traditions and institutions repeatedly confront Gulliver, they decompose him. The *Travels* record his attempts to recompose himself according to new cultural imperatives. In one sense, Gulliver's abhorrence of his self-styled Yahoo reflection negatively ratifies the social context theory of personal identity, yet in another sense it challenges it. The episode emblematizes the face-to-face encounter of self with self.[19] Its unmediated nakedness is powerful and frightening, as if Swift feared that the self stripped of social definitions would be loathsomely demonic.

The episode also emblematizes the search for the specular name, the unifying concept of self that heals fragmentation. Throughout *Gulliver's Travels*, Gulliver never refers to himself by his proper name; instead, he dons a succession of names given by the people he encounters. *Quinbus Flestrin* (Great Man Mountain), *Grildrig* (mannikin), and *naiah Yahoo* (gentle Yahoo) serve as proper names although they are actually generic descriptions, whereas *Nardac* (honored courtier), *Splacknuk* (weasel-like animal), and *Relplum Scalcath* (freak of nature) classify Gulliver within a set of cultural norms.[20] The only self-naming occurs in book 3 when Gulliver calls himself a Hollander, even making up names for fictitious Dutch parents (which, however, he does not reveal to the reader), in order to facilitate his travels in Asian waters. Such politically expedient nomination clearly equates name with disguise; it also reflects one of the motivations for Swift's use of pseudonyms and anonymous authorships. Gulliver is identified as Captain Lemuel Gulliver only on the title page and in the letters prefatory to his *Travels*, a ploy necessary to Swift's idea of travel-book verisimilitude and to Swift's own need for nominal disguise. The prefacing proper name also acts as a prescriptive authorization against which Gulliver's textual search for his specular name can be measured, and against which his final acceptance of the specular name *Yahoo* can be judged an act of folly.

Gulliver has confused metonymy with metaphor; he has mistaken physical proximity for conceptual similarity. By clinging to a specular name at best only somewhat applicable in the limited context of Houyhnhnmland even when he changes venue to the contexts of the Portuguese ship or Redriff, he absconds with the signifier and replaces the original signified with a belated and essentially bogus one—himself. In this way, he binds himself into a single, partial, and arbitrary fiction, a textual imprisonment that Swift's succession of authorial specular names avoids. Furthermore, Gulliver's errors are sins of interpretation. He reads his own text as a Laputan would: one eye on abstract metaphor, one eye on himself.

Although Swift allows Gulliver to be lost in his own interpretive blind spots, Swift does act as a flapper for the extratextual reader. Repeated emphasis on Gulliver's clothes, cleanliness, cooperation, and communicative ability reminds us of the profound differences between man and Yahoo. We are tempted to overlook these differences on metonymic grounds; since it is a fictional human, Gulliver, rather than a fictional animal, like an intelligent baboon or orangutan, that is set down in Houyhnhnmland, we conclude that Yahoos are metaphors of degenerate humanity.[21] When we follow Gulliver further, hardening the metaphor from resemblance to identity, we are captured by our own interpretation. Thus readers who label men as Yahoos do not prove that men are really like Yahoos but that they are like Gulliver. Swift's satire is of course designed to make us ask, "Is this my reflection in the text?" However, it is not designed to give a straightforward answer. Instead, it exposes how our self-centered delusions operate, how they lead us into misreading or erasing the multiple contexts that give meaning to our existence.

Yet in the last chapter of the book, when Gulliver makes his concluding vows "to behold my Figure often in a Glass, and thus if possible habituate my self by Time to tolerate the Sight of a human Creature" (*GT* 4.7.295), it seems that his search for the lost name may continue, that he may try to rewrite his humanity over the fearful Yahoo image that his indulgent fancy has inscribed upon his own reflection. Perhaps his final answer to the question of "Who am I" is not final at all, and Swift has designed Gulliver's search for the specular name that will unify his identity as a guide to interpretation. Gulliver's stubborn habitation of a stolen signifier shows the consequences of self-authorized textual trespass. The hint that he may ultimately abandon it is a reminder that metonymy is not necessarily metaphor, even though the pressures of the text tend to squeeze one figure into another, and that metaphor is but a partial and potential reflection of truth.

J.S.D.S.P.D. HOSPES IGNOTUS

Similarly, Swift's riddle poem ends with an open question, "[W]hat am I[?]" and the surface answer is challenged by the subsurface answer. Yet both solutions, mirror reflections and textual words, may be inadequate because they are, like Gulliver's textual names, generic habitations of the vacant personal pronoun, "I." The riddle quite obviously refers to Swift's own tropes, fictional constructs, and authorial habits through its references to clothes, Brobdingnagian and Lilliputian sizes, and pseudonymity:

> Sometimes imperial Robes I wear,
> Anon in Beggar's Rags appear;
> A Giant now, and strait an Elf,
> I'm ev'ry one, but ne'er my self.
> [*SPW* 635.20–23]

But the self is disclosed in the poem. The riddle is composed of rhyming couplets, yet it is twenty-seven lines long, Swift uncharacteristically having fashioned lines 6–8 into a triplet. The triplet highlights line 14 by situating it in the exact middle of the poem so that readers will notice its pun: "Swiftly I come, and enter there." In this way, Swift prescribes his own name in his specular text and makes visible his vested interest in his own works; it is his proper specular name that derives its propriety not from an accident of birth but from deliberate authorization.

Even here the name is disguised, punningly embedded in a trivial poem about identity. Swift's entire career records a frustrated search for the specular name, accompanied by evasions of his proper name. Since Swift was named after his dead father, he inherited the burdensome status of being a revenant,[22] of having a name not only previously claimed but also closed to contention for possession by death. Swift's biographical fragment asserts that his earliest known ancestor "passed under the name of

Caveliero Swift" (*PW* 5:187); although the questioning of the name's authority probably refers to the title of cavalier, it spreads doubt upon the name of Swift as well. The biographical fragment also states that in his youth, Swift was supported by his uncle Godwin Swift. Godwin's other fatherless nephew, Thomas, was approximately the same age as Jonathan Swift, and the two boys attended the same schools. Therefore, Swift grew up as sort of a dependent twin, a confusion of identity corroborated by the tangled records of Trinity College that make it difficult to tell whether it was Jonathan or Thomas Swift, for example, who was fined for off-campus carousing.[23] As we have seen, this confusion of identity extended to the authorship of *A Tale of a Tub*; in this case, Swift's anger at his cousin may also have stemmed from Thomas's employment by Sir William Temple, which Swift perhaps considered competitive. Swift's ambivalence about his own name, about whether it signified "He, or You, or I," is mirrored by his dissembling about his birthplace. Evidently he told many people that he was born in England;[24] he also frequently repeated the account of being spirited away from Ireland to England as a baby, a story that the normally uncritical Laetitia Pilkington thought resembled a fairy tale.[25] Whether or not the transplantation actually occurred, Swift recounted it as fact, and it contains the psychological truth of a child's questioning his identity, wishing for a corrective birthright to authorize an imagined self.

Creating a family romance seems to be an imaginatively logical response to the Oedipus complex. Whatever Swift's sexual feelings toward his mother may have been, his irritation at both parents' imprudence and failures is quite clear. Since his mother lived for forty-two years after his birth, Swift was able to come to some sort of acceptance of her weaknesses; when she died, he was able to praise her "piety, truth, justice, and charity" ("Swift's Account of His Mother's Death," *PW* 5:196). Swift had no opportunity to modify his anger at his father for dying "so suddenly before he could make a sufficient establishment for his family" ("Family of Swift," *PW* 5:192). Swift's relationships with older men like his uncle Godwin and Sir William Temple may have been intensified by his desire to feel established psychologically and monetarily with a substitute father, but neither man offered Swift the degree of dual support he demanded.[26] Since Swift's attempts to translate a family romance into actual terms failed, he took refuge in the fantasy of exile, a family romance with one sole actor stranded in an alien setting. The happy exile of childhood, in which the baby is taken by an unnamed nurturer to England where he precociously learns the Bible because he is unencumbered with the exigencies of family life in Ireland, turns into the unhappy exile of adulthood. Swift, unestablished in England, is banished to Ireland; when he revisits England, it is not as the lost son returned but as a stranger, and when he establishes himself in Ireland, it is not as a native but as an outsider.

Thus Swift's bleak and shrunken family romance indicates a stubborn compensatory desire to remake the self, independent of family and national ties. It encodes a rewriting of the self; it fights passive acquiescence to the received biographical text by defacing it—by writing one's own message on its surface. This is the subject of the strange series of poems, "On seeing Verses Written Upon Windows in Inns," which Swift composed while he was making his way back from London to Ireland in 1727, when Stella was critically ill in Dublin. The context is important, because Swift is in transition from one exile to another, one that threatens to become unbearable because the compensatory family he created (Esther Johnson as adored child and comforting sister, Swift as both father and brother, and Rebecca Dingley as cousin or maiden aunt) is in danger of dissolution. Inns are temporary shelters for wayfaring strangers, and their inscribed windows also record their own history of transience. Many of Swift's poems decry the scrawls, since "The glass, by lovers nonsense blurr'd, / Dims and obscures our sight" ("Window Poem 6," *SPW* 314.1-2), yet they exhibit Swift resolutely engaged in the same activity, writing himself onto the textual glass:

> Thanks to my Stars, I once can see
> A window here from scribbling free:
> Here no conceited coxcombs pass,
> To scratch their paulty drabs on glass;
> No party-fool is calling names,
> Or dealing crowns to George and James.
> ["Window Poem 7:
> Another, written upon a
> Window where there was
> no Writing before,"
> *SPW*, 314]

Swift is thankful that the window is empty because it provides him a clear field upon which to inscribe his own specular name. This inscription appears in the last poem of the series—untitled, and written in Latin:

> *J.S.D.S.P.D. hospes ignotus,*
> *Patriae (ut nunc est) plusquam vellet notus,*
> *Tempestate pulsus,*
> *Hic pernoctabit,*
> *A.D. 17 ——*
> ["Window Poem 12," *SPW*, 316]

> [J.S.D.S.P.D., an unknown guest,
> Known most for being plucked from his country (as it now is)
> Beaten by bad weather,
> Here passed the night,
> A.D. 17——] [my translation]

The specular name is cryptic: a sequence of initials, jumbling name and title, designate a wandering stranger uprooted from the fatherland, lost in a stormy blank of time. The name defines the self through absence and defeat; it performs its own defacement; its Latin form masks an epitaph for the terminal hidden name.

Just as Swift's fantasy of exile structured his concept of himself and involved a quest for the specular name, so did his succession of pseudonyms, nicknames, and other nominal substitutions like titles and initials. They go beyond reinventing the self in the text to reinvesting the self with independent authority—to refathering the self, being both father and son, and concurrently sowing oneself in one's texts so they, the "Children of the Brain," will show forth their lineage and not become orphaned. But Swift's nominal self-authorizations, even in trifles like the window poems and the mirror riddle in which he could afford to inhabit his proper specular identity, are paradoxical. Swift's works are pieces of his specular image, prescribed with different names that tend to smudge the unified text they attempt to write.

These names do have the function of authorizing future readings of the name of Swift, of uniting it with Swift's desired textual identity. In effect, the family of specular names works to turn an accident of history into an act of will, Swift into "Swift." The nominalizations thus make "Swift" an overdetermined signifier; they invest the "I" with prescribed meanings so it cannot be confused with "he" or "you." Conservative textocentric strategies, the names operate like other varieties of Swiftian textual apparatus: revisions disguised as introductions, denials masquerading as dedications, notes that block unauthorized interpretations presented as notes that offer unauthorized interpretations. In other words, Swift's awareness of the possibilities of liberal textocentrism—the undefinable play of meaning allowed, in part, by the decentered textual self—leads him to usurp its enabling devices for himself in order to bar the reader from the game. Swift's verbal divestitures are ultimately conservative and exclusionary. The fact that they have not succeeded, that readers have disagreed about the meaning of Swiftian texts and the personality and intentionality of Swift for almost three hundred years, attests more to the impossibility of the task than to Swift's conscious or unconscious ambivalence toward it. Swift is perhaps the most radically deconstructive Augustan writer precisely because he is the most energetically engaged in constructing defenses against the tendency for texts to deconstruct their own meaning. His texts thus evidence a busy and restless activity that undercuts fixed verbal significance. Similarly, the composite textual self he worked so inventively to create is profoundly unstable; it cracks under its own accumulated weight and fractures back into its discrete specular identities. The onomaclasia necessary to prescribe the name for posterity ends up shattering the glass.

Nevertheless, the result should not be taken for the intent; the decomposition of the Swiftian text is also a product of the change from a criticism of cultural guardianship to ones of linguistic scientificism, psychoanalytic refabrication, creative collusion, and explicit literary politicization.[27] Swift's original exclusionary intent is nowhere more apparent than in his epitaph. By their very natures, epitaphs inscribed on surfaces at burial sites are paradigms of perfected linguistic fixity, icons of enduring verbal form. They join signifier and signified in their proper place and redress the soul, its physical clothing decaying through the inevitable process of corruption, with engraved verbal vestments. For generations of students and admirers of Swift, his own epitaph at St. Patrick's Cathedral, Dublin, has made exterior and present the interior and absent, the lacerated heart and the savage indignation that tortured and inspired a man now long dead.[28] Inscribing the meaning of his life in a solid and impenetrable text was Swift's final strategy to authorize the terms by which personal immortality would endure in historical memory. Moreover, the epitaph's last lines embed a protective, exclusionary gesture in the change from the traditional *siste viator* to the less common *abi viator*. Swift's words do not invite the traveler, the mobile representative of time, to stay, to meditate, to draw independent and personal meanings from the written text. Instead, they command him to go away: to emulate virtuous action, certainly, but also to leave the charmed spot where words and meanings exist in harmony, in perpetuity. The epitaph, authorized by the self-authorized *genius loci*,[29] thus wards off interpretive intrusions that would rob the grave.

Swift is not an unknown guest at this terminal shelter. It is the rest of the world that is transient and banished. But the defiant defenses in his words spell their own defeat even as they gain a sort of permanent presence. Swift has resurrected his own name, stretching it out over the palimpsest of skeletal initials and alternative nominalizations, in conventionally formalized, third person wording; yet the empty "I" remains unfilled. The name belongs to the body, and the body is dead: *hic depositum est corpus Jonathan Swift.*

HEAPS OF NEVER-DYING WORKS

To Swift, as to Christian teachers dating back to St. Paul, the body is the beggar's badge we all wear to mark our mortality and signify our sinfulness, a constant reminder of the unregenerate side of man's mixed nature. The received name that labels the body is also the legacy of corruption; its words affiliate us with the originating sin of ancestral sexuality. Since a specular image resides in the mirror and in the mind, however, it is not bound to physical corruption. It can function as a substitute body, as a self protected from corporeal decay. Similarly, a specular name lives through the inherited name, rewriting and purifying the self. As a specular name affixes the specular image to the mirror surface, it turns mirror into text and text into an inscribed monument to commemorate and to contain the vested interests of the reconstituted self. The problem, however, is that words are subject to and productive of their own corruption.

When Swift as a young man asks in "Ode to the Athenian Society" how personal fame can be achieved through one's written words, his concern is not immediate recognition but postmortem memory. Near the end of his writing career, Swift directly attacks this issue in *Verses on the Death of Dr. Swift, D.S.P.D.* by writing mock memories of a deceased Swift into the mouths of those who outlive him and by canceling these incomplete assessments with the words of a neutral commentator who draws the complete "idea from th'empty name." Yet this poem also problematizes its own confident reconstitution of the textual self. Almost halfway through the poem, Swift envisions a perverse disinterment and resurrection in which his words are brought back to life through machinations of inept and unauthorized reconstructors:

> Now *Curl* his Shop from Rubbish drains;
> Three genuine Tomes of *Swift*'s Remains.
> And then to make them pass the glibber,
> Revis'd by *Tibbalds, Moore, and Cibber.*
> He'll treat me as he does my Betters,
> Publish my Will, my Life, my Letters.
> Revive the Libels born to dye,
> Which POPE must bear, as well as I.
> [*SPW* 503.197–204]

Order is inverted; the books, and Swift's fame, soon sink into oblivion, cast out by changing tastes that no longer value his "antiquated *Stuff*" (*SPW* 505.267). As Edward Said has pointed out, Swift realized that a writer's death occurs as a function of language; accordingly, artistic immortality is a prearranged "verbal protrusion into the future."[30] Nevertheless, such an act of textual self-engenderment is threatened by its medium. The book contains the body; the tome is the tomb; and the authorized, genuine textual self, like the physical body it replaces, can be transformed into waste matter.

Partially, the devolution of books and words into waste matter is a function of extratextual devaluation. As Swift's mirror riddle implies, specular texts need an exterior presence to keep alive their signifying power. However, inimical or tyrannical exterior presences can destroy signification and re-reify the text, as do Curll and his ghoulish revisers. Swift employs the language of evacuation ("Rubbish drains," "make them pass") to show that the bookmen are sons of the Goddess Criticism in *The Battel of the Books*, bibliophages interested only in the end product of consumption. Swift's own notes to *Verses on the Death* indicate that he also had portions of the *Dunciad* in mind here, tapping into Pope's mock mythic metaphor as well as attacking the same target. In book 2 of the *Dunciad*, Pope had presented Cloacina as revivifying Curll with effluvia from her nether regions so that the power to convert food to excrement homeopathically enabled the power to rename, to publish bad writers' rubbish under good writers' imprimatures. Cloacina exclaims:

> Be thine, my stationer! this magic gift;
> *Cook* shall be *Prior*, and *Concanen*, *Swift*;
> So shall each hostile name become our own.[31]

Although these lines specify Concanen partially because the minor Irish author attacked Pope as well as Swift, this section of the *Dunciad* displays neither personal animosity nor personal anxiety, these emotions having perhaps been swallowed by the playful and overtly parodic scatological movement informing book 2. Swift's lines about Curll, however, convey personal anguish about the fate of the invested textual self. The puzzling stridency of the impartial voice at the end of *Verses on the Death* may be attributable to Swift's need to create a textocentric guardian strong enough to ward off the outrages predicted by the poem, and by the *Dunciad* as well.

This sort of reactionary yet ultimately conservative textocentrism is at work in "A Panegyrick On the Dean in the Person of a Lady in the North," written the year before *Verses on the Death*. Part of a group of poems composed to tease Lady Acheson, "A Panegyrick" lauds Swift's abilities as jack-of-all-trades; the supposed narrator, Lady Acheson, hails Swift as "Dean, Butler, Usher, Jester, Tutor" (*SPW* 453.39), an obvious revision of the *Dunciad*'s "*Dean, Drapier, Bickerstaff,* or *Gulliver*,"[32] a tribute with which the honoree was apparently dissatisfied. Swift's poem goes on to devote its last 149 lines to his crowning accomplishment at Market Hill: the erection of two outhouses. Although usually considered in terms of Swift's other scatological poems of this period, "A Panegyrick" can also be read as a response both to Pope and to Swift's own fears of textual loss. Swift reclaims Cloacine's favors through his architectural act of devotion; these "Temples of magnifick Size" (*SPW* 458.201) seem to be Temples of Fame built for Swift himself, to safeguard satirically his name, his texts, and his memory. He has replaced Curll as favored son and removed Cloacine from a subterranean sewer to a Palladian shrine in which he can incorporate his textual self into rites of worship:

> Here, gentle Goddess *Cloacine*
> Receives all Off'rings at her Shrine.
> In sep'rate Cells the He's and She's
> Here pay their Vows with *bended Knees*:
> . . . .
> Ye who frequent this hallow'd Scene,
> Be not ungrateful to the Dean;

> But, duly e'er you leave your Station,
> Offer to him a pure Libation;
> Or, of his own, or *Smedley*'s Lay,
> Or Billet-doux, or Lock of Hay[.]
>   [*SPW* 458.205-8, 217-22]

Recording verbal echoes from *The Rape of the Lock*, travestying the topos of the *Temple of Fame*, and appropriating the *Dunciad*'s tutelar deity are all ways Swift cannibalized Pope in the attempt to create a sense of mock-sublimity. But Swift's method here actually cancels the mock-sublime towards which the poem aspires.[33] Instead of suggesting the end of the natural order by stretching and breaking the limits of the sensible imagination to release a comic apotheosis, the procedure Thomas Weiskel has identified as characteristic of the mock-sublime,[34] Swift displays natural order as natural ordure, contracts the sensible imagination, and turns its products into disposable material things. "A Panegyrick" ingests bits and pieces of Pope, for example, in order to void them or to use them, along with remnants of Swift's own texts, to erase the excremental traces and then be sent not upward but downward. All the making in this poem is revealed to be defecation. History and language have devolved, too: the urogenous gold of Saturn, described by the speaker in the "raise[d]" (*SPW* 459.227) style filled with images of ascension, is succeeded by the dark droppings of the usurping Jove and his gluttonous minions; the speaker finally returns to her own kitchen and the "lowly Style" (*SPW* 461.329) that suits her mediating role in honoring Cloacine, the role of keeping guests' plates filled so they must visit the Goddess's temple. The fall of language thus comically parallels the fall of excretion. As the vision of open pastoral innocence is replaced by the reality of confined domestic commodity, poetic flights give way first to mundane words about meals, then to no words at all as the speaker must show her "wit" by carving meat that cannot enter her mouth (see *SPW* 461-62.329-41). The emptying-out of language is further emphasized by Swift's footnoted allusions to Horace and Virgil in this section of the poem. Like his allusions to Pope's poetry, these semicitations gesture halfheartedly toward the mock-sublime or the mock-heroic but end up pointing to dingy and dirty actuality. Instead of humorously lifting up the commonplace, they are debased and dragged down by their trivial context.

"A Panegyrick" undresses the desire for enduring artistic fame to disclose the bare fears shivering beneath—fears of debasement and of loss, two conditions that also shape the poem's structure and determine the ritual activities of the temples' devotees. The poem's strained wit appears to be a compensatory redressing similar to that informing "Death and Daphne" or "Apollo: Or, A Problem Solved," works in which textual immortality is dealt out at the expense of sexual potency.[35] Yet the bloated joke militating against the urgency of "A Panegyric" argues against a compensatory reconciliation or resolution. The poem constitutes a preemptive strike; it does to itself what others may do to it in the future. It is Swift who uses his texts to wipe the world's posteriors, Swift who has defiled his own temple of fame.

Such defilement may be literally unavoidable because excrement is a tangible daily reminder of mortal corruption. One thinks of Gulliver in Lilliput confined in a temple, "polluted some Years before by an unnatural Murder" (*GT* 1.1.27), compelled by feelings of guilt, shame, offense, and uneasiness (see *GT* 1.2.29).[36] Certainly in book 4, Gulliver loses the sense of his own humanity in a perceived bond of the bowels between humans and brutes; the Yahoo baby's spontaneous fecal anointing of Gulliver's clothes seems to signal an interior kinship that annuls exterior difference. Gulliver smears his specular text with filth. His image of himself and of others is the same as that recorded in "A Digression Concerning Madness":

> [B]ehold a surley, gloomy, nasty, slovenly Mortal, raking in his own Dung, and dabling in his Urine . . . like other Insects, who having their Birth and Education in an Excrement, from thence borrow their Colour and their Smell. [*Tale* 9.178]

This constellation of images occurs other places in *A Tale of a Tub* and, indeed, throughout Swift's writings, from early works to late. For example, "The Ode to the King" of 1691 portrays the King of France as spawned "From the worst Excrements of Earth" (*SPW* 6.126) and predicts that his quest for Fame will "end as it began, in Vapour, Stink, and Scum" as he "Falls sick in the *Posteriors* of the World" (*SPW* 6–7.129, 147); *The Legion Club* of 1736 presents some stinking politicians quaffing their own urine, condemns others to be "Souse[d . . .] in their own Excrements" (*SPW* 607.186), and shows Clio, the muse of history and historical commemoration through art, fleeing in disgust. As in *A Tale of a Tub*, excremental origins and ends are countercharms to Fame, but paradoxically they are also tropes for the works and words with which man hopes to purchase immortality. "A Panegyric" attacks this paradox through the architectural metaphor: the textual temple sanctions and sanctifies the base material around which it is built; it also serves as sanctuary for its builder against the corruptive spirit it nominally enshrines. Defecation cleanses by removing impurities, but it also recontaminates, if the waste matter is not itself removed. In "A Panegyric" there are no Lilliputians with wheelbarrows to carry away the dung from the temple. The dung remains, an endlessly deepening substructure, mirroring and mocking the pretensions of art and artists.

The goal of delivering oneself to history through writing oneself in one's specular text is even more bitterly challenged in another of Swift's riddles, "The Gulph of all human Possessions," and its challenge also uses excrement as a mirror for misplaced human pride. This jerky and violent poem, written in 1724, is spoken by a sentious moralist, a maneuver probably designed to screen the suffocating sense of inevitable corruption and irretrievable loss. The speaker exhorts vain mankind to:

> Take wise Advise, and *look behind*,
> Bring all past Actions to thy Mind.
> Here you may see, as in a Glass,
> How soon all human Pleasures pass.
>
> . . . .
>
> The *foul Corruptions* of Mankind
>
> . . . .
>
> . . in their proper Shape and Mien.
>
> . . . .
>
> A Treasure here of *Learning* lurks,
> Huge Heaps of never-dying Works;
>
> . . . .
>
> Where each Supply of *Dead*, renews
> Unwholesome *Damps, offensive Dews*:
> And lo! The *Writing on the Walls*
> Points out where each new *Victim* falls.
> [*SPW* 621–23.3–6, 16, 21, 39–40, 55–58]

This depository of "never-dying Works" is, of course, a privy. But the privy is a textual edifice where specular words spell out sin and death, where specular images exist only en passant, on the way down to the gulf. Artistic immortality is a question of material bulk; the more huge the heap, the more time it will take to decompose. "The Gulph" darkly elaborates the posterity/posteriors pun that motivated the second dedication to *A Tale of a Tub*: an appeal to posterity is just what it says it is, and fame is, at bottom, a fecal matter.

Self-contextualization in a network of privacies and privations and privies threatens to come to a dead end. Even as it reaches out to what comes after, it retracts in upon itself. Etymologically, *dung* means a covering, a prison; Swift's habit of cloaking his specular texts with cloacal images has caused, in part, the incarcerating excrementalization of the textual self he has bequeathed to posterity. It is not necessary to rehearse in detail the attention paid to Swift's excremental vision, but from the measured disapproval of Johnson, the shocked condemnation of Thackeray, and the fulminations of Huxley to the inventive probings of Greenacre, the reconstructive analysis of Brown, the conspiratorial deconstructions of Rawson, and the historical apologetics of Fabricant,[37] serious readings of Swift have filled the empty name with meanings drawn from Swift's verbal manipulation of excrement. The "Swift" that we try to retrieve from his texts is inextricably bound to this centuries-long dispute, and the dispute undeniably springs from the excremental strategies Swift deliberately employed. Gulliver ingenuously tried to "justify [his] character in Point of Cleanliness to the World" (*GT* 1.2.29) by describing at great length how he dealt with problems of defecation. Swift could not have been that ingenuous, and he must have known that he put his own character at risk when he wrote of Gulliver's excremental adventures, or when he used feces as an objective correlative of spiritual corruption, or when he satirically bespattered pastoral or courtly love conventions with ordure. Why would Swift court these enormous risks to his posthumous reputation? What compensating gains did he hope would ensue? Answers derived from a single excrementalized text or textual group will be insufficient. Instead, the texts should be read as a fragmented, chiasmic allegory both of writing and of reading.

THE CURE PRESCRIBED

Working from plentiful evidence, most psychoanalytic critics of Swift agree with Phyllis Greenacre's observation that there is "a kind of linking of the written or printed word with excretory functions."[38] Their critical interest lies mainly in understanding Swift's psyche, his compulsions and neuroses. Such an orientation avoids two other directions for inquiry. First, there is a difference between Swift as a historical human being and

"Swift" as a series of textual investments. Although we can find much biographical information about matters such as Swift's ambivalence toward women or toward Ireland, we find none that indicates attitudes towards personal cleanliness and bodily routines that are anything but normal or healthy.[39] Swift's excremental strategies are published textual acts, not private fantasies, and we are on firmer and probably more useful ground when we examine them in terms of planned self-revelation mediated and directed by the specular text. Second, the implied metaphor can be read in two directions: excrement stands for words, as when the Yahoos's fecal aggression disguises the satirist's verbal aggression; words stand for excrement, as when Enthusiast cant or artistic imagination is caused by displacement of anal vapors. The metaphor's ubiquitous intertextual dispersion gives it the appearance of disjointed allegory, but the continual revolution of terms de-allegorizes. Interpreter becomes interpreted, and moral gloss becomes material dross. Therefore, the process of reading the constantly turning trope is highlighted, and meaning resides not only in the oscillating, mirroring, double reflection but in the interpretive gyrations required to read it at all. Swift's excremental words form a deconstructive allegory of writing, problemizing the filial textual self composed in the text by the father-author by having it bear a double moral message: the contextualizing excremental word is both corruptive and salutary. The successful transmission of these vested interests is dependent upon the accompanying allegory of reading, Swift's anticipatory deconstruction of the reader by means of the excremental semiotics he embeds in his texts.

Earlier in this chapter, I suggested that Swift's succession of specular names is designed to send a composite intertextual authority into history, to fill the empty name of "Swift" with prescribed meanings. Such a plan necessitates blurring and multiplying of the specular image projected upon the text. According to contemporary psychoanalysts, people who lack a firm specular identity tend to have fixations upon what Melanie Klein calls "part objects." These are portions or products of the body like the penis, the breast, or feces, that become externalized loci for interior psychic investments, "the very lining, the stuff or imaginary filling of the subject itself, which identifies itself with these objects."[40] One could argue that Swift's textual attention to excrement represents a part-object fixation symptomatic of psychic fragmentation, but such a diagnosis applies much more directly to Gulliver, who wanders through his fictional world recording his excremental adventures, looking for his specular name, becoming estranged from his body, and finally staring at a mirror in order to see who and what he is. Swift's specular search is enacted within words, the body of language providing materials for atemporal textual embodiment. Whereas excrement is an externalized inside of physical bodies, words are the externalized inside of textual bodies. Psychic uncertainties directed toward the textual self can cause not obsessive bowel habits but obsessive linguistic habits, efforts to conserve and control that resemble part-object fixations such as anal retentiveness but are not sublimations of them.[41] But words have filling, too; they contain meaning, and meaning can be externalized only through other words, other texts. Swift's excremental words recapture, objectify this leakage. Their textual dispersal moves towards allegory, the objectification through extended metaphor of subjective truth that can be compared structurally to obsessive neurosis.[42] Swift's subjective truth is the willed truth of his textual self as subject for posterity, a subject that must always be represented verbally as object. Swift alludes to this paradox in *Verses on the Death*: "[F]rom Discourse of this and that, / I grow the Subject . . . while they toss my Name about" (*SPW* 506.301–3). As part of an allegory of writing, excremental words collect spilled and expelled significance so the textual self can germinate and flourish.

Since the strategies of presentation necessarily contaminate the objectified subject, Swift must involve contamination chiasmically in the entire allegory and extend the allegory beyond authorial vested interests, unhinging it from the narrative time that falsifies its quest for atemporal permanence. Swift had only to look to the New Testament as a source for the double allegory of word and excrement flowing through the body, acting above and below, inside and outside, to contextualize individual human bodies into an eternal body. In particular, First Corinthians, an epistle Swift most certainly knew well, provides both an origin for, and a commentary on, Swift's strategies. Addressing himself to the gnostic tendencies of a Greek congregation, Paul chooses irony and paradox as rhetorical weapons to combat the Corinthians' intellectual pride: God appears foolish to the wise, and apostles "are fools for Christ's sake," a "spectacle unto the world" (1 Cor. 1:20–25; 4:10; 4:9). Paul presents himself as a satiric text. He is a sight, separate from the beholder, a site towards which to direct laughter; he is also a mirror reflection that thrusts into view what no one cares to contemplate or claim, the truth that "we are made as the filth of the world, and are the offscouring of all things" (1 Cor. 4:13). Like Paul, Swift allows his excremental imagery to spill onto his contextualized self because, despite his nominal divestitures, Swift is engaged in a power struggle for the truth of his own text. Paul too waged a battle for interpretive custody; First Corinthians confronts the problem of false nominalizations, as congregations baptize themselves in the names of Apollos or Cephas or even Paul. As Swift would advise ironically in *On Poetry: A Rapsody*, Paul denies the authority of his name, the authority of the word itself, but then reasserts the generative, paternal power that he claims through the word: "For though ye have ten thousand instructors in Christ, yet have ye not many fathers: for in Christ Jesus I have begotten you through the gospel" (1 Cor. 4:15).

Paul's method, like Swift's, is to vex rather than to divert, and his authority for clothing himself textually in filth and foolishness stems from God. God's text—our world—is a satiric construction or, actually, a satiric deconstruction; Paul explains that God selected "the base things of the world" and "things which are not to bring to naught things that are" (1 Cor. 1:28). The similarity of stance, mode, and wording between First Corinthians and book 4 of *Gulliver's Travels* suggests that the epistle may be Swift's hidden authorizing text. The groups that inhabit Houyhnhnmland annihilate Gulliver's pride; the Yahoos's nastiness and Gulliver's unreasonable words destroy readers' vanity. Even the Houyhnhnms are "things which are not," and the textual exposure of their ability to seriously consider castration and genocide to purge their society of "base things" and lies in order to save "things that are" also attacks extratextual faith in the perfectability of reason. To accomplish these layered, deconstructive exposures, Swift follows the distinctive New Testament pattern and offers a limited valorization of filth and fiction. They are privileged not as means of self-expression or celebrations of corporeal humanity or accesses to the sublime but as antidotes to the basic evils that are their mirror images: the excrement that defiles is not belly-bred feces but heart-born words (Matt. 15:16–18); the fiction that defiles is not imaginative fancy but dependence on things that are (Phil. 3:8). But whereas the Gospels and the Pauline Epistles offer alternatives to the corrupt kingdom of earth, Swift does not. He is trapped in the degenerate world of language, separated by the fall from the originating and redemptive Word. Therefore, his cures are all contaminated.

Swift's dilemma as satirist and moralist is encapsulized when Gulliver relates that, in Houyhnhnmland, only Yahoos contract disease and that they sicken because of their innate disposition toward and greedy indulgence in nastiness. The Houyhnhnm language has but

> a general Appellation for those Maladies; which is borrowed from the Name of the Beast, and called *Hnea Yahoo*, or the *Yahoo's Evil*; and the Cure prescribed is a Mixture of *their own Dung* and *Urine*, forcibly put down the *Yahoo*'s Throat. [*GT* 4.7.262]

Filth is causative and curative. It is a textual prescription, the specular "Name of the Beast." Swift's unstable scatological allegory has the same function: it uses a "general Appellation" for man's basic corruption and forces it into readers' perceptions by quite literally divesting texts of conventional decency. But such semiotic coercion de-allegorizes itself as it reverses its terms, revealing the posterior salutary power of excrement and therefore questioning its status as an adequate appellation for essential baseness. Nevertheless, its anterior reality remains, and the reality reeks of corruption and sends its contamination forward.

Like the pharmaceutical words in Plato's *Phaedrus*, Swift's pharmaceutical excrement, which exists only in words, simultaneously poisons and purifies according to how it is received.[43] Swift's suspicion that readers are not receptive to the double nature of seemingly indecent language lies behind Gulliver's redemptive urination in book 1. The palace of Lilliput is saved, but the Queen reads only the interdicted pollution and withdraws her favor from Gulliver. The episode probably refers to Swift's belief that Queen Anne turned against him after discovering his authorship of *A Tale of a Tub*. Thus Swift again links physical secretions with verbal secrets, and, through the prolix legalism of the formal charges against Gulliver that ensue, he shows how a secretive text can engender a despotic countertext. Gulliver, however, fights hostile interpretation with his own renegade interpretation (he cannot discover the self-proclaimed leniency and gentleness behind the king's sentence) and authorizes himself an escape into a new fictional context that enables a new life.

Gulliver's urination expresses in phallocentric terms the paradox of masculine creativity. Evacuation substitutes for insemination, literally displacing the female as the Queen retreats to the farthest corner of the palace. Even more common in Swift's work is the analization of masculine creativity.[44] Swift's texts can be both offspring and offal, as was the dream birth of Martinus Scriblerus in the form of a huge and overflowing inkhorn.[45] *A Tale of a Tub* frequently labels artistic creativity and masculine power politics as anal generations, and the Spider in *The Battel of the*

Books is the emblematic reductio of this process. These images and explanations also usurp the female generative role. The Spider "*Spins and Spits wholly from himself*" (*Battel*, 234); male Aeolists manually inspire themselves into communication by applying bellows to each others' behinds. Even in *The Memoirs of Martinus Scriblerus*, the text focuses on the dream of the inkhorn rather than on the natural birth that follows, and Martinus's first word is "Papa," which his father interprets as "paper"—a contradiction that may be a tautology. These exclusions of the female point to two other, conservative impulses behind the excrementalized text. First, such a text guards against unchecked proliferation of words and meanings, like the "masculine" style of Brobdingnagian authors who "avoid nothing more than multiplying unnecessary Words," a style commensurate with a legal code written in so few, plain words that readers cannot "discover above one Interpretation" (*GT* 2.7.136). Second, as it hoards its secreted materials, the excrementalized text forms a defense against linguistic depletion,[46] against the exhaustion of matter.

Although fear of linguistic depletion can cause efforts to cure the diseases of language as a whole, efforts such as Swift's *Proposal for Correcting . . . the English Tongue*, it is rooted in individual compositional anxiety. Artistic impotence can prevent generation of new texts and enduring textual selves, and artistic impotence is prefigured in every authorial endeavor that arouses intentions, builds to a climax, and ends.[47] When Swift's Tale-writer follows comments about man's ascending and descending thoughts with the conjecture that "Fancy, flying up to the imagination of what is Highest and Best, becomes over short, and Spent, and weary, and suddenly falls like a dead Bird of Paradise, to the Ground" (*Tale* 8.158), he uses the vocabulary of detumescence to describe creative collapse. One solution, of course, is to liberate the signifier from the signified, to free writing through the agency of the specular pen[is] from its textual ground and its duties to matter and meaning. For example, Swift's Tale-writer ends his text with the attempt "to *write upon Nothing;* When the Subject is utterly exhausted, to let the Pen still move on; by some called, the Ghost of Wit, delighting to walk after the Death of its Body" ("The Conclusion," *Tale*, 208). An alternate solution is, simply, to be a satirist, to write about the offscourings and waste products of human thoughts, words, and acts. As Swift stated to Gay, "new Follyes and Vices will never be wanting any more than new Fashions. Je donne au Diable the wrong Notion that Matter is exhausted. For as Poets in their Greek Name are called Creators, so in one Circumstance they resemble the great Creator by having an infinity of Space to work in" (20 Nov. 1729, *Corr.* 3:360).

Swift metaphorically analizes and sexualizes the process of writing in order to puncture dreams of unbounded and irresponsible authorial power, reified in the *Tale* as an apotheosized part-object and debased in the letter to Gay by circumscription within the space of human corruption. Even rewriting oneself is a bound activity, as Swift maintains in *The Progress of Beauty*, a poem that is grouped with the scatological works because it vividly emphasizes physical decay. Celia still strolls the streets, but her face is rotted by time and by sexual excess until it metamorphoses into a death's head. The narrator explains that Celia's pencil can no longer reinscribe lost beauty upon the image peering back from the mirror:

> But, Art no longer can prevayl
> When the Materialls all are gone,
> The best Mechanick Hand must fayl
> Where Nothing's left to work upon.
>
> Matter, as wise Logicians say,
> Cannot without a Form subsist,
> And Form, say I, as well as They,
> Must fayl if Matter brings no Grist.
> [*SPW* 174.61–68]

The textual self is created in corruption, through corruption, through the process of writing that mirrors the process of physical secretions, depletions, evacuations, decompositions. The only defense is to make another chiasmic switch and turn excremental words into an allegory of reading.

Therefore, Swift's excremental semiotics, like so many of his other verbal divestitures that use textocentric license for ultimately conservative ends, can guard the precarious integrity of the text by exposing the follies of interpretation. Readers find themselves in the uncomfortable position of deciphering excrement, a practice that Swift reveals to be both silly and stupid and one that he specifically sets up as an analogue to irresponsible and unauthorized criticism. For example, a 1732 pamphlet entitled *An Examination of Certain Abuses, Corruptions, and Enormities, in the City of Dublin* focuses on street vendors' cries—some meaningless, some mendacious. As in *A Modest Proposal*, Swift's humor castigates the abused along with the abusers, the fools along with the knaves: a hawker may lie about the freshness of his fish, but a buyer who accepts an old, chopped-up salmon advertised as "Alive, Alive-O" deserves what he gets. In the middle of this pamphlet, the anonymous narrator discusses the phenomenon of those who determine national origin from the shape and texture of human feces left in the street. Little heaps of waste reflect the shape of the anus that reflects diet that reflects environment and so on; this diseased mirroring series is cured of its cancerous proliferation by an ironic appeal to a Physician "Well versed in such profound Speculations" who distinguishes excrement not by form but by smell (*PW* 12:220). Again the target is twofold: the waste maker and those seduced into finding the waste significant. The placement of this apparent digression implies a relationship between debased language and debased matter; the streets of Dublin are doubly polluted, and people are foolish enough to assign arbitrary meanings to both types of defilements. In fact, the narrator himself is seduced by excremental interpretation and spends the rest of the pamphlet deciphering meaningless street cries into calls for treason and deconstructing signposts on public houses to uncover seditious meanings. His final act is to decode the simple abbreviation "G.R.II" into a plot to restore the pretender, and he pleads for interpretive ratification: "I appeal to all Mankind, whether this be a strained or forced Interpretation of the Inscription, as it now stands in almost every Street" (*PW* 12:232). But the "it" has a triple referent: a sign, a pile of dung, an interpretation.[48] Swift's excremental strategies implicate readers as well as that which is read, and they enmire the body politic and the body linguistic in the body physical.

An Examination elaborates upon a passage from *Gulliver's Travels* in which a Lagadan professor explains how to discover plots against the government. The projector advises investigators "to take a strict view of [subjects'] Excrements, and from the Colour, the Odour, the Taste, the Consistence, the Crudeness, or Maturity of Digestion, form a Judgment of their Thoughts and Designs: Because Men are never so serious, thoughtful, and intent, as when they are at Stool" (*GT* 3.6.190). This plan to seize and examine a man's excrement provokes a parallel plan; Gulliver suggests the seizure and examination of a man's writing. Both types of "leavings" are human products, and in each can be read man's "deep Designs." Before Gulliver recounts the anagrammatic and acrostic methods of decoding, he asserts that Tribnians "dextrous in finding out the mysterious Meaning of Words, Syllables, and Letters" use puns and synecdoches to diagnose diseases of the body politic:

For Instance, they can decypher a Close-stool to signify a Privy-Council . . . the Plague, a standing Army. . . the Gout, a High Priest . . . a Chamber pot, a Committee of Grandees; a Sieve, a Court Lady . . . a bottomless Pit, the Treasury; a Sink, a C[our/un]t . . . an empty Tun, a General; a running Sore, the Administration. [*GT* 3.6.191]

Gulliver's choice of examples indicates that verbal interpretation digests and assumes fecal interpretation rather than merely replacing it. It also shows that the text-to-be-read is sick: it oozes and leaks from its cavities and ruptures; the images of emptiness warn of unauthorized and unsavory fillings. The cure prescribed not by Gulliver but by the excremental subtext is to plug up the gaps so meaning cannot escape—to reincorporate waste matter in order to prevent final and fatal evacuation. The cure prescribed by Gulliver despite himself is to make clear that arbitrary interpretation, as it feeds upon decomposition and waste, becomes in itself a corruption.

Both the Lagadan project and *An Examination* are based in specific political satire. Accused of treason, Bishop Atterbury was imprisoned and Bolingbroke was forced into exile; exploited by British laws and economic policies, poor Irish citizens faced starvation. As parts of the larger, intertextual allegory, these passages imply that totalitarian interpretation can bring political oppression, real physical harm, and eventually death to those bodies made legible by their words or, hyperbolically, by their excrement. The threat extends to any author who seeks fame through a specular image created from textual selves and to any work that lays itself open to interpretive violation. The vulnerable, naked body is the channel through which passes the chiasmic allegory of excremental words; clothing the textual body thus can divert allegorical motion into one that either encircles protectively or one that exposes *ab extra* rather than *ab intra*. Therefore, Swift covers one allegory with another. His ubiquitous vestmental metaphors act as transvestitures for the problems of meaning and survival inherent in the body of language and in the personal and political vested interests that language embodies.

5 / TRANSVESTITURES
Swift and the Parallel Sign

A POEM Swift wrote to vilify his political enemy Richard Tighe demonstrates how clothing can reflect and define its wearer. In an ugly compression of the macrocoatic process described in *A Tale of a Tub*, clothing transvests the body that transvests the soul:

> Foulest Brute that stinks below,
>   Why in this Brown dost thou appear?
> For, would'st thou make a fouler Show,
>   Thou must go naked all the Year.
>   .   .   .   .
> 'Tis not the Coat that looks so dun,
>   His Hide emits a Foulness out,
> Not one Jot better than the Sun
>   Seen from behind a dirty Clout:
> So Turds within a Glass inclose,
> The Glass will seem as brown as those.
>
> Thou now one Heap of Foulness art,
>   All outward and within is foul;
> Condensed Filth in e'ry Part,
>   Thy Body's cloathed like the Soul.
>   ["Clad all in Brown,"
>   *SPW* 349–50.1–4, 7–16]

Tighe's coat conceals an even more disgusting inner foulness, performing a screening function like the dirty cloth masking the sun. It also transparently reveals an interior state, performing a disclosure like the turd-filled glass. The clothes are an excrementalized text, a covering and a filthy mirror for the corruptions of the host body. As such, they run parallel to and comment upon the excremental linguistic text that contains them, a text that in its parodic transformation of Cowley's "Clad All in White" is concerned as much with language and writing as it is with Richard Tighe.

In Swift's work, any semiotic system that can be excrementalized may disguise the system of language. As has been observed in chapter 4, bodily waste is an objective correlative of man's fallen nature and of the corrupt structures, including language, he has erected to guard against complete collapse. Waste also signals textocentric fear that meaning can seep away from written words and provides protection against plundering interpretation. When a nonverbal network of signifiers is subjected to the same risks of loss and strategies of conservation as is language, it becomes what can be called a *transvestiture*, a figural exploration of language activities that uses terms drawn from nonlinguistic discourse. A Swiftian transvestiture is an elaborate intertextual trope that conveys meaning through the communication of its own components and through its metaphorical or allegorical relationships with language. Two of Swift's major transvestitures are clothes and money.

Swift develops the vestmental trope most fully; body, clothes, and fashion point to meaning, words, and language in different ways throughout his career. But during the height of his writing about Irish political matters, he juxtaposes against language another semiotic system, that of money. Money too can be excrementalized; a burlesque piece written to lampoon a plan to establish an Irish Bank, for instance, turns on the depiction of the bank as the posteriors. Financial schemes are described in terms of intestinal contractions, and money is ultimately excrement. The Bank-Rump

> has the Reputation to be a *close, griping, squeezing* Fellow; and that when his Bags are *full*, he is often *needy*; yet, when the Fit takes him, as fast as he gets, he *lets it fly* . . . He hath discovered from his own Experience the true *Point*, wherein all human Actions, Projects, and Designs do chiefly *terminate*; and how *mean* and *sordid* they are *at the Bottom*. [*The Wonderful Wonder of Wonders*, PW 9:281–84]

The language of this broadside closely resembles Swift's "Riddle on the Posteriors," in which the rump's "*Words* . . . spoke with *Sense*" punningly shift to scents and cents, enabling the equation of the intestinal exchange of food and feces with the economic exchange of receiving and spending (*SPW* 617–18.4ff.), a joke that also patterns "The Gulph of all human Possessions." Furthermore, the style of *The Wonderful Wonder* deliberately parodies that of advertisements for traveling freak shows and monstrous births[1] in order to make deceptive writing a corollary subject of humorous attack. Both money and language are man-made orders of signification marred by internal corruptions exacerbated by the circulatory process. Shared corruption allows reciprocal interpretation; the concerns Swift has about meaning, words, and language can be transvested into discussions of value, coins, and economics.

With money, transvestiture is a matter of theme, whereas with clothing, transvestiture is a matter of theme and of form. Swift's vestmental metaphor figures his texts in such a way as to become a structural component in his writing. In *The Battel of the Books*, combatants' clothes signify literary affiliations and artistic merit; clothes function more as commentary on the base allegory than as allegory per se. *A Tale of a Tub* uses the trope as a somewhat coherent narrative allegory in which one set of textual events refers to another set of events or ideas.[2] Fashion and textiles create allegorical ground for examination not only of the Divine Word but also of the nature of writing and reading. The *Tale* thus builds a model for Swift's exploitation without allegorical narrative of the clothing metaphor in later works. As it continues to refer to how words work and what authors do, the clothing metaphor refuses to fragment into isolated tropes; even without the time sequence of narrative, it keeps inhabiting the space of allegory in the sense that Maureen Quilligan defines the genre, the species of text that has as its subject the signifying power of language.[3] Swift's transvestitures of language problems into clothing commentary, and later into economic discourse, reveal themselves by impressing the verbal surface with rhetorical devices that call attention to the work's textuality. Techniques of divestiture like pseudonymity and wordplay as well as rhetorical repetition become part of conservative textocentric tactics. The demands Swift's language makes on readers dictate the rules and set the boundaries of interpretation, as does the presence of allegory itself, since allegory prescribes and includes its own allegoresis.

If Swift's extended clothing metaphor helps control the centripetal relationship of reader to text, it also mediates the centripetal relationship of writer to text. The ancient notion of the woven word is a trope for the graphic transvestiture of speech, speech that is often prohibited or violently suppressed.[4] Clothing negotiates nakedness: vestmental figures allow Swift to write about violation and contamination, about sexual threat and social danger; they locate and prescriptively redress wounds on linguistic, natural, and political bodies. After controversies in Ireland made clothing a real political issue, intertwining it with economics and collapsing its metaphorical or allegorical space, Swift resuscitated the trope by clothing himself in it and applying it to authorial work. M. B. Drapier is the fabricator and purveyor of texts about the parallel semiotic system of money that reflects, finally, the system of language. Since money is the subject of the works written to defeat William Wood's scheme of flooding Ireland with brass halfpence, specifically economic language cannot be used as overt metaphor. The figure is woven into the textual background, however, via the common tradition, articulated by authors ranging from Boethius to Sir William Temple, of comparing words to coins.[5] In the foreground, the vestmental trope and the Drapier persona set up a structure that allows problems of economics to be read in terms of problems of fashion or problems of language. Coins and clothes and words are all counters in larger systems, signifiers threatened by transmission and circulation, markers of worth and corruption.[6]

In the *Drapier's Letters*, Swift's figural transvestitures shape a third relationship, the centrifugal one of text to reader, not to the reader reading but to the reader after he has read. Questions of desire and value, coercion and resistance, appropriation and propriety, initiate the letters, propel their rhetorical motion, and direct their effects on their audience. The précis on the title page of the first letter makes these concerns clear; this pamphlet will be one

> Wherein is shewn the Power of the said PATENT, the Value of the HALF-PENCE, and how far every Person may be oblig'd to take the same in Payments, and how to behave in Case such an Attempt shou'd be made by WOODS or any other Person. (Very Proper to be kept in every FAMILY.) [*PW* 10:1]

Due in large part to Swift's efforts,[7] Wood's patent finally was revoked. The letters and the attendant poems and prose pieces had mobilized the people of Ireland into a united opposition to the debased coins; the power of language has enabled the power of political action. This success also enabled a fourth relationship, the centrifugal one of reader to author or, in other words, of author to history. Swift's life-long desire to be a historian was manifested in antiquarian endeavors like his unfinished *Abstract and Fragment of History of England* (*PW* 5:1–78) and in contemporary political documents like the *History of the Last Four Years of Queen Anne* (*PW* 6).[8] Yet ultimately Swift wished to make history through writing and to make himself and his reputation through writing history. The *Drapier's Letters* are Swift's most fully realized historical works because in them he is constantly aware of the shaping power of fiction on history and because he uses this awareness as a means of control; as Frank Lentricchia notes, a "writer is most historical not when he tries to make some calculated leap into the past . . . but when he attends most assiduously to the problematic 'present' in its fissured sociolinguistic 'immediacy.'"[9] Swift saw the present as problematic because he witnessed firsthand the results of abused institutional authority, as Walpole's ministry continued to support schemes that would drive Ireland to economic disaster. And Swift's prediction in *Verses on the Death*, that he would be remembered most as the Drapier who defended Irish liberty, at least in part has been fulfilled; today his portrait and a passage from the *Drapier's Letters* are engraved on the twenty punt (pound) bill issued by the Republic of Ireland. The bill is a transvestural artifact, combining the parallel discourses of clothes-making, economic exchange, and writing on a portable, negotiable, and reduplicated text. A visual trope of the *Drapier's Letters* themselves, it serves as a semi-ironic memorial to the period in Swift's career when he most effectively manipulated language to serve private and public purposes.

MY CLOTHS VERY ILL MADE

In *A Tale of a Tub*, the three brothers' eagerness to adapt their coats to prevailing fashion, and to adapt the words of the will so that they can authorize change, shows that Swift understood how fashion in dress confers meaning on the meaningless. Shoulder knots, for example, do not have any meaning, save their tautological naming of a bundle of braid, unless a social group decides that they do. If that collective decision is made, shoulder knots communicate the agreed-upon significance (e.g., elegance) and invest wearers with visible insignia of rank within a social order (e.g., members in good standing of the fashionable, cosmopolitan set). They therefore function as intertextual signs, reaching beyond their host textile to link with other orders of meaning. They act, in other words, like words.

If clothes are transvested words, Swift's explorations of garments and fashion and their relationships to body, world, and act comment upon his explorations of language and meanings. Such analogous significatory systems anticipate the modern project of Roland Barthes, who theorizes that fashion and literature are "homeostatic systems" signifying "nothing"; "their being is in signification, not in what is signified."[10] For both

Swift and Barthes, actual fashion details are valueless in themselves. Swift, however, does value, negatively, the rapid arbitrariness with which points of fashion or points of language are assigned meaning, the usurping violations that time and history impose upon texts. Whereas Barthes celebrates the energy with which fashion elaborates meanings out of empty distinctions[11] and thereby devaluates the basic garment, Swift fears it. Textiles and texts are ruined by perpetual alterations and interpretations, or they are entombed and ignored—as when the brothers buried their text in a strongbox of unintelligible language—so that the business of complying "with the Modes of the World" can proceed unencumbered, to "an infinite Number of *Points*" (*Tale* 2.89–90). Textocentrism goes mad under the weight of its own signifying potential, collapses in upon itself. It turns textile to shroud, text to epitaph, the play of meaning "delighting to walk after the Death of its Body" ("The Conclusion," *Tale*, 208).

A Tale of a Tub, therefore, denies its own end just as it disguises its own origins through anonymity and through the inverted relationship of ancient to modern authors (e.g., *Tale* 5.129–30). Avoiding closure is one of the many subversions of form that constitute the book's most striking characteristic, and such subversion is encoded in the clothes allegory as the brothers incessantly deform their coats. Even in the first edition of the *Tale*, before inclusion of the prefatory material and of Wotton's notes, ruptured form is signaled by the interweaving of base allegory with digression and the deliberate breakdown of symmetrical alternation that occurs in the final chapters.[12] A similar breakdown occurs in the clothes allegory itself, as Jack treats the written Will as "Cloth . . . working it into any Shape he pleased; so that it served him for a Night-cap when he went to Bed, and for an Umbrello in rainy Weather" (*Tale* 11.190). The coat and the word are finally indistinguishable, as are Jack's rags and Peter's finery (*Tale* 11.200). This overlapping and fuzzing of discourses, and the formal insinuation that discourses can be multiplied indefinitely, call into question the adequacy of all interpretive systems.

If there is a central subject that unites the disparate elements of *A Tale of a Tub*, it is exegesis, the transmission and interpretation of texts. Swift seems to start from the same premise that Dryden articulated in *Religio Laici*, that originating Divine Will is clearly and sufficiently manifest in the Biblical word;[13] Swift, however, seems much more skeptical than Dryden of the possibility of correct reading in the temporal context of non-Edenic history. If clothing, discrete languages, even the necessity of written testaments are consequences of the Fall, so is semiotic interpretation. The fractured and finally fallen form of *A Tale of a Tub* enacts its own message: the multiple, layered discourses enhance the rhetorical repetition necessary for allegorical meaning, the repetition that can never coincide with the original signified[14] and that therefore testifies to the permanent belatedness of the written word; the structural collapse of the *Tale* announces its author's lack of control and hints that no text can fully withstand the onslaught of interpretive wills unleashed in the postlapsarian world.[15] Formal disintegration, as well as the elaborate and self-conscious rhetoric with its insistence on the vestmental trope, draws attention to the *Tale*'s status as a text threatened by the burdens that history will impress upon it. It also invites the reader as representative exegete to try again, to reconstruct this self-deconstructed book, to reweave the textile and make it fit. Swift thus covertly enlists his own historical context, in the form of the prevailing Augustan virtue of fitting measure or proportion, in the struggle to save the shredded text, but he makes proper fit the duty of the reader rather than the property of the written word. The Tale-writer ends "A Digression in Praise of Digressions," for instance, by explaining that

> THE Necessity of this Digression, will easily excuse the Length; and I have chosen for it as proper a Place as I could readily find. If the judicious Reader can assign a fitter, I do here empower him to remove it into any other Corner he pleases. [*Tale* 7.149]

Despite the ironic tone, the writer divests himself of authority; the reader is "empowered" to structure the text in accordance with his own desires and with the mediations of his historically determined literary values, and placement entails "assignment," the fitting of meaning to sign that constitutes interpretation.

In broad terms, then, the clothing allegory helps dictate the formal structure of the *Tale*, and the structure discloses the theme of interpretation. This theme necessarily is directed at the reader, and the clothes allegory centers not on garments as things but on garments as investitures of authority and transvestitures of will. Therefore, Swift's attention to clothing is humanistic in a way that Barthes's is not. Throughout Swift's works, clothes signify within their relationship to body and spirit. Proper dressing can be "read" as accurate commentary upon the dressed person; improper dressing sets up a tension between the outside and the inside, a conflict of orders that carries valuative meaning. Swift is not interested, as

Barthes is, in the syntagmatic codes of clothing per se; one imagines Swift would consign an attempt to fit garments to the model of structural linguistics to the tailor shops of Laputa. It was there that Gulliver, ill-clad according to the fashion language of Laputa, was outfitted properly by a tailor who

> first took my Altitude by a Quadrant, and then with Rule and Compasses, described the Dimensions and Out-Lines of my whole Body; all which he entred upon Paper, and in six Days brought my Cloths very ill made, and quite out of Shape, by happening to mistake a Figure in the Calculation. [*GT* 3.2.162]

As in the *Tale*, man is again an inverted microcoat; his body is to be mapped mathematically, human dimensionality—a product of inner space —reduced to flat "Out-Lines." In Laputa, the tailor-God of the *Tale* has sunk to the status of a bad author, one who takes six paleogenetic days to exercise metaphorically his divine creative powers through the fallen medium of arbitrary, ill-fitting graphic marks. The tailor writes Gulliver upon paper, and the resultant textile text is deformed, "quite out of Shape," because a formal system of figures replaces the human figure as origin and end of vestmental art. Barthes, perhaps unconscious of the critique he was delivering against his own fashion systematics, called such a substitution a disease of costume; a healthy costume must "favor human stature," "serve the human proportion," and agree with the human face.[16] Gulliver's ill-made clothes are not only badly fabricated; they also are made ill, rendered sick, by the mechanical operation that produced them.

Swift's early prose satire, *The Battel of the Books*, shows clothing in the process of moving from referential sign to functional metaphor, the core of verbal activity that directs relationship between the physical or experiential realm and the world of ideas[17] and that can be extended into complex allegory, as happens in *A Tale of a Tub*. The *Battel* includes many diseased costumes, and one of the most memorable is Dryden's combat outfit. Virgil, "in shining Armor, completely fitted to his Body," is approached by a stranger:

> [L]ifting up the Vizard of his Helmet, a Face hardly appeared from within, which after a pause, was known for that of the renowned *Dryden* . . . the Helmet was nine times too large for the Head, which appeared Situate far in the hinder Part, even like the Lady in a Lobster, or like a Mouse under a Canopy of State, or like a shrivled

Beau from within the Penthouse of a modern Perewig: And the voice was suited to the Visage, sounding weak and remote. [Dryden, calling Virgil "Father," proposed exchanging his rusty Iron armor for Virgil's gold apparel.] However, this glittering Armor became the *Modern* yet worse than his Own. [*Battel*, 246–47]

Dryden's ill-fitting clothes indicate the sickness of presumption. The huge helmet smothers his words just as his grandiose literary projects overwhelm his talent. As is so often the case in Swift's works, smallness gives evidence of corruption and spatializes diachronic deterioration; the shrunken Dryden is kin to the *Battel*'s diminished and degenerate Modern Cavaliers who cannot pick up Pindar's javelin (*Battel*, 249). Trying to wear Virgil's gold armor intensifies the illness, piling presumption upon presumption, assigning Dryden to the category of poseurs most deserving of satirical exposure. Although not above gratuitous ad hominem jabs, Swift would like to think that his satire was humane and salutary, a prescription against foolishness and vice; as he wrote of himself over thirty years later, again equating fashionable fops with literary pretenders:

> He spar'd a Hump or crooked Nose
> Whose Owners set up not for Beaux.
> True genuine dulness moved his pity,
> Unless it offered to be witty.
> Those who their ignorance confessed,
> He ne'er offended with a jest;
> But laughed to hear an idiot quote
> A verse from *Horace* learned by rote.
> [*Verses on the Death*,
> *SPW* 512.471–78]

Dryden's supreme prince of true genuine dullness, Mac Flecknoe, at least had the sense to be taciturn, even stupidly silent; Dryden, Swift suggests, aggravates his flights of dullness with wordy justifications. His offense, then, is not in being an occasional pea-brain but in claiming false filiation that ignores the distances imposed by time and in trying to clothe himself with borrowed glory, just as he tried to legitimize his works with a host of dedications and prefaces (see *Tale* 1.72).[18] The metaphor of clothing, then, transvests an author's relationship to history as it is woven through the fabric of his texts.

Dryden's offense may also lie in what Swift perceived to be a double rivalry for literary supremacy in a particular historical moment and for literary legitimacy in an unfolding historical tradition. At the time Swift wrote *The Battel of the Books*, Dryden was England's greatest living satirist. Swift's energetic attacks upon Dryden in *A Tale of a Tub* and in the *Battel* seem directed towards usurping Dryden's place by diminishing his territory. Destructive ridicule of Dryden's religious writings, panegyrics, and translations reduces the base upon which his reputation rests, making his satire (which Swift did not criticize overtly) more vulnerable. Swift's extended lampoon of Cowley, a fine instance of intratextual dispersement of authorization that mitigates the denigration of Cowley's odes through a contradictory footnote rehabilitating them (*Battel*, 250), also indicates that in the *Battel* Swift was waging a personal campaign with near-contemporaries for his own literary reputation, since at that time Swift was writing Pindaric Odes in Cowley's manner. The struggle, fought in a text that represents a library, the world of written words, unfolds in two directions. On the one hand, Swift wishes to be invested into the tradition fashioned by the ancient authors and their legitimate progeny. On the other hand, he needs to divest himself of his precursors and their possibly fatal influence;[19] the library is also a "Cemeter[y]," and books that seek to affiliate themselves with the ancient tradition may be "buried alive in some obscure Corner" (*Battel*, 222, 225). The skirmishes with Cowley and more particularly with Dryden, who actually was a relative of Swift's, can be characterized as fraternal. Dryden is not so much a precursor as he is a competitor for proper filiation.

In this early text, Swift has not perfected the ability to engender textual selves, to act as his own literary father, that I discussed in chapter 4. Proper filiation is an issue in the *Battel*, and the fatherless Swift, just beginning his authorial career, must choose his literary progenitors. Allying himself with the ancients is safe and desirable; distance as well as original arrangement of and inventions upon inherited materials can counteract the anxiety of influence. But the choice of the ancients compels the choice of Sir William Temple, whose scholarly controversies are the occasion for *The Battel of the Books* in the first place. Textually treating Temple as a father confers two benefits: Swift can be protectively legitimized, and he can be a dutiful son, guarding the chosen father against the death that overtook the biological father. It also confers the liability of collapsing the space of influence into unbearable proximity. In *The Battel of the Books*, Swift's manipulation of clothing images reveals the competing claims of filial guardianship and filial renunciation.

Since they challenged Temple's literary authority, Bentley and Wotton are made Swift's prime satiric targets. Bentley wears a diseased costume: like Dryden's, his armor emblematizes the shortcomings of his writings; unlike Dryden's, it is sick because it is contaminated by its wearer, not because it is ill-fitting.

> His armour was patch'd up of a thousand incoherent Pieces; and the Sound of it, as he march'd, was loud and dry, like that made by the Fall of a Sheet of Lead, which an *Etesian* Wind blows suddenly down from the Roof of some Steeple. His Helmet was of old rusty Iron, but the Vizard was Brass, which tainted by his Breath, corrupted into Copperas. [*Battel*, 250–51]

The corruption and fall mark Bentley as a scion of the spider, the emblem of the diseased writer-weaver whose poisoned and meaningless word-web is the natural issue of his filthy body. Wotton's filiation is similarly impugned. His clothing is not described, but that of his mother, Criticism, is. The malignant metamorphosis of the Goddess Criticism into a book has been discussed in chapter 2; her textilic composition and covering are the text itself. In addition, after her change she appears "undistinguishable in Shape and Dress from the *Divine B-ntl-y*" (*Battel*, 243). Swift also defends his desired affiliation with Temple by exposing Wotton's corrupted heritage: a bastard born of Criticism and an unknown mortal father, Wotton cannibalizes his own sibling before setting off with Bentley, being lured by Philaris and Aesop's "shining Suits of Armor" (*Battel*, 253), and fighting to the death with Temple's champion Boyle, "clad in a suit of Armor which had been *given him by all the Gods*" (*Battel*, 256).

The language of clothing proves a visualizable diacriticism upon the battle between the ancients and the moderns, as well as between Swift and his rivals or precursors. On one level, the system is transparent, resembling the conventional sign functions of clothing in society (e.g., a jester's costume, a chef's hat, a bishop's robe). Shoddy, ill-fitting garments indicate villains and fools, while true heroes are literally knights in shining armor. On another level, the system complicates the battle. Only the ancients and the gods possess healthy clothes. The ancients' allies, whom the *Battel* was written to support, either are given clothes, as was Boyle, or wear clothing that remains undescribed, as does Temple. The allies thus have indeterminate status, dependent on the real hero-fathers, the ancients. Their derivative or indistinguishable clothing demotes them from fathers to sons.

As manipulator and resolver of this multiple family feud, Swift can place Temple in a horizontal kinship pattern, reordering the large, impersonal structures of history into smaller, more controllable organizational units that depend upon Swift's placement within them. Swift and Temple both become children of the ancients, but Temple is virtually helpless and must be saved by Boyle—and by Swift. Swift's strategies reduce Temple, even as they rescue him. They also consolidate Swift's claims to direct filiation with the unthreatening amalgam-fathers, the combined excellencies of ancient authors. In *The Battel of the Books*, Swift clothes himself as much as he clothes his characters. By borrowing tactics such as the Homeric extended epithet from the ancients and inverting them through mock-heroics, Swift arrays himself in their finery yet protects himself from the presumption symbolized by Dryden's oversized helmet. Similarly, the Aesopian-Baconian origins of the Spider and the Bee allegory or the Spenserian pattern for the Goddess Criticism indicate Swift's attempt to enact his theory of good writing; one should gather high-quality raw material but then transform it into something new.

The balance between pretentious imitation and presumptuous solipsism, however, is difficult to maintain. Since both poles produce diseased verbal garments, the middle ground should generate healthy substances, symbolized by the sweet honey of the bee. Swift accordingly tries to detoxify his invective, the gall that corroded Bentley's helmet, by adopting the pose of a disinterested chronicler, but the fiction cannot stand the assaults of his own vested interests. The labored patness of the sustained allegory of the *Battel* itself is anomalous in Swift's writing; it comes not from the earliness of the work, which is contemporary with the layered and ultimately exploded allegory in *A Tale of a Tub*, but from the need to invest himself into a literary hierarchy unfolding in time. Such an investment, the process of which can be read through the clothes, necessitates annihilation of sibling rivals, glorification of literary fathers, and simultaneous demotion and retrieval of the most personally problematic figure, Sir William Temple. It seeks the good fit of filiation that wraps body, word, and meaning in the protective armor of self-determined history. Constructing verbal armor, however, invites writing a closed text; Swift's last minute passes at dis-closure, such as the narrator's ironic eulogy of Bentley and Wotton or the terminal hiatus ending in *Desunt caetera*, are defeated by the risks of dis-clothing.

After *The Battel of the Books*, Swift's works increasingly exploit the knowledge that a clothed text is not synonymous with a closed text, that textocentric fabrications are in fact necessary to dis-cover meaning, even as they shield significance from interpretive assault. For Swift, the paradoxical properties of clothing—protection and exposure, investiture and divestiture—enable it to stand metaphorically for writing. Swift employed this rather commonplace figure in a particularly intense and comprehensive way. Contemporary and near-contemporary authors like John Gay, John Locke, Samuel Butler, Ben Jonson, and Shakespeare used the trope, but it originated in Biblical homily[20] and in classical antiquity, perhaps in the notions of weaving fate and of the fatal fabric as legible narrative. The figure's ancient origins contribute, I suspect, to its attractiveness, allowing Swift to bind himself in filiation to the church fathers, Homer, Plato, Aristotle, Sophocles. As Geoffrey Hartman suggests, the textilic text—in Sophocles' phrase, the "voice in the shuttle"—may be the archetype of metaphor itself.[21] Samuel Johnson's pronouncement that Swift's "few metaphors seem to be received rather by necessity than by choice"[22] may contain a psychological truth that Johnson did not intend; Swift's fascination with his transvestural metaphor of clothes and words reveals a compulsion to explore the twinned origins of language and self.

Sophocles' phrase comes from a lost play, *Tereus*, based on the myth of Philomela: raped by Tereus, who cuts out her tongue to prevent discovery of his crime, Philomela weaves a robe in which is figured the story of her attack. A covering, the woven textile, promotes discovery. The myth presents the primal textual scene: writing engendered by violation, necessitated by absence and loss. Philomela, the androgynous author, was raped and symbolically castrated; her semic robe is a transvestiture of desire that reinscribes the story of the self into the text, a compensatory self-begetting. Ovid continues the Philomela legend by changing her into a nightingale, thereby recovering her voice. Swift revises Ovid by putting into question Philomela's regained power of speech in "A Love Song in the Modern Taste," a parodic pastiche about amatory melancholia. After running through classical clichés on the subject of pining and dying for love, the poem concludes:

> Thus when *Philomela* drooping,
>   Softly seeks her silent Mate;
> See the Bird of *Juno* stooping.
>   Melody resigns to Fate.
> [SPW 586.29–32]

The overload of sibillants in lines 30 and 31 emphasizes the pun on "resign" in line 32: poetic song not only submits to the preweavings of the fatal sisters emblematized in the gaudy and watchful garments of the peacock, it also re-signs itself to its prior condition, when meaning was silently and textilically bound. The shuttling of signs shows that speech is transvested by writing, and the naked gap between desire and articulation—Philomela looking for her lost love, Juno trying unsuccessfully to guard against her husband's philandering, the auditor's wish to hear and say supplanted by the reader's mute ability to see—is left unclosed and unclothed.

Aristotle refers to "the shuttle's voice" in the section of *The Poetics* devoted to "discovery," the portion of the plot that discloses the interior passage from ignorance to knowledge through exterior signs, additional texts, surprising incidents, and excavations of memory or reasoning into material buried in the subconscious.[23] Discovery recovers lost truth, and written words repeat the work of Philomela's woven fabric, revealing what is concealed by wrapping silence in folds of form. The textilic figure thus describes the classical idea of metaphor as a trope of transference, the unknown made visible by the known.[24] It also conveys the context of violence and coercion essential to making metaphor: suppression and emphasis, the warp and woof that organize the transvestiture of attributes from one thing or concept onto another.[25] All writing and weaving is this sort of violation. It imposes pattern on raw material; it covers the matrix, the mother tongue, to create patronymic issue.

The microcosmics of metaphor are contained in the mutually defining relationship of clothes and words; the macrocosmics of metaphor resonate through the systems that contain clothes and words—the systems of fashion and of language. Swift's visitations to the scene of transvestiture extend from *A Tale of a Tub* and *The Battel of the Books* to the late Irish tracts, and the site of meaning is ultimately the body: created by and creative through corruption, swathed in clothes and words that share its illnesses and can effect homeopathic cures, transvesturally represented every time the self is incorporated within the body politic, the body of history, the body of language. Each return to the central textilic trope unravels and rewinds the mysteries of metaphor. Swift covers, discovers, and recovers the body that is metaphor's matrix, and continues the line of linguistic engenderment that is metaphor's meaning.

THE LEXICON OF FEMALE FOPPERIES

In *The Battel of the Books*, clothing is a metaphor for words. Both can give form to, disguise, or make manifest unstable, shameful, or invisible interiors. A diseased costume, like bad writing, can indicate a clash of orders—outward indices of meaning that do not correspond with inner reality—or the workings of internal corruption. A different sort of metaphorical relationship exists between clothes and words in a 1720 pamphlet, *A Proposal for the Universal Use of Irish Manufacture*. Here, Swift metaphorizes the figural ground: the physical body is the body politic, yet this tired trope is revitalized by literal somatocentric emphasis. Swift also utilizes his habitual technique of chiasmus, reversing tenor and vehicle of the metaphor generated by this bodily matrix. Clothes, not works of literature, are the pamphlet's subject, since Swift is asking Irish citizens to wear and use domestic cloth to combat England's oppressive economic policies. Nevertheless, Swift portrays clothes as words, as keys to the meaning under the outer form:

> What if the House of Commons had thought fit to make a Resolution, *Nemine Contradicente*, against wearing any Cloath or Stuff in their Families, which were not of the Growth and Manufacture of this Kingdom? What if they had extended it so far, as ultimately to exclude all Silks, Velvets, Calicoes, and the whole *Lexicon* of Female Fopperies; and declared, that whoever acted otherwise, should be deemed and reputed *an Enemy to the Nation*? [*PW* 9:16]

The clothes produce verbal metaphor in the Aristotelian sense of cross-naming: fops become traitors. They also metaphorize themselves; they constitute a visible vocabulary of the sick spirit. In this particular political context, therefore, costumes of imported fineries are diseased. They exemplify what Barthes has termed the "disease . . . of money, the hypertrophy of sumptuousity or at least its appearance"[26] that vulgarizes by mendacious imitation the wearer and the play. The Marxist orientation of Barthes's critique of theatrical costume is not inappropriate to Swift's *A Proposal for the Universal Use*. To Swift, Ireland is the stage for a political drama of oppressor and oppressed, a tragedy motivated by the former's greed and fueled by the latter's stupidity. Ireland can gain, if not independence, at least some self-sufficiency by casting off costly alien textiles and substituting simple homespun. Clothes were actually a political issue; Swift wishes to make them a clearly legible manifesto.

Swift's Irish patriotism is not a simple championship of the downtrodden. As he wrote to Pope, "your kind opinion of me as a Patriot (since you call it so) is what I do not deserve; because what I do is owing to perfect rage and resentment, and the mortifying sight of slavery, folly, and baseness about me" (1 June 1728, *Corr.* 3:289). Swift's self-interest, authoritarian inclinations, and hatred of Irish exile further complicated his efforts on behalf of Ireland. But in the 1720s, historical events such as passage of the Declaratory Act[27] and physical location (St. Patrick's was in the center of Dublin's weaving district) joined with two private factors: a strong preexisting trope, the fashion/language metaphor developed in the *Battel* and most completely articulated in the *Tale*'s allegory of the coats and the vestmental religion; and a personal preference for simplicity of dress.[28] This collocation of public and private interests made clothing an ideal polemic text. Such a text also carried the extra benefits of allowing Swift to win the goodwill of his parishioners, to urge the use of outer form to check deterioration, and to turn exilic necessity into incendiary virtue. Swift recounts an observation "*that* Ireland *would never be happy 'till a Law were made for* burning *every Thing that came from* England, *except their* People *and their* Coals"; such legislation would reauthorize the interpretation of fashion, as "a *Stay-Lace* from *England* [would] be thought *scandalous*, and become a Topick for *Censure* at *Visits* and *Tea Tables*" (*PW* 9:17).

Thus clothes become cures, the diseased lexicon of female fopperies translated into a salutary pharmacopoeia. Swift often lamented that women acted as if "the whole Business of [their] Lives, and the publick Concern of the World, depended on the Cut or Colour of [their] Petticoats" (*A Letter to a Young Lady*, *PW* 9:90). If *A Proposal for the Universal Use* were followed, tea-table fashion prattle necessarily would be replaced by substantive discourse. But elevating feminine discourse is only one effect of wearing domestic materials. Using the same logic of absolutist outer forms as he does in *A Proposal for Correcting . . . the English Tongue* and *A Proposal for the Advancement of Christianity*, Swift envisions reinterpreted fashion coercing recuperation into widespread reformation. Molded by newly fashionable clothes and their newly authorized significances, the populace would display signs of patriotism and become, in fact, more patriotic; motivated by new demand, weavers would produce better merchandise and merchants would trade more ethically. Curative clothes may even provide remedy for clergymen unhappily marooned in the impoverished country of Ireland: "*[T]hose among them who are so unfortunate to have had their Birth and Education in this Country, will think themselves abundantly happy when they can afford* Irish *Crape, and an* Athlone *Hat*" (*A Proposal for the Universal Use*, *PW* 9:18–19). So Swift addresses himself, and ironically redresses, for the moment, the wounds of exile.

Redressing, cross-dressing—the transvestural activities of metaphor—

return to the body and forcibly reform the spirit. Swift's Irish tracts play upon the bodily matrix, weaving figured robes of discovery for the violated and voiceless Hibernian Philomela. His earliest tract, "The Story of an Injured Lady" (1707, but published posthumously), metaphorizes Ireland as a sexually victimized woman, enslaved then cast off by her British despoiler, and consigned to "the Office of being Semptress to his Grooms and Footmen" (*PW* 9:8).[29] The propaganda pieces of the 1720s, particularly the *Drapier's Letters*, deal with properly clothing the body politic. By 1729, in *A Modest Proposal*, the body is stripped of its protective or curative coverings and exhibited as consumable commodity, to be "dressed" for the table; perhaps this is a bizarre prefiguration of the late Irish political writings concerning the repeal of the Sacramental Test, in which under cover of irony Swift argues (as he had in 1709–11) that adherence to Anglican teachings about transubstantiation maintains the kingdom's health (*Reasons . . . for Repealing the Sacramental Test*, *PW* 12:291). That Swift ends up addressing the legislative body about the ecclesiastical body is largely a function of historical events, but that he begins his Irish political writing with a metaphor of physical violation is a product of authorial choice.

Physical violation also marks *A Proposal for the Universal Use*, and it appears in conjunction with figural redefinition. In the middle of the pamphlet, Swift transvests the metaphorical spider from *The Battel of the Books* with new meaning. No longer the venomous, solipsistic modern, spinning out words, the spider now appears as an Irish Arachne, spinning out nothing. Although the spiteful British Pallas has condemned Arachne "to *spin* and *weave* for ever, *out of her own Bowels*, and *in a very narrow Compass*," she has also violently deprived her of the right to make her own textiles; as Swift, speaking for the weavers, insists, "the greatest Part of *our Bowels and Vitals* is extracted, without allowing us the Liberty of *spinning* and *weaving* them" (*A Proposal for the Universal Use*, *PW* 9:18). The passive voice ("is extracted") implies forcible entry and conquest—it implies rape.[30] The pronoun "us" identifies author with victimized subject, yet the purpose of the pamphlet—to use words to redress injuries—sets the author above the subject; he still has the liberty of fabricating discourse. That Swift deliberately conflates literature with fashion is clear both from his earlier use of the spider metaphor and from a passage following the Arachne episode in *A Proposal for the Universal Use*. In this passage, Swift berates Irish preference for English writing and oratory. Such diseased taste can perform feats of metaphorical transvestiture, as an author who "hath been the *common Standard of Stupidity in England*" can in Ireland become "the Pattern of *Eloquence* and *Wisdom*" (*PW* 9:20); conversely, it poisons the reputation of Irish-born writers. Therefore, curative clothes and curative words rehabilitate not only the body politic but also the body authorial, perhaps of Swift himself.

Through the Arachne vignette, Swift threads together writing and weaving in an intertextual web. The self-citing, self-amending, self-promoting variation on his own earlier metaphor dresses the spider in classical garb in order to invoke the time when textiles were texts. In his call for new clothes, Swift can play Penelope, weaving the fabric of political narrative from wandering words; he can speak of truth and violation, like the tongueless Philomela, through the voice of the shuttle. And his call for patriotic wearing is also a call for patriotic reading, for the Irish audience to heed and act upon his words. Swift's involvement in his own trope resembles traits Wayne Booth assigns to rhetorical historians such as Edmund Burke and Norman Mailer: "Such immense metaphoric identifications of a constituted self and a constituted cause ... [form] self-advertisement as a passionately concerned, distressed citizen ... [that] implies that the fate of a whole nation depends on embracing a national character that will match the personal ethos of the speaker."[31] Actually, however, Booth's observation applies more aptly to M. B. Drapier than to the personae of *A Proposal for the Universal Use* or "The Story of an Injured Lady." In these two tracts, authorial identification is bifurcated. It extends to the passive, feminine victim as well as to the active, masculine redemptor. It is as if Swift substitutes himself as the bodily matrix of his layered metaphors, embodying the tenors and vehicles of each: weaving and writing, the violated and the liberator, the female and the male.

In *A Proposal for the Universal Use*, Pallas is not only an adversary; she is a metaphorical double. She may represent Swift's transvested desire for British origins and his scorn for the partially self-victimizing Irish. She is the British Swift, whereas Arachne is the Irish Swift.[32] But in a variety of works Swift wrote around this time, Pallas is given positive as well as negative powers. In *An Epilogue* for a 1721 theatrical benefit on behalf of Dublin weavers, Swift answers a rhetorical question with what seems to be an arbitrary iconological assignment:

> Perhaps you wonder whence this Friendship Springs,
> Between the *Weavers* and us Play-House Kings.

> But Wit and Weaving had the same beginning,
> *Pallas* first taugh[t] us Poetry and Spinning.
> [*An Epilogue, SPW* 215.35–8]

Pallas, whose traditional attributes do not include patronage of poetry, here shows an unusual double nature that mirrors the dual role Swift assumed in Ireland.

Interpreting Pallas as a metaphorical projection of Swift involves asking why Swift would choose a female rather than a male deity as a figural alter ego. One answer may be Pallas's almost ontogenetic and androgynous nature. Born an adult, dressed in armor, from a father's head rather than from a mother's impregnated womb, Pallas circumvented the corruptive process of procreation; like Swift the offspring of a single parent, she could function as a mythic correction of Swift's childhood. Furthermore, her traits and gifts are mostly masculine: goddess of wisdom and war, protector of heroes, she bestows learning and decorum, strength and honor. Not surprisingly, Swift presents Pallas as the tutelar divinity of the two women for whom he acted as patron. In *Cadenus and Vanessa*, Pallas is tricked by Venus and:

> Mistakes *Vanessa* for a Boy;
> Then sows within her tender Mind
> Seeds long unknown to Womankind,
> For manly Bosoms chiefly fit,
> The Seeds of Knowledge, Judgment, Wit.
> Her Soul was suddenly endu'd
> With Justice, Truth, and Fortitude.
> [*SPW* 119.201–7]

Nevertheless, Vanessa, "tho' by *Pallas* taught / By *Love* invulnerable thought," was "betrayed" by Venus's early influence into loving Cadenus, "Whom *Pallas*, once *Vanessa*'s Tutor, / Had fix'd on for her Coadjutor" (*SPW* 127.488–89, 491; 126.465–66). If Pallas had not been thwarted, the pure friendship between Esther Vanhomrigh and Jonathan Swift would not have been spoiled by physical and emotional demands. More enduring and protective was Pallas's insemination of virtue into Esther Johnson. Swift's 1720 poem, "To Stella, Visiting me in my Sickness," explains that Pallas's gift to Stella was a noble sense of honor that purified her body and soul, decreed that "All Passions must be laid aside" (*SPW* 181.36), kept her words and friendships sacred, and helped her attend and comfort her sick friend. Pallas's weavings, similarly, are curative coverings for the diseased body. Her female charges dress modestly and, in terms of modish fashion language, are nearly illiterate. Enacting Swift's desire, Pallas immunizes against female foppery (e.g., "Verses to Vanessa," *SPW*, 189–90). The political disease symbolized by extravagant clothes in *A Proposal for the Universal Use* is a variant of a more personally disturbing contagion: the disease of physical sexuality, the threatening promise of what lies under the clothes.

If Pallas teaches vestmental modesty, women under Venus's care dress showily and filthily. The young coquette clad in "French brocades and Flanders Lace" becomes unfaithful and diseased through Venus's stratagems ("The Progress of Marriage," *SPW* 224.65); the "*Venus*-like" Chloe turns incontinent in boudoir deshabille (*Strephon and Chloe, SPW* 521.87); Strephon follows the trail of Celia's smelly clothes to her water closet, allowing comparison between the nymph and "the Queen of Love" who "rose from stinking Ooze" (*The Lady's Dressing Room, SPW* 480.129–30). As if playing with Pope's line from *An Essay on Criticism*, that "*True Wit* is *Nature* to Advantage drest,"[33] Swift shows that foolish lovers lose their wits (e.g., *Cassinus and Peter, SPW* 531.117) when they discover the undressed, true nature of their nymphs. In addition, the nymphs' vestmental and cosmetic impostures signal their own corrupted wit, particularly in the area of language (e.g., *Strephon and Chloe, SPW* 526.267–82), just as the burlesque of pastoral convention[34] shows that these poems are about language as much as they are about love or sexuality or scatology. Swift's dirty ladies are not Popeian Belindas, dressing and expressing themselves to advantage and inviting ironic admiration of their artistry.[35] By letting readers spy on their undressing (e.g., "The Progress of Beauty," *SPW*, 172–75; *A Beautiful Young Nymph Going to Bed, SPW*, 517–19), or peer over the shoulder of a prying Strephon or Cassinus, Swift peels away the pretense that fashion artists or language artists can permanently amend corrupted nature. The anger that infuses what Ehrenpreis has called "the comedy of sexual prosthesis"[36] may derive from the inevitable failure of art: parallel semiotics and the meanings inlaid through their transvestural relationships are crushed as one system falls into the other. For example, Corinna's body becomes her crystal eye, her reeking plumpers, and her steel-ribbed bodice. As her metaphor implodes, neither memory, painstaking craft, nor inspiration can help her recreate it so that she can interpret herself in accordance with her desires:

> The Nymph, tho' in this mangled Plight,
> Must ev'ry Morn her Limbs unite.
> But how shall I describe her Arts
> To recollect the scatter'd Parts?
> Or shew the Anguish, Toil, and Pain,
> Of gath'ring up herself again?
> The bashful Muse will never bear
> In such a scene to interfere.
> [*A Beautiful Young Nymph Going to Bed*,
> *SPW* 519.65–72]

The narrator's refusal to answer his own questions, to participate in artistic reconstruction of corrupted materials and disintegrated figures, corroborates the impotence of language. The refusal also shifts the burden onto the reader, who will then be stripped of his interpretive pretensions just as the disadvantaged nymphs have been stripped of theirs.

In many ways, *The Lady's Dressing Room*, focusing on diseased clothes confined in a claustrophobic chamber, is the most disturbing of Swift's scatological poems. It suppresses the satiric spirit that infuses poems like *Cassinus and Peter* with good-natured silliness and emphasizes the grim work of discovery and interpretation. Strephon's penetrating survey of the feminine sanctum sanctorum presents an excrementalized vestmental text that becomes another allegory of reading. He assigns meaning to Celia's body through her clothes; they bear the tale of physical corruption, but the text is decomposed, as sweaty smocks and stained stockings are scattered among cosmetic pots, combs, and mirrors. Strephon's reconstruction reinterprets Celia: she is now a disgustingly dirty woman rather than a clean one. Although the evidence presented in the poem confirms Strephon's reinterpretation, it casts doubt on his groping efforts to find profound meanings under disguising exteriors; his investigation of Celia's closed excremental cabinet reveals "Things, which must not be exprest" (*SPW* 479.109). Strephon's punishment for such destructive reading affects his ability both to express and to suppress. Like readers caught in Swift's textocentric traps, he is locked within his own interpretive trope, a prisoner of his own metaphor:

> His foul Imagination links
> Each Dame he sees with all her Stinks:
> And, if unsav'ry Odours fly,
> Conceives a Lady standing by:
> All Women his Description fits,

> And both Idea's jump like Wits:
> By vicious Fancy coupled fast,
> And still appearing in Contrast.
> [*SPW* 479–80.119–26]

Swift's brief recapitulation of contemporary theory about the poetic imagination suggests that metaphor can tyrannize and despoil, that it can reenact its ontological violation. The lines read like self-criticism, particularly in the context of this group of poems, but they are followed by the emergence of a corrective persona who pities Strephon and bids him "think like me," rejoicing to see "Such Order from Confusion sprung" (*SPW* 480.139, 141). Through this voice, Swift divests himself of responsibility for Strephon's metaphorical fixation. He revises Strephon's re-reading of Celia into a universally applicable synecdoche by substituting tropes: now women resemble "gaudy Tulips rais'd from Dung" (*SPW* 480.142). Simultaneously, Swift de-authorizes his figural reinterpretation, emphasizing the excremental part of the image through the order/ordure pun, assonance, and terminal placement of the word *Dung*. The tell-tale clothes, shed like serpent's skin, have exposed woman's body, man's metaphorical imagination, and Swift's radical ambivalence toward both.

Samuel Johnson was surely mistaken when he called Swift the kind of a "Rogue" who "never hazards a figure."[37] Swift not only creates and uses metaphorical figures, he puts them at risk. As his career progresses, the early clothes/words trope is exposed to new interpretations, new extensions, new perils. To wear is to bear the burden of discourse. But as the truth-telling cloak of Philomela or the diseased costumes of Venus's devotees indicate, wearing also bares the burden. Therefore, the transvestural metaphor must turn again. Pallas is superseded by her function as drapier, and this personified function can prescribe the remedies that will turn a "Nation of Ideots" (*An Humble Address to Parliament*, *PW* 10:133) into something wiser, cover unpleasant realities with curative clothes, mask metaphor's capacity for reviolation, and enable yet another parallel semiotic system to refer both to itself and to language.

THE BEST IRISH WOOL

Swift begins and ends the *Drapier's Letters* with explicit references to his *Proposal for the Universal Use*. The introductory section of the first letter,

To the Tradesmen, Shopkeepers, Farmers, and Country People in General, mentions not only the previous pamphlet but also the violent suppression it provoked, implying that the Drapier's words will put him at risk of physical harm (*PW* 10:3). The seventh letter, *An Humble Address to Parliament*, closes with suggestions for the betterment of Ireland in which are discussed the same proposal, the entire issue of wearing domestically manufactured clothing, and the attendant hostile and threatening reactions of the ruling interests to such proposals (*PW* 10:135–39). Here the Drapier explicitly couples coinage and clothing, setting them up as parallel political texts. He wants "the same Power" to legislate against use of Wood's halfpence and against wearing imported textiles, and he notes that at present "there is no *Law* of this Land obliging us either to *receive such Coin*, or to *wear such foreign Manufactures*" (*PW* 10:135). Wood's scheme, therefore, is treated as a transvestiture of the earlier economic scheme, specified by the Woolen Act and strengthened by the Declaratory Act, to weaken the Irish body politic. Both schemes work as semiotic systems through which can be read the purposeful degradation of Irish liberty, and the second system is interpreted in terms of the first. Swift's linguistic transvestitures reflect and play through his perception of the political situation, and he attempts to make the message of power encoded in coins and clothes the property of his own language.

Such an interchange of signs controls the striking image of the Drapier as David and Wood as Goliath that concludes the third letter, *Some Observations upon . . . the Report of the Privy Council*. Apologizing for the simple, forthright style with which he has presented complex legal issues, the Drapier compares himself to David, unable to "*move in the Armour of Saul*" (*PW* 10:48), choosing therefore to divest himself of cumbersome apparel and weaponry in order to fight stripped to the bare essentials. Accordingly, Wood appears as Goliath, wearing a formidable but diseased costume:

> For *Goliah* had *a Helmet of* BRASS *upon his Head, and he was armed with a Coat of Mail, and the Weight of the Coat was five Thousand Shekles of* BRASS, *and he had Greaves of* BRASS *upon his Legs, and a Target of* BRASS *between his Shoulders*. In short, he was like Mr. *Wood*, all over BRASS. [*PW* 10:48]

Wood's clothes are his coins, and they imprison and immobilize him in his own avaricious schemes. The reductively logical outcome of earlier English economic sanctions against weaving and wearing domestic textiles, the clothes wreak vestmental vengeance against those who would deprive Ireland of her cloth or her currency. They are diseased not because they fit badly but because they fit too well—so well, in fact, that they replace the wearer. Reified outer form displaces its own contents, and identity shrinks to tautological iconographic presentation.[38] Accordingly, this emblematic allusion denies money its exchange value; significance lies merely in metallic mass. Wood as Goliath embodies an objectivist theory of money just as the Laputans who haul around sacks of word-things embody a referentially objectivist theory of language.

It is objectivist theory that accounts for much of the parodic humor of the first letter. If Wood's halfpence enter Ireland, shoppers will be followed by "five or six Horses loaden with *Sacks* [of coin] as the *Farmers* bring their Corn," a rich squire will need 250 animals to carry half a year's tax payments, and the Drapier will revert to the barter system, trading his textiles for meat and drink (*PW* 10:6–7). The first letter's rhetoric of exaggeration and repetition, which includes skewed computations of buying power and personal diatribes against Wood as well as burlesque scenes of transacting business using the new halfpence, is a form of mock-sublime, a programmatics of hyperbolic excess that Pope would formally identify two years later in *Peri Bathuos*.[39] By the third letter, however, the Drapier has pushed the comic elements of his political sublime to the background.[40] Wood dressed as Goliath is not funny; he is a frightening tautology, the starkness with which the inert dis-signification of money is presented anticipating the relentless objectification upon which *A Modest Proposal* is based. The Drapier's plan is to deprive Wood's coins of any meaning at all, and he does this by setting up a conservative textocentric system of exchange that tries to define and delimit signifying potential.

The description of the brassy Philistine follows the Biblical source closely except for one detail: 1 Sam. 17:7 records that Goliath's spear was the size of a "weaver's beam." On a loom, a heavy beam anchors the warp threads that are wound around it so that the woof threads can pass through. Without the beam's strength and stability, the shuttle would be voiceless and the textile would be a tangle of flaccid fibers. The Drapier naturally denies to Wood the power of the weaver's beam, instead silently appropriating it for his own use. For his work is weaving the text, empowering words so they can disempower Wood's brass, and the clothing metaphor that anchors his discourse about coinage also defines the discourse itself.

It is in the fifth letter that Swift brings to the surface how the vestmental metaphor controls the production of his texts. Addressing himself to Viscount Molesworth, the Drapier begins this letter with a "little Account of my self" (*PW* 10:82) designed to counter legal charges against him and to explain the nature of his writing. Simply put, writing is weaving. The first textile mentioned is a "Piece of *black and white Stuff*," the colors referring to print on paper, which was the *Proposal for the Universal Use*. The next goods mentioned are the previously published *Drapier's Letters*:

> [T]he *lower and poorer Sort of People* wanted a *plain, strong, coarse Stuff, to defend them against cold* Easterly *Winds; which then blew very fierce and blasting for a long Time together*, I contrived one on purpose, which sold very well all over the Kingdom, and preserved many Thousands from *Agues*. I then made a *second* and a *third* kind of *Stuffs* for the *Gentry*, with the same success ... This incited me so far, that I ventured upon a *fourth* Piece, made of the best *Irish* Wool I could get; and I thought it grave and rich enough to be worn by the best *Lord* or *Judge* of the Land. [*PW* 10:82–83]

Curative coverings, the textilic texts protect their reader-wearers from sickness by offering prescriptions against threatening contaminants. Protection is based on an opposite quality of clothes and words, the ability to expose that which cannot be said effectively, or said at all.

Exposure may devolve upon those who try on the texts as well as upon exterior dangers described by the texts. Referring to his fourth letter, *To the Whole People of Ireland*, the Drapier explains that "some *great Folks* complain, as I hear, that when they had it on, they felt a *Shuddering in their Limbs*, and have thrown it off in a Rage; cursing to Hell the poor *Drapier*" (*PW* 10:85). Alluding to the Shirt of Nessus allows the Drapier to involve in his little allegory of fabric and pamphlets broad problematics of written language that go beyond the immediate situation. In Greek myth, the poisoned garment was originally designed to preserve Hercules's life as long as he remained faithful to his wife. Hercules, however, was unfaithful, and when he donned the shirt it stuck to his skin, prophylactic turning to poison that ate into his flesh and drove him mad. The myth reverses the normal relationship between clothes and body, between the outside and inside, and, since Swift applies it to written texts, between words and meaning: external coverings have power to draw out the secrets of the interior, to coerce hidden truth into showing itself. Authority to do so is based not only on power but also on priority, since the judgment woven into the garment or the words exists prior to the act that calls it forth. The Shirt of Nessus is a trope of Swift's conservative textocentrism, his continual strategies to control the play of linguistic meaning by trapping and exposing unfaithful interpretation.

The specific unfaithfulness revealed by the *Drapier's Letters* is the betrayal of country by those who acquiesce to Wood's halfpence scheme. Hercules's rage and pain at being exposed drove him to throw Lichas, the messenger who had brought the centaur's shirt to him, from the summit of Mt. Oeta. Similarly, the fifth letter mentions how the "great Folks" curse the Drapier, a threat that joins the network of implied violence fretted throughout these pamphlets. As in the myth of Philomela, words reenable what violence has tried to suppress. Accordingly, the Drapier explains the necessity compelling him to write:

> It is a known Story of the Dumb Boy, whose Tongue forced a Passage for Speech by the Horror of seeing a Dagger at his Father's Throat. This may lessen the Wonder, that a Tradesman hid in Privacy and Silence should *cry out* when the Life and Being of his Political *Mother* are attempted before his Face. [*PW* 10:89]

This frightening primal scene of violence has engendered writing.

The Drapier returns to the subtext of sexual violation in his final letter. *An Humble Address to Parliament* concludes with a list of "*Wishes* of the Nation, which might be in our Power to attain" (*PW* 10:138), the Drapier having initially set himself up as the transvestor of silent public desire into articulated written will. The first two items on this six-part list concern coinage, the third dredges up the issue of wearing Irish manufacture, and the fourth proposes that "the poorer Sort of [Irish] Natives" be taught the English "Language and Customs" (*PW* 10:139).[41] Thus the Drapier again juxtaposes the orders of money, of clothing, and of language, suggesting that they are parallel systems whose taxonomies reflect the dominant will-to-power. But the final two items concern not the body politic but the body natural, in the sense of the World's Body, the land itself. The Drapier asks for agricultural and ecological reform by exposing common abuses of the Irish land: over-extensive pasturage, deforestation, and unchecked turfcutting. Turfcutting in particular is described in terms of physical violence. It "is flaying off the green Surface of the Ground," divesting the land of "many Skirts of Boggs, which have a green Coat of Grass," so that it can be "mangled for *Turf*" (*PW* 10:140). The placement of this indictment at the very end of the *Drapier's Letters* series suggests that the continual and brutal rape of the earth lies behind Ireland's economic and political troubles. The dagger is not just at the Motherland's throat; it has cut away her clothes and carved up her flesh. The Drapier's filial duty is to "cry out,"[42] and his letters are the textilic record of his cries.

Rituals of violence performed on the land work two ways. They can ensure fertility, as do different varieties of sparagmos such as Dionysian revels, or they can spread sickness and death, such as the plague visited upon Thebes by Oedipus's killing his father and violating his mother. The multiple rapes of Ireland are of the second sort. The *Drapier's Letters* constantly compare Wood's plan for economic despoliation to a sickness, the coins to carriers of contagion. For instance, the fourth letter begins with the notion that Ireland is sick and that the Drapier's writings are "Cordials" to revive "weak Constitutions, *Political* as well as *Natural*" (*PW* 10:53). The medicinal letters are actually prescriptions, not cures. They are prior written documents showing the way to guard against a diagnosed disease. The Drapier sees his texts as engaged in a battle of prescriptions because Wood has transvested his coinage scheme back into words. Wood "prescribes to the NewsMongers in *London*, what they are to write" (*PW* 10:53), but these writings resemble the wind forced into the unfortunate Lagadan canine and are nothing more "than the last Howls of a Dog dissected alive" (*PW* 10:54); they are materials issuing from the diagnostic process, not a diagnosis or a cure. It is the Drapier who is the true doctor-apothecary: dissecting, diagnosing, offering remedies. Wood himself is at best a charlatan, like a discoverer of "the *Universal Medicine*" (*PW* 10:36). At worst he is a disseminator of death and destruction who threatens to have Walpole "*cram his Brass down our Throats*" and make Irishmen "*swallow his Coin in Fire Balls*," a plan that would necessitate 50,000 medical assistants to force the populace to take their deadly nostrum (*PW* 10:67–68).

Wood's coins participate in false homeopathy. They cannot cure because they are themselves the disease, and they will spread sickness unchecked until they destroy the host body. The Drapier maintains that if "that execrable Coin . . . once enters, it can be no more confined to a small or moderate Quantity, than the *Plague* can be confined to a few Families; and that no *Equivalent* can be given by any earthly Power, any more than a dead Carcass can be recovered to Life by a Cordial" (*PW* 10:60–61). Economic plague is also a type of moral corruption, and again

Swift's metaphor gathers power through its intersection with historical reality. A plague on the continent had ruined the French linen trade, and Spain had been eager to buy textiles from Ireland; ignorant merchants and dishonest weavers, however, had produced bad quality, overpriced goods and the incipient Hibernian-Hispanic linen trade died. The Drapier notes in his seventh letter that such a "foul and foolish Proceeding" poisons the entire country. He even wishes that the plague itself had traveled to Ireland from France, if it "could have been confined only to those who were *Partakers in the Guilt*" (*PW* 10:136–37). Plagues, however, do not discriminate. The Drapier knows this, so he tries to write his prescriptions to keep the body politic free from fatal infection before it is too late.

The medical terminology that links the economic system with vestmental and linguistic systems relies on the common trope that compares the circulation of money in a nation with the circulation of blood in a body. Hobbes had used this analogy in *Leviathan*,[43] and Swift had used it during his earlier involvement in other fiscal controversies, the establishment of an Irish Bank and the debacle of the South Sea Bubble:

> Money, the Life-blood of the Nation,
> Corrupts and stagnates in the Veins,
> Unless a proper Circulation
> Its Motion and its Heat maintains.
> ["The Run upon the Bankers,"
> *SPW* 192.9–12]

Swift's opposition to the Bank stemmed from its being an English economic scheme, thus automatically suspect in terms of Irish welfare, and from the very conception of money he perceived to lie behind it, a conception that also underlay such disastrous projects as the South Sea Bubble. Just as Swift denies that bullion has an intrinsic value in itself, as the Yahoos' useless pursuit of shining stones and the harsh objectification of Wood and his coins make clear, he denies in his economic writings what might be called a liberal textocentric theory of money, that money's substance and meaning are arbitrary designations capable of limitless and chaotic signifying potential. Any economic theory that uproots money from its signifying origins is dangerous: Swift lumps together paper money, lines of credit, stock schemes, and Wood's halfpence as products of "monied interests" that either randomly assign meaning or substitute valueless objects that tautologically signify only themselves for valuable goods and the bullion that in a stabilized context can reliably signify market worth.[44] Therefore, Swift believes that money's value is determined by its exchange value in relation to products of the land. Land is the physiological matrix for the meaning of money, serving as a conservative textocentric guarantee for the signs that move across it (e.g., "Some Arguments Against Enlarging the Power of Bishops," *PW* 9:51).

Swift understands the necessity of circulation—of goods, of money, of words—but he also is aware of the relativity of value that circulation produces. For example, one of the papers he contributed to *The Tatler* shows how the meaning of money changes as it moves through space and time; a personified shilling relates how he is variously worth a pint of sack, a shoulder of mutton, a play book, or a milkmaid's favors. Eventually reduced to a mere token by the passage of history, he is invested by his gambler-owner with arbitrary meanings, "being in a few Moments valued at a Crown, a Pound, or a Sixpence, according to . . . Fortune" (*The Tatler* #249, *PW* 2:245), only to be divested of all meanings when a coin artist completely disfigures him. The piece ends as the shilling is reminted through language into the hero of *The Splendid Shilling* (and, of course, of *The Tatler* essay), until he is finally devalued through being misread by a blind man. Thus both money and language are subject to Gresham's Law: the wider the circulation, the greater the devaluation.

Devaluation is the curse of history upon semiotic systems. Swift has a tendency, as we have seen in chapter 2, to construe such threats as inevitable and to counteract them through rigid investitures of prescriptive authority. Thus many of Swift's writings about money mirror his writings about language at their most conservative. Signifying power must be stably situated; the authoritarian thematics of property underlining the *Proposal for Correcting . . . the English Tongue* are transvested onto Swift's economic discourse (e.g., "A Letter on Maculla's Project About Halfpence," *PW* 12:98–102) because the same mob that threatened to destroy proper linguistic usage with its unauthorized coinages is assaulting Ireland's monetary system. As the Drapier's seventh letter asserts, "When the Value of Money is *arbitrary*, or *unsettled*, no Man will be said to have any Property at all: nor is any Wound so suddenly felt, so hardly cured" (*PW* 10:128). Similarly, in "Some Arguments Against Enlarging the Power of Bishops," Swift champions controlled circulation so that money and goods will not get lost in some remote vein, breaking the entire arterial system as happened in the Roman Empire, to the detriment of language as well as currency (*PW* 9:48–51; see also *Proposal for Correcting . . . the English Tongue*, *PW* 4:14). When Swift calls devaluation "the Fall of Money" (*PW* 9:55), he links it to the necessary falls of all other human orders of signification; each is marked with innate corruption and marred by the corruptive process of history. But just as transvestural exchange reveals through economic discourse Swift's fears that words and meanings will fall prey to devaluation, it offers a way to reappropriate questions of value into language and settle meaning into the circulatory system itself.

The way involves prescribing words within the field of writing. By retransvesting economic issues into verbal ones, Swift as the Drapier trades an essentially negative and passive view of the devaluations time and interpretation visit upon semiotic significance for a hopeful and active one in which he fights false paper with true paper, illusions with reality, abuse with justice. Writing of Wood's collusion with the Duchess of Kendall to obtain the Royal Patent, Swift recapitulates the tactics that underlie all the *Drapier's Letters*:

> When late a Feminine Magician,
> Join'd with a *brazen* Politician,
> Expos'd, to blind the Nation's Eyes,
> A Parchment of prodigious Size;
> Conceal'd behind that ample Screen,
> There was no Silver to be seen.
> But, to this Parchment let the *Draper*
> Oppose his Counter-Charm of Paper,
> And ring *Wood*'s Copper in our Ears
> So loud, till all the Nation hears;
> That Sound will make the Parchment shrivel,
> And drive the Conj'rers to the Devil.
> ["A Simile on Our Want of Silver,"
> *SPW* 287.19–30]

In the texts surrounding the Wood's halfpence crisis, Swift exploits, with full self-awareness, the potential valuations of linguistic power politics, becomes an active participant in the prescriptive war for Ireland's national health, and wagers the value of his own words upon their enactment by history.

I WONDER WHERE YOU STOLE 'EM

The *Drapier's Letters* constitute Swift's most extended and most successful overt engagement with language as a mode of political praxis. Swift viewed these pieces not as works of art but as works of work, the *organon* for the *ergon* arising from present historical necessity; as he wrote to Worrall, stopping publication of the seventh letter because Wood's patent had been surrendered, "The work is done, and there is no more need of the Drapier" (31 Aug. 1725, *Corr.* 3:266). In the rush of current events, M. B. Drapier could be dismissed as a merely reflective function of exigency, although, as we have seen in chapter 4, Swift will reappropriate this specular identity into his composite textual self, thereby conscripting the Drapier from service to Irish economic interests into service to Swiftian reputational interests. But even in 1724 and 1725, the Drapier —the voice in the shuttle, the supplier of texts—defined through his own personification of a dominant Swiftian metaphor a strategy of signification that enabled not the politicization of written texts but, rather, the textualization of politics. This strategy in turn activates the affective power of language.

Swift's task involves transvesting monetary issues into linguistic ones. The Drapier treats history and legal precedent as texts from which he assembles an authoritative canon concerning coinage. Its authority derives from proper reading, reading determined both by present and by past interpretation ("the plain Meaning of the Words" as well as, for instance, Coke's construals of ancient charters and laws, *PW* 10:9–12). Such an assemblage of texts forms a specular prescription (the first work cited is the *Mirror for Justice*) that diagnoses current events; these events are transformed into supplicant texts, begging admission to the canon, by being transvested into key terms and words. Throughout the letters, the Drapier attempts to stabilize and restrict the meanings of key terms: "Lawful Metal" and "*Wood*'s Half-pence" in letter 1, "obligatory" and "voluntary" in letter 3, "Prerogative" and "Dependence" in letter 4. The terms are defined through differences disclosed by their binary relationships, as well as through their similarities and dissimilarities to the canonical texts against which they are measured.

In addition, Swift reconstitutes the institutional framework that generated his written body of prior authority. Because the legal institution had failed the Irish people, he appropriates the judicial system as the narrative structure for his texts, and this appropriation gathers power and urgency as it coincides with the extratextual event of judicial intervention in the publications of the letters, resulting in a price being put upon the Drapier's head, illegal manipulation of the Grand Jury, and imprisonment of Harding the printer.[45] Thus by the sixth letter, *To the Lord Chancellor Middleton*, this institutional substructure rises to the surface. Deposing Chief Justice Whitshed for crimes against verbal meaning, the Drapier sets himself up as judge in a trial of interpretation (*PW* 10:109). The verdict is delivered throughout the letters: Wood's halfpence as objects are determined to be trash, Wood's patent is determined to be non-binding, Wood's scheme to inflict his money upon Ireland is determined to be economic assault and battery, and Wood himself is determined to be a Highwayman (*PW* 10:20), a robber (*PW* 10:54), a counterfeiter (*PW* 10:32), a slanderer (*PW* 10:61), and a traitorous destroyer of the kingdom (*PW* 10:19, 87). Therefore, the new halfpence is not admitted to the canon of legal coinage. Economic discourse, like the ideal verbal discourse Swift sought to safeguard from renegade new coinages in a *Proposal for Correcting ... the English Tongue* and like the authorized bibliotic discourse at issue in *The Battel of the Books*, is protected against corruption.

Swift's textualizing seizure of the judicial institution and his decision to contest Wood's scheme through verbal definition indicate a politico-linguistic awareness that anticipates twentieth-century thinkers. The *Drapier's Letters* show that Swift was cognizant not only of the nature of what Antonio Gramsci would identify as hegemonic control—the way ruling interests achieve educative domination by saturating their values into all aspects of a culture[46]—but also of what Kenneth Burke was to call the "stealing back and forth of symbols," the struggle to redefine and thereby appropriate the key terms of political and social discourse.[47] The success of this endeavor can create a counter-hegemony by turning ruling discourse against the rulers; thus, according to Michel Foucault, is produced a historical "event."[48] The historical event that Swift helped bring about through his textual warfare was not a full-fledged revolution, although the references in his fourth letter to possible Irish rebellion against England in the cause of their common king understandably provoked violent and oppressive reaction from the ruling authorities.[49] His verbal tactics were revolutionary, however; they were conceived from a hegemonic awareness of how the institution of constitutional monarchy—which previously had commanded Swift's full support—could use language to help pervert orderly rule into crippling colonial domination.

Swift's verbal tactics also grew from his textocentric outlook, one that recognized and feared the prolific significatory capacity of words, and the corollary conviction that determining meaning is a way to transvest the exercise of power.

The method of stealing verbal symbols so important to the *Drapier's Letters* was first employed regularly by Swift in *The Examiner*, another textual group that participated and tried to precipitate events in current history. *The Examiner* frequently presents words as possessions of political and literary factions; even factions themselves are linguistic entities, determined by the custodianship of hostage words forced to carry the message of dominant power, as in the case of "the Words *Whig* and *Tory* ... having been pressed to the Service of many Successions of Parties, with very different Idea's fastened to them" (*The Examiner* #43, 31 May 1711, *PW* 3:163). When Swift as the anonymous Examiner shifts from noting to entering the battle of verbal appropriation, he treats words as essentially hollow and unattached signifiers. Asking whether the words "Popery," "Arbitrary Power," and "the Pretender," for instance, which have "by dextrous Management, been found of mighty Service to their Cause," can be "adapted to more proper Objects" (*The Examiner* #40, 10 May 1711, *PW* 3:150), he is not uncovering truth but is substituting one set of meanings for another. Like style, political discourse is a matter of propriety and appropriation. As the Examiner explains about the term "Passive Resistance": "Let us therefore see what this Doctrine is, when stript of such Misrepresentations; by describing it as it is really taught and practiced by the Tories" (*The Examiner* #33, 22 Mar. 1710, *PW* 3:113–14). Stripping must precede reclothing, and describing must precede reinscribing. The reality is not original meaning: there seems to be none or, if there is, it is irrelevant. Instead, meaning is a function of political praxis, and it is inculcated through education, the operative and fundamentally linguistic mode of hegemonic dominance.

The Examiner supports a political faction currently in power; it speaks quasi-officially to educate the public about the words and concepts this faction has attempted to appropriate. The *Drapier's Letters* oppose an economic faction currently seeking to usurp power; part of their function is to speak from the public to the government in order to educate the rulers about the misappropriation of discourse. Yet even when Swift has withdrawn from most active political engagement, he uses the verbal and transvestural tactics honed in his overtly political writings to show how seizing discourse can cause social change. A late work like *Directions to*

Servants (1733), written in the context of household hegemony, is putatively addressed to the powerless strata within that structure to indicate how to gain power over their superiors and covertly addressed to those superiors in order that they can retain power over their domestic domains. In it, Swift utilizes the knowledge that words are vehicles of dominance. Amidst the tedious instructions for household sabotage and self-serving chicanery occurs advice about how to appropriate language. Doing so allows servants to control masters: "[W]hen you are chidden, complain as if you were injured" (*Directions to Servants, PW* 13:8), thereby putting masters on the defensive and reducing the probability of future accusations. It can also allow penetration and destabilization of the hierarchy itself. Footmen, for instance, should learn "all the new fashion Words, and Oaths, and Sayings, and Scraps of Plays that your Memory can hold" (*Directions to Servants, PW* 13:35) so that they can rise in the world and maybe even gain the lasting attentions of a high-born lady. Such hierarchical mobility is the premise upon which the courtesy books that Swift parodies in *Polite Conversation* are based. It is also the same process as that outlined for bad poets who want to become successful critics in *On Poetry: A Rapsody*; learning by rote terms of art, modern jargon, and critical clichés enables total dominance over other poets and lesser wits (*SPW* 576–77.239–76). Here again, the issue is not the significance of the words but the ownership of them. Possession allows them to be passports to power.

At the time of the *Drapier's Letters*, Swift was writing on behalf of the partially dispossessed who feared they would become totally and permanently dispossessed. Therefore, the Drapier not only struggled for possession of ruling discourse; he also had to expose its illegal and unreasonable possession by enemies of Ireland in order to galvanize the Irish into active political combat while there was still time to avoid "utter Ruin" (*PW* 10:100). William Wood, of course, is the prime target, and the Drapier carefully shows how Wood transforms a word like *oblige* into an instrument of extortion (*PW* 10:19), or a word like *exigency* into license to steal (*PW* 10:47). But another target is Chief Justice Whitshed, who arbitrarily discharged the Grand Jury for refusing to return a presentment of libel against the Drapier, who imprisoned Harding, and who had given Swift and his printer Waters similar trouble over the *Proposal for the Universal Use*. The operative word in Whitshed's case is *freedom*, fortuitously inscribed extratextually in the motto on his coach: *Libertas & natale Solum*. The sixth letter refers to this ironic usurpation, as Whitshed literally absconds with the word *freedom* after he has tried to enslave the entire people of Ireland by oppressing its spokesman (*PW* 10:100–01), treating the kingdom as his private estate. But the poem Swift wrote on the same subject makes even more clear the theft and tyrannical misuse of empowering words:

> *Libertas & natale Solum*
> Fine Words; I wonder where you stole 'em.
> . . . .
> But, let me now the Words Translate;
> *Natale Solum*; My Estate;
> My dear Estate, how well I love it,
> My Tenants, if you doubt, will prove it;
> They swear I am so kind and good,
> I hug them till I squeeze their Blood.
> ["Whitshed's Motto on his Coach,"
> *SPW* 280.1–2, 5–10]

The rest of the poem dissects Whitshed's readings of the word *Libertas*, ones that allow him, among other things, to override juries, enrich himself, replace political enemies, and "humble that vexatious Dean" (*SPW* 280.20).[50] The tacit answer to the question posed in the second line is given by the intertextual network of *Drapier's Letters* and Wood's halfpence poems: the words have been stolen from the responsible people of Ireland. Therefore, Swift as Drapier must steal them back.

Swift's strategy of stealing involves drawing William Wood into the *Drapier's Letters* as a literary character rather than as a historical figure looming outside the text. This task is accomplished partially by setting Wood in opposition to the Drapier.[51] Even in disguising his own fictionality, the Drapier cannot resist asserting the textuality of his existence through self-definitional allusions to other texts, allusions that also implicate William Wood. If the Drapier is David, Wood is Goliath; if the Drapier is Midas's barber, Wood is the money-bound and asinine Midas; if the Drapier is the madman in *Don Quixote*, Wood is the spaniel hit by a stone. The literariness of the descriptions of Wood functions as a form of control; the Drapier as author exercises ultimate power over all elements in his texts. Furthermore, the allusions define Wood by prediction through analogy based on previously written authority. Wood's textual prototypes were all losers, beaten in struggles for supremacy. Similarly, the halfpence poems compare Wood to such presumptuous mythological failures as Prometheus and Salmoneus or textualize him by analogizing him to characters in contemporary comedies, old folktales, and religious fables. The works' insistence upon their own literary status becomes a form of dominance: the very uttering of these garrulous mock-epics puts Wood in his place, and his place is the allusive intertext of the defeated, the exposed, the ridiculed, and the powerless.[52] Glossing history through fictional narratives provides the texts with the authority of self-awareness and with an arsenal of rhetorical controls.

Swift's more familiar tactics for gaining textual control over William Wood are ridicule by inflation and deflation. Wood resembles a Lilliputian courtier, blustering threats against the giant body politic of Ireland. The sheer pretentiousness of such a posture provokes anger; it also provokes amusement, since it is hard to take seriously as a danger to the nation's welfare a figure presented as a crazed tinker, an insignificant mechanic, and a diminutive hardwareman.[53] But this comic technique quickly loses its humor as jokes about size are eclipsed by synecdochal conflation of Wood with his work. Thus the Drapier's name-calling is not gratuitous; it functions as essentialist definition, reductively reading Wood's significance in terms of his occupation, just as the hapless Partridge was lampooned as a lunatic cobbler lacing together the messages of the stars into a text equally useful "for *Almanacks* or *Shoes*" (*An Elegy on Mr. Patridge, SPW* 67–69.46). This definitional approach draws strength from existing social and political hierarchies: Wood's assigned status as a historically powerless artisan makes his grandiose scheme to seize power a design against the properly ordered relationship of all levels of society.[54] Swift's awareness of the need to activate the power inherent in the existing Irish hierarchy is apparent from the various audiences the individual letters explicitly address and by their frequent references to the discrete effects of Wood's halfpence on royalty, on nobility, on gentry, on clergy, on merchants, on farmers, even on beggars. And the instrument for awakening the sleeping hegemonic structure is language, the good Irish cloth offered by the Drapier, figured with the reflective message of power that can make power aware of itself.

Swift also activates the affective power of language by exploiting figural repetition. The poems on Wood's halfpence and the prose burlesque, *An Account of Wood's Execution*, for instance, rely on the pun. Unlike integrative metaphor, the pun disintegrates coherent meaning by stealing the signified out from under the signifier. William Wood becomes the site of radical transvestitures: his name refers not to a living man but to a bug or to an inert piece of lumber; he exists not in the historical world but in the texts that Swift controls. A work like *A Serious Poem*, for example, runs through a sequence of terrible puns: Wood is a "*Son of a* BEECH," a "*Block-head*," and a "*Groaning Board*" who will meet tautological extinction by being hanged from a tree (*SPW* 270–73.28, 42, 84, 110–22). Unlike Baucis and Philemon, who are shown in the process of metamorphosis in Swift's 1706–09 poems, Wood is subject to distinctly un-Ovidian dendrification through the cascade of puns that reinforce his static and speechless existence as a wooden object. Part of the persuasive power of Swift's halfpence writings may come from implied analogy: the texts' unsympathetic treatment of Wood as an object to be manipulated reminds readers that Wood wishes to treat the people of Ireland in the same way.[55]

Power also wells from Swift's textocentric ability to hold Wood captive in a net of self-conscious and pressuring rhetorical figures. Textual dominance provides a model for reader reaction to Wood's scheme; the Irish people must disempower the projector by exposing his imposture, immobilizing the flow of his debased currency, and exerting control over their own economic destiny. And this strategy of dominance depends on a strategy of rhetoric, a series of figural shifts that Swift sets into motion through the text. He exploits one variety of pun—antanaclasis, the repetition of a word with a slippage in meaning—in order to generate two other varieties of the trope. In *A Serious Poem*, for instance, the word *Wood* variously denotes a raw material, a forest, a plank, a single tree, a gallows, and a halfpence coiner. Repeated antanaclasis conditions the reader into interpreting all mentions of the word *Wood* as syllepsis, the type of pun in which a word contains two simultaneous meanings; it also sets up extratextual asteismus, the punning dialectic in which a speaker replies to another, using the first man's words in a different sense. The ultimate goal of Swift's puns on Wood's name is thus to have readers come away from the text with a syllepsic sense of *Wood* that will cause them to question and resist asteismically any nonpejorative invocation of his name and his scheme.

Addison had indicted the pun as "false wit,"[56] and even Swift, fond as he was of punning, recognized the difference between good puns and bad and humorously affirmed the supposedly debased origins of the figure by tracing the word's origins first to "*Fundum*, a Bottom," and last to "*Punaise*, which signifies a little stinking Insect that gets into the Skin" ("A Modest Defense of Punning," *PW* 4:205–6). The pun is an appropriate figure with which to entrap and expose Wood not just because one of the punning identities Swift bestows on him is a Wood Louse ("Wood, an Insect," *SPW* 284.3) but also because the pun is false and debased word usage. It stands to language as Wood's adulterated, easily counterfeited coins stand to economics.[57] And Wood is defined by his coins as well as by the punningly literal readings of his name. The equivalence runs throughout the *Drapier's Letters* and is explicitly stated in *An Account of Wood's Execution*: "Then appeared William Wood, Esq . . . Upon his Face, which looked very dismal, were fixed, at proper Distances, several Pieces of his own Coin, to denote who he was, and to signify his Calling, and his Crime" (*PW* 10:147). Identity is not merely skin-deep—or, here, bark-deep, as in this burlesque Wood is constructed from an old piece of timber. Wood's unprepossessing background included having been charged with perjury; Swift comments in a sermon delivered during the halfpence crisis that Wood's debasement of words makes him a "proper instrument" for "the pernicious project now in hand to reduce us to beggary" ("Doing Good: A Sermon," *PW* 9:236) and explains that Wood's methods to "bind us with fetters of brass" are, fittingly, spreading lies and false arguments (pp. 237–38). Corrupted language and corrupted coinage once again define each other and define their user, and both are sired by Satan's fall from heaven and subsequent temptation and betrayal of man (e.g., *The Examiner* #14, 9 Nov. 1710, *PW* 3:8; "On False Witness," *PW* 9:182).

Conflating the perjurer Wood with his adulterated coin implies that money and language have meaning as marks of human worth, of the value of their possessors. But Swift's elaborate transvestural tactics in the service of verbal praxis, his textual weavings and symbolic thefts, suggest that the mark is a hollow sign waiting for action to fill it with meaning. Possessing, or as in Wood's case, literally making money, parallels possessing verbal ability and making texts. The token or sign itself is value-neutral (e.g., "On the Poor Man's Contentment," *PW* 9:195); its value and that of the person to whom it belongs are determined by use (e.g., "On Mutual Subjection," *PW* 9:144–46). As Swift wrote in his "Ode to William King":

> Him for an happy Man I own,
> Whose Fortune is not overgrown;
> And, happy he, who wisely knows
> To use the Gifts, that Heav'n bestows.
> [*SPW* 195.15–18]

Swift appears to have honestly tried to put this belief into practice in reference to both money and words. Thrifty management of his moderate income enabled public charity, private subsidies, and an estate arranged to benefit the Irish people as well as his own friends and relatives.[58] Yet the gift of wealth bestowed on Jonathan Swift was outweighed by the gift of writing ability, and the success of the *Drapier's Letters*, designed for the public good, ratified the deceptively simple concept that all meaning and value are functions of use. Therefore, Swift not only allowed himself pride in the Drapier's accomplishments; he also defined himself as the Drapier for the rest of his life and authorized this self-definition into history.

But even as the "neutral" commemoration in *Verses on the Death* focuses on the twin legacies of the *Drapier's Letters* and funds for the Steeven's asylum, it reveals that both writing (even as civic duty) and wealth (even as charity) are transvestitures of power, fashioned to make contemporaries and future generations Swift's "Debtor[s]" (*Verses on the Death*, *SPW* 513.487). And the debt works in two directions. W. B. Yeats, one of a long line of Irish writers and patriots who have kept Swift alive as a defender of Hibernian liberty, explains that Swift incurred his own debt to the nation when he transvested the desire that took form in writing onto the Irish politico-economic situation: "Swift found his nationality through the *Drapier Letters*, his conviction came from action and passion."[59] Identity and belief, discovered through the agency of the written word, cast debts back into language that language ultimately cannot meet. The word may triumph in the *Drapier's Letters*, but the triumph is fleeting, disconnected from language's customary ineffectiveness and betrayal, from its tragic failure to repay its human investments.

6 / INVESTMENTS
Swift and the Tragedy of Language

IN THE *Drapier's Letters*, the transvestiture of clothes explored the nature of writing and the transvestiture of money explored the nature of meaning and value. These exploratory tropes interwove with historical events to make Swift's epistolary text an activist success. Nevertheless, the success of the *Drapier's Letters*, limited to the particular issue of debased coinage, magnified Swift's sense of the failure of his other political writings to effect changes in Ireland. This sense of failure grows out of the behavioral theory of language upon which all polemic and didactic texts, including satire, are based, a theory that is itself predicated on a textocentric recognition of verbal polysemy: such texts can only create meaning outside themselves. The defeat of Wood's halfpence radicalized this theory by demonstrating that the potential of meaning inscribed in words is realized not only by readers' interpretations but also by their subsequent actions. And if texts are conduits rather than containers, secondary stations along the production line of meaning, the author is tertiary. He dissolves into a spectral initiatory figure whose status as originator is challenged both by the temporal process of usurpative responses and by the suspicion that accumulated historical pressures and current cultural demands authorized and in effect produced the text in the first place. He is victim of the process described by the clothing metaphor organizing *A Tale of a Tub*, that authorial will passes into textual word that is superseded by reader "wearing."

To avoid being sacrificed to a localized reception-aesthetic that circumscribes significance within the horizon of a particular historical moment,[1] Swift industriously reinvested the Drapier and the Drapier's triumph into subsequent texts and composite textual selves. He tried, as we have seen, to dictate the terms by which history would know him and to multiply these terms so that his textual identity would transcend any particular interpretive appropriations or fulfilling actions. This is a grand textocentric strategy, conceived as are Swift's other textocentric countermoves to preserve the significatory vitality of the written word as a function of controlling authorial will. The investitures, divestitures, and transvestitures characterizing Swift's work are thus responses to the inexorable logic of linguistic behavioralism, that meaning must ultimately leave writer and work behind.

The *Drapier's Letters* highlight the double bind forged by even a limited commitment to linguistic behavioralism. If on the one hand people act on Swift's political proposals or reform themselves after reading his satires—or if on the other hand no one acts and no one reforms—Swift's reason for writing disappears and his words are rendered meaningless. Like all serious satirists, Swift believed that the world's fund of vice and folly would never be depleted; unlike many political reformers, he did not believe that society's evils could be completely eradicated by utopian projects. The rescission of Wood's patent, however, offered a tantalizing instance of how his words could diagnose and cure at least one societal illness. Thus, subsequent works undertaken to heal the political and moral sicknesses that continued to fester around him but that were not effective in doing so are racked with the heightened, indeed the tragic perception of the failure of words and the uselessness of writing.

As a whole, therefore, Swift's Irish writings fall into a tragic pattern. This pattern can demonstrate a coherent trajectory of language use, illuminate the intensity with which Swift invested himself into political and reformative writing endeavors, and show through its changes in tropes and tone the magnitude of Swift's demands upon language and the personal anguish caused by the failure of language to meet these demands. Certainly the darkening of Swift's linguistic practice after the *Drapier's Letters* may also be attributable to personal misfortune,[2] but the idea of writing as inevitable betrayal is latent in Swift's earlier works as well. As we have seen, *A Tale of a Tub*, written when Swift's world lay all before him, predicts the tragedy of language. So does book 4 of *Gulliver's Travels*, written at the height of Swift's mature authorial power, just before the *Drapier's Letters* translated desire into momentary fulfillment.

Looking at *Gulliver's Travels* from the perspective of tragedy requires reading the adventures in Houyhnhnmland against the various investitures, divestitures, vested interests, and transvestitures that comprise the ways in which Swift creates the vested word. Previously, we have considered how the specific linguistic satires in book 3 and Gulliver's communication difficulties in book 4 furnish material for investigation of Swift's flexible and conflicting attitudes toward contemporary theories of language. We have seen how the Lagadan language machine and the Struldbruggs's loss of speech coherence implicitly criticize Swift's early desires to invest language with authorized fixity it cannot possess, yet how Gulliver's narrative voice, Swift's handling of ironic space, and the book's orchestration of various types of parody demonstrate successful investitures of authorial control into unruly, risky fictional constructs. The concocted languages of *Gulliver's Travels* have given evidence of Swift's techniques of divestiture, the playful tortures he inflicts on words so that significance remains open and seductive; they also have displayed how divestitures turn into traps for interpretation, tricking readers into misassignments of meaning that snarl the circuits of communication transmitted through the text and that mock hermeneutic desire. We have examined how Gulliver's search for the specular image inscribed with his proper specular name resembles, yet ultimately diverges from, Swift's own search for his textual self, as Gulliver's specular identity is further complicated by his metonymic mistakings and by his excrementalizing of his own text. Finally, we have remarked how Gulliver's geometrically fashioned garments exemplify a disease of costume that is a component in a larger transvestiture, Swift's intertextual metaphor of the vestmental word. Obviously, however, Gulliver's involvement with apparel does not begin and end in Laputa. Therefore, we can resume consideration of *Gulliver's Travels* with the transvestural system of clothing. It comments upon Gulliver's crisis of language and demonstrates the tragedy encoded in Swift's transvestitures of money into words that is explored and, finally, enacted in Swift's Irish political writings.

Perhaps the compelling force in Swift's intense struggle with and through language is his own sense of history, the tragedy of time that will mangle texts and forget their authors. In "The Epistle Dedicatory" to *A Tale of a Tub*, time is Prince Posterity's governor, the grim reaper of history who "intercept[s] and devour[s]" writing so that it is as if writers never existed (*Tale*, 34). But time has another tragic dimension. Rather than eradicating words and meanings, it can fulfill them, simultaneously confirming truth and uselessness. Swift lived long enough to see many of his predictions come true, and he knew that meant his written warnings had had no effect. A disguised autobiographical poem written in 1729, the year of *A Modest Proposal*, blends Swift and St. Patrick into a single angry voice of wisdom crying out the tragic lessons of history, from Ireland's mythic beginnings under the protection of Pallas to its endangered present:

> WRETCHED *Ierne*! with what Grief I see
> The fatal Changes Time hath made in thee,
>
> . . . .
>
> With Omens oft I strove to warn thy Swains,
> Omens, the Types of thy impending Chains.
>
> . . . .
>
> To din thine Ears with unharmonious Clack,
> And haunt thy holy Walls in white and black.
>
> . . . .
>
> Emblems of Insects vile, who spread their Spawn
> Through all thy Land, in Armour, Fur, and Lawn.
>
> . . . .
>
> Soon shall thy Sons, the Time is just at Hand,
> Be all made Captives in their native Land.
> ["St. Patrick's Well," *SPW* 388–89.33–34, 41–42,
> 47–48, 55–56, 89–90]

Swift read his own history as a rejection, as a non-reading of the omens, types, and emblems he had given it, as language-in-time failing to accomplish the tasks he put to it. Swift's greatness as a writer perhaps lies in his refusal to submit to the tragic inadequacies of language that his own texts expose and in his dedication to clothing the naked bodies of self and experience, imagination and prophecy, in words that insist on a mutual vesture of significance with history.

WHAT WILL IT IMPORT?

Between the publications of *Gulliver's Travels* and *A Modest Proposal*, Swift produced a series of political tracts that indicate the failure of language through declarations of personal despair and through calcification of habitual tropes and images. In *A Short View of the State of Ireland*, for instance, he paints a patently false picture of his country's beauties and then admits that "my Heart is too heavy to continue this Irony longer" (*PW* 12:10); the rhetorical resources of language are not adequate to describe or to prescribe to social ills. In "Answer to Several Letters from Unknown Persons," linguistic behavioralism underpins assessment of verbal efficacy. Responding to letters from "unreasonable well-meaning people" asking him to deliver his thoughts, which "I have often done in vain," Swift asks:

> What will it import that half a score of people in a Coffee-House may happen to read this paper, and even the majority of those few differ in every sentiment from me. [*PW* 12:77]

The "well-meaning people" are unreasonable to suppose that words with such a restricted audience can have any meaning at all. Moreover, people will not even pay attention to the admission of language's failure to cause beneficial change. Swift asserts in a "Letter to the Archbishop of Dublin, Concerning the Weavers" that all schemes for improvement "are idle and visionary... as I have told the publick often enough, and with as little effect as what I did say at present is likely to produce" (*PW* 12:65–66).[3] Again, ineffectiveness engenders personal frustration about stillborn writing endeavors; Swift comments, "I am weary [of] so many abortive Projects" (*PW* 12:66), and he in fact aborts his project himself by not publishing this letter or its companion pieces ("Answer to Several Letters from Unknown Persons," "Answer to Several Letters from Unknown Hands," and "A Letter on Maculla's Project About Halfpence"). He also abandons faith in the healing powers of the linguistic pharmikon: "I freely own it a wild Imagination that any words will cure the sottishness of men, or the vanity of women... My meaning is that a consumptive body must needs dye" (*PW* 12:68, 71). Such a bald declaration of intended signification tries to reclaim meaning from a consumptive readership that turns words to waste and to redefine the function of polemic texts. If these texts cannot change anything substantially, their meaning cannot be located in extratextual reception or reaction, and their function is merely to point out and to condemn. Of course, refusal to publish represents an extreme of protecting personal investitures of meaning, but the post-*Drapier* political pieces that are published also conserve meaning by addressing their own powerlessness and insufficiency.

The Legion Club, written seven years after *A Modest Proposal*, shows how the fear of fugitive meaning can shrink language to demonstrative diatribe. Its speaker tours the hellish parliamentary asylum, detailing degradations and cursing the already damned.[4] Many readers believe that this poem employs invective as a sort of magic ritual,[5] but although the name-calling does exploit the nonrational power of language to evoke emotion, it does not share nomenclative magic's purpose, which is to bring about changes in the person or entity addressed. Swift's language is powerless to cast out the Legion Club's demons, or to reform them, or to destroy them. Instead it piles abuse upon abuse, trying perhaps to find power in the sheer accumulation of words, but the excessiveness of the accumulation announces the impotence of its parts. The names of evil are legion, and language can never enumerate them. The poem ends in exhaustion, disgust, defeat, and damnation; the appeal to Hogarth to paint the bestial politicians implies that language cannot fulfill its limited task of representation, much less of communication or of reform.

Exasperation with language's inadequacies may account for the hardening of the tropes in Swift's post-*Drapier* works, as if Swift suspected that figural turnings were vertiginous delusions, rhetorical mockeries of authorial hopes that words can move in and through texts and readers. *The Legion Club* encases its targets in bestial and excremental images, denying them even the reduced and ironic chance of societal reincorporation offered to Gulliver through his unwilling return to England, and to the Bedlamites in "A Digression Concerning Madness" through the suggestion that they be assumed into the army or the Inns of Court or the Royal College of Physicians. Similarly, the tracts immediately preceding *A Modest Proposal* present an uncompromising picture of Irishmen as "animals . . . with two legs and human faces, clad, and erect," a status ratified by their relationship with language: their animality can be exposed by asking them "to define what they mean by Law, Liberty, Property, Coinage, Reason, Loyalty, or Religion" ("A Letter to the Archbishop," *PW* 12:65). They fail Swift's test not only because they cannot speak English but because it is supposed that "the size of a native's understanding [is] just equal to that of a dog or horse" ("Answer to Several Letters from Unknown Hands," *PW* 12:88–89). The vestmental metaphor also petrifies into apocalyptic fact. Irishwomen's lust for imported clothing moves from being symptomatic of pernicious vanity to being an instrument of God's wrath:

> [Women] under their present corruptions seem to be a kind of animal suffered for our sins to be sent into the world for the destruction of families, societies, and kingdoms . . . [and who] spend the revenue of a moderate family to adorn a nauseous unwholesome living carcase. ["Answer to Several Letters from Unknown Persons," *PW* 12:80]

This language recalls Isaiah's condemnation of the daughters of Zion, whose love of luxury will be punished by revelation of their physical sordidness and by the destruction of Israel (Isa. 3:16–26), but it withholds Isaiah's consolation that seven women who promise to "wear [their] own apparel" (Isa. 4:1) can help restore the remnant of Jerusalem. It also withholds the New Testament consolation that the word incarnate in the second Eve can purify inherited corruption. Since neither hope nor humor nor irony softens Swift's denunciation, his statements in these letters present a universal evil broken free from culpability and running rampant, embodied in all women and aided by all men: "It is absolutely so in fact that every husband ... is nourishing a poisonous, devouring serpent in his Bosom" ("A Letter to the Archbishop," *PW* 12:68). Such utter calumniations of women and of human physicality cast an ominous shadow over the contemporaneous scatological poems and *A Modest Proposal*, just as the vilification of the Irish as animals retroactively darkens the fiction of *Gulliver's Travels*, book 4. Being human seems to be a tragic disaster visited upon beings helpless to avert it.

George Steiner suggests that the difference between Hebraic and Hellenic perspectives on man's misfortunes can be understood as the difference between justice and tragedy. In the Old Testament, punishment follows crime in a rational, though often harsh, manner; there is always hope that one person's obedience or goodness can avert catastrophe. In Greek epic and drama, punishment surpasses guilt in an often incomprehensible way; fate seems to be capricious, and disaster is irreparable.[6] By this standard, Swift's quasi-Biblical tone in many of his late political writings denies the authority it seeks to invoke. Divine Justice, in the sense of discernible causal connection between guilt and retribution, disappears. It is replaced by revenge and abandonment. Jehovah becomes an unreasonable and irascible Jove, washing his hands of poets, for instance, in *On Poetry: A Rapsody* (*SPW* 582.489–93), or damning all humanity in *The Day of Judgement* (*SPW*, 516). Swift does not invoke the Christian mystery of redemptive sacrifice, and so the entire Irish people—frivolous women, greedy men, demoniac politicians, dishonest merchants, brutish cottagers, subhuman beggars, and foolish writers—are condemned through language that refuses to speak of salvation to a hellish world of tragic determinism.

Swift's Irish writings taken as a sequence arrange themselves into a tragic plot. The tragic hero is not the people of Ireland but Swift's language and the personal investments it carries. The origins of the tragedy (Ireland's history of exploitation by England, Swift's peculiar childhood in Ireland, the early but unpublished "Story of an Injured Lady") lie outside the main structure, as do the sources of action in classical drama; they are concerned, as are the origins of so many Greek tragedies, with polluted and endangered kingdoms, sexual transgression, parentage and accidents of birth. The play proper begins with the *Proposal for the Universal Use*, its flexible and witty rhetoric demonstrating an Oedipus-like confidence that language can solicit solutions to extra-linguistic problems and setting out the metaphors that will bear the burden of discourse. Rising action develops through the poems and pamphlets of the early 1720s and culminates in the *Drapier's Letters* of 1724–25; language triumphs and the kingdom is saved. Triumph brings recognition of two types. First, disguised identity is penetrated as Swift's authorship of the letters became widely known. Second is the rethinking of the losses entailed by achieving a goal, with the attendant knowledge of how successful fulfillment of demanding words alienates and condemns the invested textual self they have revealed. Triumph also brings about reversal, a returning or re-troping that Swift enacts by reconstituting his functional metaphors into grotesque and unmoving metaphysical condemnations. And unlike aspiration, triumph sets a standard by which defeats are measured and experienced. Thus when the kingdom's ills resurface and language cannot heal, denouement unravels in a double strand of anxiety and failure, through the choric lamentations of the Holyhead Journal and the excoriating pamphlets of 1727–29 to the catastrophe marked by *A Modest Proposal*.

The vocabulary of political arithmetic used to some extent in the *Drapier's Letters* and to a greater extent in subsequent tracts like "A Letter on Maculla's Project About Halfpence" (*PW* 12:98) dominates *A Modest Proposal*, as if dehumanized people have lost the right not only to be discussed but also to be addressed in terms of human discourse. The flat, mechanistic diction of the speaker indicates the exhaustion of language in general and the specific exhaustion of authorial faith in the power of words to articulate or to influence the will. In *A Modest Proposal*, trans-vestural systems implode as metaphor folds back into its bodily matrix. The body *is* money when human carcasses enter economic circulation; the body *is* clothes when flayed skin is made into gloves and boots of unimpeachable domestic manufacture. The figure of animalistic man is shaped into obdurate, monstrous reality, enabling the text to offer a universal Thyestean banquet in a ceremony of revenge. The beastly feeding signals the loss of communion and communication, and since the proposed banquets of children's flesh are particularly suitable for civic and sacramental occasions, "a Lord Mayor's *Feast*, or . . . *Weddings* and *Christenings*" (*PW* 12:116), they are dark inversions of the ritual gestures that end many Classical tragedies and, indeed, that transform the sacrifice of the Son of God, both child and Word, into hope for redemption.

Like Thyestes' far-reaching curse upon the house of Atreus, Swift's denunciation extends to all participants in the drama: the self-victimizing Irish, the passive Anglo-Irish gentry, the rapacious English exploiters, and the imprecator himself. The multifocused anger that allows *A Modest Proposal* to retain its shock value and to avoid a pigeonholing that would fix blame on some and therefore exculpate others[7] gains urgency and authority by refusing to absolve language from responsibility for its own failure. The lesson of the Drapier's victory echoes through the famous passage detailing Swift's earlier and serious written proposals for the betterment of Ireland: linguistic behavioralism necessitates the tragic failure of language because people do not act in accordance with authorial will. Before the Modest Proposer admits his weariness "with offering vain, idle, visionary Thoughts," he repeats: "[L]et no Man talk to me of these and the like Expedients; till he hath, at least, a Glimpse of Hope, that there will ever be some hearty and sincere Attempt to put them in Practice" (*PW* 12:117). But Swift offers no hope. Language is suspended in the gap between lexis and praxis, and there it will die.

Finally, the tragedy culminates in *The Legion Club* of 1736. This poem operates as an exodos, the moment in Classical tragedy when the mediating choric voice turns to the audience, asking it to look at the tragic scene and to bear it from the domain of fiction into collective historical memory and current political application. Swift's poem, however, specifically denies its own historical effectiveness. Clio, the muse of history, initially tells the narrator that the club members belong not to reality but to imagination:

> These, she answer'd, are but Shadows,
> Phantoms, bodiless and vain,
> Empty visions of the Brain.
> [*SPW* 604.100–102]

Then as she enters the club, odious reality assaults her. Fearing imminent death, "In a Fright she crept away" (*SPW* 605.131), leaving the narrator alone in an a-historical hell that no cathartic ritual can cleanse and no humanitarian effort, not even Swift's actual endowment of "Schools / For his Lunatics and Fools" (*SPW* 602.31–44; cf. lines 35–36) can replace. Language curses not just the politicians but its own desertion by history and its own fatal and final tragic inadequacy.

Language also curses its user. In *The Legion Club*, the welter of allusions to the *Aeneid*[8] situates the poem in a realm of anti-epic where language seems not parodic but used up; linguistic resources having run out, the poet cannot rise from his infernal descent and is trapped in his own verbal construction. Swift accordingly invokes his own verbal eschatology by referring to one of his first major works (*The Battel of the Books* is recalled in lines 206–14) and to his actual last words (his will, that includes bequests for Steeven's asylum), but the invocation fails to deliver him from evil. Even the poem's title hints at the failure of the language user. Jesus' words successfully cast a legion of devils into a herd of swine, but according to St. Matthew, Jesus' accomplishment made the people afraid and they drove him out of the city (Matt. 8:28–34).[9] Exorcism expels the exorcist, and the title of Swift's last major poem suggests his feelings of abandonment by his audience and victimization by his words. This is the tragedy of an author who has invested much and perceived little dividend, who has questioned the significatory value of his texts—the texts that bear life in language as pledge to history—and has been forced to conclude that they "import" next to nothing.

I BOLDLY PRONOUNCED YAHOO

This conclusion is also Gulliver's. He has invested his desire for significance into successful enactment by his readership, and he has used this hope to assuage the "Mortification" that attends knowledge that History will produce new texts "to jostle me out of Vogue, and stand in my Place; making the World forget that ever I was an Author" (*GT* 4.12.292). The result of his writing, according to his letter to Sympson, has not been action or reform. The yield has come in words—usurping, conflicting, destructive "Libels, and Keys, and Reflections, and Memoirs, and Second Parts" that have falsified or denied his authorship; further, Gulliver asserts that "I hear the original Manuscript is all destroyed, since the Publication of my Book. Neither have I any Copy left" ("Letter to Sympson," *GT*, 7). Investments in writing ultimately annihilate text as well as author, and Gulliver is the protagonist in a linguistic tragedy that Swift arranged to disclose language's potential for betrayal. Using the powerful trope established in his earliest prose works, Swift transvests verbal discourse with vestmental discourse in order to dress and address problems of the textual word, problems that coalesce in book 4 of *Gulliver's Travels*.

Throughout books 1 and 2, Gulliver gives a great deal of information about the state of his clothes and his efforts to remain decently attired: readers enjoy vignettes of 200 tiny sempstresses stitching shirts (*GT* 1.6.63) or of faithful Glumdalclitch outfitting her living toy with handmade doll clothes (*GT* 2.2.95). Such scenes, which include the Laputan tailors' arbitrary creations, depict one side of an acculturating trade of clothes and words. Host societies try to accommodate Gulliver's sartorial needs, although he never sews for the people he visits; he returns their efforts by learning their language, and they never try to learn his. Making clothes is an epistemological activity because, as the *Drapier's Letters* reveal, it stands figurally for making texts.[10] All the peoples whom Gulliver meets attempt to read him, and they do this by examining his garments, measuring his body, deciphering the mysteries therein, and then sewing the textile of "Gulliver" according to their interpretations. Gulliver reciprocates by cracking the codes of the linguistic fictions Swift has fashioned and, subsequently, by writing the text of the cultures he encounters.

The trade, however, becomes one-sided in Houyhnhnmland. Gulliver dutifully learns the horses' difficult language, but they do not respond by supplying him with new apparel when his old wears out. Gulliver instead makes his own clothes from animal hides and his own shoes from wood and "the Skins of *Yahoos*, dried in the Sun" (*GT* 4.10.276).[11] Gulliver's industriousness, of course, parodies catalogues of individual entrepreneurship in books like Defoe's *Robinson Crusoe*, as do many of Gulliver's descriptions of diet and personal sanitation,[12] but the unbalancing of the words-for-clothes equation in book 4 hints at the fundamental and disastrous schisms facing Gulliver and at the failure of language these schisms demonstrate to the reader.

What Gulliver calls the "Secret of my Dress" does indeed "distinguish [him] as much as possible, from that cursed Race of Yahoos" (*GT* 4.3.236), but when Gulliver's equine keepers find him half-exposed in his sleep, the secret identity is uncovered. Gulliver's devastation by this vestmental betrayal indicates a failure of metaphorical imagination; in this realm of objective signification, he takes the man-as-microcoat metaphor literally. His devastation also indicates a failure of contextual interpretation because his earlier travels had foreshadowed the unreliable function of clothes as protection and concealment. His strong buff jerkin had insulated him from Lilliputian arrows (*GT* 1.1.22), yet his dignity was penetrated when marching soldiers peeped up through a hole in his breeches (*GT* 1.3.42) and one plot against him by the courtiers of Lorbrulgrud entailed reenacting the Shirt of Nessus myth by dousing his clothes with "a poisonous Juice . . . which would soon make you tear your own Flesh, and die in the utmost Torture" (*GT* 1.7.69). In Brobdingnag, where the citizens, like those in Houyhnhnmland, first thought his clothes were part of his body, Gulliver was trapped in a field because the beards of fallen grain "pierced through my Cloaths into my Flesh," preventing escape (*GT* 2.1.86); his sturdy coat lappet was the instrument with which the marauding monkey dragged him out of his room to the terrors of primate domesticity (*GT* 2.5.122). Thus it appears that Swift complicates the role of clothes before Gulliver reaches Houyhnhnmland; he valorizes them by presenting them as part of a transvestural acculturating trade, and he denigrates them by showing how they can inflict harm on their wearer. Clothes then become indeterminate signs; their meaning lies instead in investitures and divestitures by reader and wearer alike.

Gulliver himself overdetermines the meaning of clothing; in fact, he invests his humanity in it. When the Sorrel Nag finds him asleep, partially naked, the horse "in a great Fright gave . . . a very confused Account of what he had seen . . . [and the Master] asked me the Meaning of what his Servant had reported; that I was not the same Thing when I slept as I appeared to be at other times" (*GT* 4.3.236). The meanings of Gulliver's clothes and Gulliver's body do not have to be fixed; the Houyhnhnms assign him not to the category of Yahoo but, if anything, to the category of incomprehensible falsehood, the thing that is not. It is Gulliver who insists on defining his own existential truth. His reservation about undressing, that he does not wish to uncover that which Nature has taught us to conceal, is overcome by Houyhnhnm logic and by Houyhnhnm indifference: his master does not understand why one should hide what Nature has freely given but says to Gulliver that "however [he] might do as [he] pleased" (*GT* 4.3.237). What pleases Gulliver is to make a difference, to show the self-determined truth of his body, and to designate that body as the axis of semantic investments; although not requested to do so, he strips naked except for a makeshift loincloth. Following his interpretive gesture, the Houyhnhnms predictably declare him to be a perfect Yahoo. Through his own will, Gulliver places himself into the rigid binary taxonomy of Houyhnhnmland, just as he does when he encourages the vague Yahoo suspicion that he is "of their own Species, which I often assisted myself, by stripping up my Sleeves, and shewing my naked Arms and Breast" (*GT* 4.8.265), just as he does when he bathes in the nude and interprets the amorous attack of a young female Yahoo as certification of his brute nature (*GT* 4.8.267).

These deliberate divestitures, then, are acts of interpretation that close off the potentialities of meaning. They are consequences of and transvestural commentaries on Gulliver's initial act of interpretation in Houyhnhnmland, one that provides an ironic terminus to his quest for his specular name and one that generates the failure of language that shapes the tragedy of book 4. Immediately after Gulliver comes ashore, he meets horses who seem to be conversing; he first addresses them in English, thinking that what must be their supernatural skills will enable them to understand him. They pay attention but do not respond, so Gulliver listens closely and tries another tactic:

> I could frequently distinguish the Word *Yahoo* . . . although it were impossible for me to conjecture what it meant . . . I endeavored to practice this word upon my Tongue; and . . . I boldly pronounced *Yahoo* in a loud Voice, imitating, at the same time, as near as I could, the Neighing of a Horse; at which they were both visibly surprized, and the Grey repeated the same Word twice, as if he meant to teach me the right Accent, wherein I spoke after him as well as I could, and found myself perceivably to improve every time. [*GT* 4.1.226–27]

Gulliver's considerable investments in language have betrayed him. He names himself, and the name is Yahoo; the Houyhnhnms, who use words as value- and ambiguity-free markers of fact, accept his self-naming as truth. From that point on, the experience in Houyhnhnmland records Gulliver's endeavor to close the gap between an initially meaningless word and the significance to which it may be attached. And the quest for stable signification precipitates for Gulliver a cosmic verbal tragedy: language not only fails to distinguish man from beast, but it also certifies that man is beast. No longer privileged, language has fallen from grace and has taken Gulliver with it. His confusion and fall resemble that of Milton's Eve, who is similarly puzzled by a speaking animal and who therefore decides to redefine her identity by misreading the authorized text of Eden.[13]

Gulliver is victimized not just by pride in language learning[14] but by denial of textocentric reality. Words are imperfect and polysemous; their multiple contexts are ignored at the interpreter's peril. Gulliver not only isolates the word *Yahoo* from the foreign discourse of Houyhnhnm language by choosing it arbitrarily as a sound with which to impress the horses with his desire to communicate, but he also refuses, as we have seen in chapter 4, to read himself in the context of his own history. Swift's textocentric strategies are designed to trap readers into fallacious interpretation, and in Houyhnhnmland, Gulliver is a paradigm of bad and dangerous reading. Swift's textocentrism, however, usually tries to make interpretive error aware of itself. Gulliver's tragedy lies in his lack of awareness that the meanings he has assigned to clothes and words, the surface signifiers of self, are not necessarily true ones and certainly not the only possible ones.

How, then, in the face of Gulliver's obliviousness, are subsequent readers supposed to discern the osmotic interchange of the fall of language and the mock ascension of interpretive desire? Swift's twofold strategy often operates by divesting the text of expected guidelines (or inserting duplicitous ones) to such an extent that the subsequent critical chaos signals its own transgression. Such appears to be the case with the multiplicity of responses to book 4, which resemble the inventive "translations" of the made-up languages in *Gulliver's Travels* in their prolix and profound lack of agreement. To elicit interpretive disorder concerning Houyhnhnmland, Swift uses not meaningless snippets of actual languages but the trapping expectations of genre. Books 1 through 3 are obviously satiric; topical, situational, and stylistic satires ground the more general satire of folly and vice. Interpretations of book 4, therefore, begin with an assumption of satire, usually to the exclusion of other genres: debates over whether the Houyhnhnms are admirable rationalists or lampooned Deists, whether the Yahoos are homiletic vice figures or hyperbolically uncivilized Irish peasants, whether Gulliver gains useful if painful knowledge of human frailty or participates in the "satirist-satirized" topos, try to fit interpretation into a set of preconceived generic demands. Genre functions as textual predestination, for the more a work conforms to type, the more clearly it prescribes its own interpretation. Obviously, the satiric genre does not prescribe a clear interpretation for book 4 of *Gulliver's Travels*. Therefore, the text may be generically polycentric.[15] Polycentrism precludes interpretational certainty by pitting the expectations of one genre against those of another; careful readers who assess Gulliver's actions at the end of the book according to the satiric mode, for instance, are aware that the prancing, neighing traveler is also highly comic. But even as Swift's generic mélange promotes perplexity, it provides materials for mapping and evaluating this perplexity. What I believe to be Swift's deliberate use of tragic structure and tragic character seems to be an attempt to prevent readers from falling completely into the snares of language that imprison Gulliver in an interpretational hell of his own making.

Although the rough shaping force of tragedy distances book 4 from the rest of *Gulliver's Travels*,[16] it provides ways to bridge the distance and it gives formal cohesiveness to Gulliver's adventures in Houyhnhnmland. In book 4 flower the seeds of tragedy sown in Gulliver's previous adventures. The Lilliputian plot to maim and starve him, for instance, predicts the Houyhnhnm threats of castration (another example of how Gulliver is menaced by his own words, for it was he who planted the idea of castration) and sentence of exile. Book 2 seethes with unfulfilled tragic potential. Gulliver's near-destruction at the claws and maws of mammals, insects, amphibians, and birds occurs so frequently that the danger becomes comically absurd;[17] nevertheless, the series of quasi-disasters sets up all branches of the animal kingdom as Gulliver's enemies and lays the groundwork for the mental devastation caused by the encounter with the very concept of animality in book 4. Even the incidents that strand Gulliver in alien settings become more and more devastating, as they move from storms to piracy to mutiny and betrayal by his own crew. The subtext of tragedy that finally breaks through reinterprets the book's earlier symmetries into a larger cyclic structure; each deliverance can only play for time, and time finally runs out.

The journey topos itself confers upon Gulliver a heroic stature suitable for tragedy; exported into unfamiliar surroundings, he can be singular, high-minded, and important in ways he could not be in England.[18] Yet in books 1 through 3, Gulliver, insofar as he is any type of hero, remains a comic one. Like Odysseus *polylogos*, he meets the perils and temptations of a strange sea journey through inventive verbal skills and through a sustained desire to go home.[19] But in book 4, Gulliver's linguistic adaptability fails him and he also no longer wants to return to England. Caught by what René Girard has called "triangular desire,"[20] Gulliver replaces his goals with those of the Houyhnhnms, substituting bare truth of word and body for verbal and vestural disguises that allow humans to function in a fallen world, sacrificing himself to determinations of meaning not his own:

> I must freely confess, that the many Virtues of those excellent *Quadrupeds* placed in opposite View to human Corruptions, had so far opened mine Eyes, and enlarged my Understanding, that I began to view the Actions and Passions of Man in a very different Light . . . I had likewise learned from [my Master's] Example an utter Detestation of all Falsehood or Disguise; and *Truth* appeared so amiable to me, that I determined upon sacrificing every thing to it . . . I entered on a firm Resolution never to return to human Kind, but to pass the rest of my Life among these admirable *Houyhnhnms* to the Contemplation and Practice of every Virtue. [*GT* 4.7.258]

Finding in Houyhnhnmland an ideal of perfection that, when rendered unattainable, plunges him into misery,[21] Gulliver therefore follows the tragic pattern of choosing a fate that will make him wretched. Yet concurrently, fate seems to single him out for extraordinarily severe treatment. The Houyhnhnms exhibit the same peculiar combination of detachment and involvement in the affairs of humans as the Greek gods do. They alternate between imparting wisdom and wreaking vengeance, like Apollo as oracle and Apollo as hunter in *Oedipus Tyrannos*; their double nature makes them agents of tragedy. They help propel Gulliver through a classic and harsh tragic plot: he seeks, he finds, he fails, he endures the blinding pain of insight. But his stage is the text, and his tragedy, as we have seen, proceeds from and is enacted through language. Reading his verbal travels as a tragic journey saves interpretation from triangular desire: it warns us not to allocate meaning to words in the way that Gulliver does, not to accept the classificatory systems that Gulliver embraces, and not to hold the unskeptical faith in language's communicative and redemptive powers that leads Gulliver to despair.

Swift also makes Gulliver trot through his tragic paces because he represents man as language-[ab]user, a definition ultimately indistinguishable from man as animal [ir]rationale. In this role, Gulliver discloses some of Swift's deepest fears about the treachery of language and his own ability to prevent it. Like Gulliver, Swift makes overwhelming investments in language; as I have tried to demonstrate throughout this study, he lived his life in and through language that he vivified in most extraordinary and demanding ways. Like Gulliver, Swift offered language as his part of an acculturating covenant with the world, whether it be the little world of Esther Johnson's friendship, the larger world of Irish politics, or the transtemporal world of historical memory. Many factors can break the covenant: the world may mistake or abandon the word, language may fail due to inherent stresses and maculations, or the author may become negligent and write without reflection. Swift knew that only the last factor was under his control, and it is precisely this control that he denies to Gulliver. Gulliver thus becomes a cautionary and cathectic character, actively promoting and passively submitting to all the broken promises and tragic betrayals that language can make.

Gulliver's reflective failure blocks his ability to understand his own use of language. In books 1 through 3, Gulliver's language acquisitions function in what Jean Piaget has termed the first stage of epistemological growth, that of simple abstraction.[22] The mind focuses on individual objects and is conscious of itself as separate from those objects; Gulliver's placement in this stage is indicated by his practice of making dictionaries or his preservation of difference by using England as frame of reference for discussing alien cultures. In book 4, Gulliver tries to enter what Piaget calls the stage of reflective abstraction, when the mind arranges objects in relational orders and also judges as well as perceives its own systematizing activity. In Houyhnhnmland, Gulliver extracts *parole* from an exotic tongue unaware that this act of appropriation changes the host language and the social relationships it articulates. Gulliver does create taxonomies, and he invests himself into them. He does not, however, reflect on the effects of this investiture—just as he cannot bear his own reflection and just as he defends the objectivity of his account by maintaining that "I never suffer a Word to pass that may look like Reflection" (*GT* 4.12.293). All forms of reflection are renounced, and Gulliver is oblivious to what today is termed the Heisenberg principle, that observation changes the observed, and the observer as well. This terrible truth lies behind Swift's own acute textocentric consciousness, his knowledge that writing and reading transform, suborn, and supplant ideas and desires.

If there is any site for textocentric consciousness in book 4, it is the Houyhnhnms. Recognizing and fearing the effect of Gulliver's participation in the closed linguistic world they inhabit, they resort to the most extreme form of conservative guardianship: they throw him out of their text. As Swift had hoped about twenty years earlier, language can theoretically be protected from corruption by prohibition, exclusion, and fixity. Perhaps, then, the Houyhnhnms represent a form of self-criticism; Swift invests them not only with the virtues of rationality and benevolence, which he undoubtedly approved of, but also with linguistic paralysis, with a denial of the sometimes unpleasant reality of historical change, and with an intolerance of fiction. For Gulliver with his deceptive clothes and usurping speech represents the intrusion of fiction into the domain of fact.[23] His expulsion from Houyhnhnmland enacts what would have happened to *A Tale of a Tub* and *Gulliver's Travels*, as well as to Swift's punning poems and bagatelles as examples of verbal play and to the *Drapier's Letters* as examples of historical tampering, had they been brought before the language tribunal Swift had urged in *A Proposal for Correcting ... the English Tongue*. But even if Gulliver challenges the exclusionary values of objectivist language, as a character in a fiction he is defeated by the verbal struggles he engages in. His boat of Yahoo skins and his refusal to accept clothes from Pedro de Mendez are clear transvestural signals that he does not escape the incarcerating imprint of the Houyhnhnms's verbal system. Back in England, he reverses the pattern of language acquisition[24] that had betrayed him and regresses to gesture (putting herbs in his nose, seating himself at the far end of the table) and to mimetic rather than meaningful vocalizations (whinnying with the stable horses). This pathetic, ludicrous attempt to break the edifice of language that had denied him shelter and security forms the last act of his linguistic tragedy.

WISDOM CRIETH IN THE STREETS

By letting embedded tragedy erupt through a satirico-comic book, Swift opposes a vision of inimical time to one of redemptive time. In comedy, time heals the wounds of language and life; in satire, time offers the only hope of linguistic fulfillment and existential reform. In tragedy, time is fearful judgment and final closure, imposing sentences of suffering and silence. *Gulliver's Travels* evades the full consequences of its tragic emplotment by its investment of language into time, by Gulliver's refusal to be silent. And this quixotic refusal, undertaken in a book that in part demonstrates the failure of language, predicts the way in which Swift preserves his own investments in language even as time deepens the fissures between will and word or between text and audience, even as time renders verdicts of exile and sends meaning off on a diaspora from which there is no return.

Gulliver avenges his tragic fall through language, the instrument that caused it. He does what the Houyhnhnms cannot do: he writes.[25] The Houyhnhnms "have not the least Idea of Books or Literature" (*GT* 4.3.235) and they "have no Letters" (*GT* 4.9.273), even though their ability to use needle and thread gives a transvestural clue that they could use pen and ink if they so chose. Gulliver's promise to spend his exile writing their praises (*GT* 4.10.281), then, presumably fails to interest or impress them. He writes not for them but for himself; he writes to fulfill his own desire to mend the torn fabric of the world as he perceives it and perceives himself in it. Despite his cantering through the fields of Redriff, his writing asserts his difference from the horses he emulates. Making a book reopens the issue of who is a Yahoo and what is a rational creature; writing gives the Houyhnhnms the history that their static society eschews (*GT* 4.9.273); the power of letters and literature propels the Trojan textual horse back into the closed world from which Gulliver has been expelled[26] and reinvests him into the time from which the dictates of tragedy have banished him.

Gulliver is closest to Swift in the last part of book 4 not because he satirizes the work of satire. The churlish letter to Sympson demonstrates no satiric self-awareness; by questioning the fate of his own text as it passed from author to printer to reader, going so far as to amend the spelling of Brobdingnag, Gulliver gives a final divestural flourish to the attacks upon the linguistic institution he began by importing Houyhnhnm accents and ideas back to England. He remains an instrument of satire, but he is a subject of tragedy. And in this subjection, he resembles his creator and embodies Swift's fears that in spite of his powerful investments of skill and passion, in spite of the exquisite balance of intricate schemes to preserve elasticity of meaning while retaining shaping authority over his texts, in spite of inventive efforts to bequeath a textual self into history, in spite of attempts to turn self-proclaimed exile into something productive and beneficial, language will fail him too. Yet because Gulliver escapes total immersion in the tragedy that words cause and enact through his commitment to writing, he tests in fiction what Swift demonstrates in fact: a stubborn refusal to relinquish the written word to the limitations and failures of language-users, linguistic institutions, and communication systems. And in this refusal, tragedy is transcended and time is reopened.

Such an opening bares the heart of articulation beneath the vested bodies of words, the absence that longs to be present, that needs to live in time through language. Today we might identify this longing as phenomenological desire; it is easy to imagine that Gulliver, before he is exiled from Houyhnhnmland, would agree with this Heideggerian credo: "The ability to speak is what marks man as man. This mark contains the design of his being. Man would not be man if it were denied him to speak unceasingly, from everywhere and every which way, in many variations . . . Language, in granting all this to man, is the foundation of human being."[27] Swift invests Gulliver with this faith, tests it, smashes it, yet skeptically resurrects it by marking Gulliver profoundly with and in language, by not denying to Gulliver the chance to speak unceasingly through the controlled medium of the written word.

Gulliver's faith in language is but a naive version of Swift's. To Swift, writing is the only way to speak unceasingly, to speak through time and to have time speak through textually bound speech. Time speaking through the openings in the text preserves the engraphed self and the meanings it tries to authorize, even as it necessarily and tragically alters them, reestablishing the difference that holds apart the claims of absence and presence so that writing can give its sacrificial and precious gift to the future. Such a phenomenological web of gain and loss is described by Wilhelm von Humboldt: "*time* . . . will often introduce into language what it did not possess before. Then the old shell is filled with a new meaning, the old coinage conveys something different . . . All this is a lasting fruit of a people's *literature*."[28] Time and literature: the latter demands trespass from the former; the former gathers fruit from the latter, fruit sweet to itself and often tragically bitter to the textual consciousness that longs for a harvesting it can never experience. In one of Swift's riddles, time explains that it "Never find[s] full Repast, / Till I eat the World at last" (*SPW* 630.3–4). This is the final and fatal harvest, when hunger is satiated and desire is fulfilled.

Swift's tragic sense of himself as writer grew stronger, as we have seen, after the *Drapier's Letters*. But he kept writing, and he increased his risks—stretching language to the breaking point in word games with Sheridan, facing physical mortality and textual frailty in autobiographical poems, declaring authorial weariness and worthlessness in political pieces, exposing language as empty fraud in *Polite Conversation*, increasing levels of excrementalization and metaphorical bloat in a variety of texts. Perhaps Swift believed that language cannot work as praxis or as persuasion, but his last years of intense linguistic engagements indicate that some bargain remained to be struck with words. A pamphlet he published in 1728, *An Answer to a Paper called a Memorial*, suggests that the conditions of the bargain have to do with fulfillment of meaning by history. In *An Answer*, Swift declares that history has circumvented audience indifference by visiting the calamities he predicted upon the people who could have avoided them if they had heeded his words. He has seen his dark visions realized, and the realization brings rage at "all the Warnings I have in vain given the Publick, at my own Peril, for several Years past," and sorrow at having "to see the Consequences and Events answer in every Particular" (*PW* 12:22). Thus meaning is estranged from communication; in fact, it depends on the failure of communication.

Swift keeps courting peril because he believes himself under the aegis of the Pallas figure, the militant weaver of wisdom who has governed his personal relationships with women, who has stood behind the Drapier, and who appears in *An Answer* as Biblical Gnosis. Borrowing the text from Prov. 1:20–26 but suppressing the verses that clearly identify the "I" as a female voice separate from the proverb speaker, Swift presents his own ignored words as the object of Wisdom's lamentations:

> *Wisdom crieth in the streets; because I have called and ye refused; I have stretched out my Hand, and no Man regarded. But ye have set at nought all my Counsel, and would none of my Reproof. I also will laugh at your Calamity, and mock when your Fear cometh.* [*PW* 12:23]

In Proverbs, Wisdom's cries are last calls for communication, directed at the audience; the chapter begins by specifically lauding the ability to understand and to interpret, and it ends with promising salvation to those who listen to the power of the word. In Swift's version, Wisdom's cries commemorate the final failure of communication and offer the presently unregarded text a compensatory reading in the future, a future where it can reread itself, where it can laugh at the bitter truths that time has confirmed and mock the belatedness of authorized interpretation.

Perhaps such a sour and solipsistic projection into history motivated Swift's last investments of himself into language. If so, his predictions about the magnitude and effect of his textual existence were much less accurate than his general predictions that human stupidity and corruption would never be eradicated. No other Augustan writer lives so fully in his texts and demands such engagement with the authorial will vested in his words. No other Augustan writer's grave is one of its city's major tourist attractions. No other Augustan writer's works have passed so fully into popular consciousness and popular culture while retaining attraction for critics, philosophers, and theologians. No other Augustan writer is still considered a hero by his country. No other Augustan writer could move as agilely among prose fiction, poetry, political polemic, philosophical tales, history, and occasional essays. No other Augustan writer so directly influenced subsequent authors and bequeathed such a variety of literary gifts: serious language games to Sterne and Joyce, the clothes philosophy to Carlyle, political and artistic commitment to Yeats, a distinctive animal dystopia to Orwell and Malamud.

Some eighteenth-century writers have achieved some of these successes. Defoe's *Robinson Crusoe* has entered popular myth; Dryden worked effectively in many genres; actual lines and phrases from Pope are more frequently quoted than ones from Swift; Fielding and Richardson shaped the development of the modern novel; Samuel Johnson's personality has superseded his writings, a phenomenon due in large part to Boswell's mediating biography. But in the combination of scope and consequence, in the tenacity with which a self-authorized textual personality has demanded the attention of future generations, in the simple fact that his works have been read and enjoyed and pondered over for two and a half centuries, Swift remains unparalleled among his contemporaries and near-contemporaries. And in these accomplishments he has few rivals in all of English literature.

Massive returns can only follow massive investments. Swift asked a great deal of language, more perhaps than it can bear. The straining seams of his texts testify to the interwoven investigations of words and meanings, to the tensions between the warp of investiture and the woof of divestiture, to the struggles of the textual selves they enwrap, to the weight of metaphorical transvestitures layered upon them, to the burden of fictional, figural, and personal investments sewn into the verbal fabric. Swift has, and we have, no guarantee that the elaborately authorized meanings have survived centuries of interpretation intact. One suspects they have not, and one suspects that Swift suspected they would not. This is part of the game: a losing game, a tragic game that fashions gains and triumphs by building loss and tragedy into its rules, but a game very much worth playing because it is so fully and achingly human. Swift's vested word embodies the human need to be heard, to be read, and to be remembered. It embodies the need to leave writing on the wall, to weave the text of printed Omens and transvested Emblems described in "St. Patrick's Well," so all can see, so all can try to interpret, so all can communicate with the textual self that lives in language.

POSTSCRIPT

I AM NOT SURE what *postscript* means. Is it "writing after"—part of a text placed behind, or composed later than, the main text, perhaps an afterbirth? Or is it "after writing"—a kind of nonwriting, a sweeping up of what is left in writing's wake, perhaps an aftermath? Swift, as we have seen, thought of texts as metaphoric children and as potential calamities, so both ideas of postscript capture something of the spirit behind Scriblerian addenda. And that spirit involves feelings of separation and responsibility. Books can be finished, ready to enter the world and have their effects (or not have any at all). Authors are not finished; they still think and rethink their material, which is about to move beyond their control.

Swift's Tale-writer wisely remarks that "there seems to be no Part of Knowledge in fewer Hands than that of Discerning *when to have Done*" ("The Conclusion," *Tale*, 208). Writing a postscript is a way to force this knowledge upon oneself; one can discern, perceive the apartness of, text and author by sending the book on its way with postpartum or postmortem last words. The real audience of a postscript is its own writer. Therefore, it seems appropriate to use this vehicle to address subjective matters that have been excised or repressed in the text proper. Allowing oneself to speak briefly in one's own voice, rather than that of an impersonal scholarly narrator, may be a way "to have done."

My preface evaded the issue of critical allegiance by claiming that this book is "informed" by various postmodern theories and more or less leaving it at that. Such a claim no longer seems adequate to me. It is dishonest to imply that "all criticism is, or can be, useful" means the same thing as "all criticism is, or can be, equal." One's practice—my practice—clearly indicates otherwise: some types of criticism are more equal than others.

Theoretical and methodological choices are not made at random. I believe they should be influenced by the texts under consideration; the form of *A Tale of a Tub*, for example, appears to demand a deconstructive approach, whereas the political situation of the *Drapier's Letters* appears to demand historicist contexts and reception aesthetics. I also realize that this belief is illusory. What a critic thinks a text demands is necessarily a reflection of his or her critical predispositions.

For instance, I wrote that "Swift is the most radically deconstructive Augustan writer" after years of reading poststructuralist studies with enthusiasm. Deconstruction appeals to my own sense of verbal play, dislike of closure, and delight in textual mysteries; more significantly, Derridean deconstruction has posed important and exciting questions about writing that—no matter what their truth value, if there is such a thing—have revitalized literary studies. A similar claim can be made for Lacan's de/reconstruction of Freud; it is not necessary to adopt the Lacanian model completely in order to profit from his interestingly redefined psychoanalytics as one circulates the model through literary history and biography. Nonetheless, personal enjoyment of these ways of thinking makes me give more credit to their partial truths and their attendant modes of revelation than I give to conflicting ones, and I consequently discover kindred operations in Swift's work.

Although I may not fully accept the truth of the theories I have in part appropriated, I do accept their value. Their value, on one level, is the pleasure I get from grappling with them and the critical issues they help to formulate. Their value, on another level, is to assist in the reintegration of eighteenth-century studies into the most challenging levels of academic discourse. This is a task to which I am truly committed, a task which demands every critical and methodological tool at our disposal.

In the main, practitioners of deconstruction have ignored Restoration and eighteenth-century texts (excluding, of course, Milton and the novel).[1] This in itself is not an irredeemable loss, but it suggests that the poems of Dryden and Pope, the prose of Swift and Johnson, the works of Thompson and the Whartons, are less accessible to one type of modern critical mind than the sonnets of Donne or the odes of Keats. Why is this so? First, the different guises of poststructuralism are heirs of earlier formalisms; as a concept like ambiguity mutates into a concept like erasure, privileged fields of demonstration, such as the lyric, tend to remain the same. These fields are not frequently found in the Augustan landscape. Second, the period that I study has been dominated by the idea of personality, the outsized figures of literary power like Dryden, Pope, Swift, and Johnson. Johnson's *Lives* present prototypes for this idea; his work is in part a product of the post-Enlightenment shift toward belief in individual human nature, and much modern work in the period is the offspring of Johnsonian critical biography. As a rule, deconstructive critics are not interested in the individual human personalities that produce texts. Third, a strong, traditional historicism has retained control over Restoration and eighteenth-century studies long after it has eased its hold upon other areas of literary inquiry. Few people today believe in the pervasiveness of the Tudor myth, for instance; we now have alternative Shakespeares and alternative myths, and these provide in Renaissance studies alternative mediations among cultural, political, historical, social, economic, and "literary" texts.[2] But many people today believe in the pervasiveness of the Augustan ideal of order, or in the organizing force of the Great Chain of Being metaphor, or in the aptness of the poetry-of-statement concept, or in other categorical pegs on which to hang Restoration and eighteenth-century writers and their works. My point is not that such categories are wrong. Rather, these categories may have outlasted their usefulness, and they now may destroy the ground they were designed to cultivate if they continue to shut out other methods of finding interest and meaning. And this *would* be an irredeemable loss.

Because the study of literature written between 1660 and 1792 has been saturated by historical considerations of one sort or another, and because this body of literature often requires knowledge of socio-political history simply to understand its overt subject matter and interior references, a scholar who takes a radically and exclusively poststructuralist approach can be regarded with suspicion. He or she suggests prima facie affiliation with Swift's mad modern Tale-writer, who proudly proclaims that "[i]n my Disposure of Employment of the Brain, I have thought fit to make *Invention* the *Master*, and to give *Method* and *Reason* the Office of its *Lacquays*" ("The Conclusion," *Tale*, 209). When one deals with texts that are in various ways *about* history, one cannot ignore history and expect to be read seriously. For deconstruction to be more than a self-indulgent game, it must scrupulously attend to historically particularized contexts as well as theoretically universal textual operations.

Thus I come to the second major body of contemporary theory that to me is more equal than others: new historicism. Because the period with which I deal has been dominated by a more traditional historicism, it seems reasonable to assume that new historicism could go where poststructuralism fears to tread. And it has, to some extent—Michael McKeon's book on Dryden, Terry Eagleton's work on periodical essays, Carole Fabricant's investigation of Swift, Laura Brown's reading of Pope, and Alvin Kernan's study of Johnson, to name a few.[3] Such endeavors present ways of focusing upon (to risk another Augustan cliché) the public, political busyness of the age as it helped produce, and was itself produced by, written texts. By questioning the existence of a monolithic zeitgeist to which all canonical works conform, new-historicist examinations affirm a multilayered and deformative palingenesis[4] of text, audience, economics, politics, and culture. By denying the superiority of one genre of text over another, they open to fruitful consideration types of writing previously regarded as minor or marginal. Moreover, a complex and skeptical historical awareness guards against the tendency for a historically oriented critic to become a custodian of a sanctified tradition[5] or an annotator of works demanding so much erudition that they are approachable only by a scholarly elite. By retheorizing the relationships between texts and contexts, new historicism resituates literature in history and culture both by refusing to privilege "literature" and by implying that literature is indispensable to the human experience.

Yet within this critical orientation there remains a certain adherence to ideological absolutism, even if the ideologies perceived by new historicists differ from those perceived by "old" historicists. The underlying assumption governing the old historicism, that there *is* a recoverable and factual history that Restoration and eighteenth-century texts reflect, that there is a truth to be found and promulgated, therefore is not adequately problematized by substituting "histories" for "history" or "subvert" for "reflect." Although in theory new historicism "discourages dogmatism, by obliging us to foreground the difference between our circumstances, aims, and language, and those of the past,"[6] in practice it often fails at this task. No matter how forthright critics may be in declaring their own political agendum or in articulating the pressures of their own historical moment, heavily ideological criticism with its emphasis on correct rather than reactionary attitudes can lead to anachronistic, slanted, or simply implausible readings. For example, much applied new historicism is Marxist; authors can be so committed to pejorative views of capitalism that polemicism risks undercutting the credibility of their claims about Addison's prose or Pope's poetry. Feminist critics who work with eighteenth-century texts tend also to use new historicism; again, the strength of their personal ideological biases can contaminate the authority of how they read writing by and about women. The line between forceful conviction and force-fed dogmatism is, of course, subjectively drawn. But when a reader of critical work starts receiving a picture of Pope as a literary

Daddy Warbucks—or of phallocentric conspiracy as the evil twin of bourgeois economics—the line, in my opinion, has been crossed.

Poststructuralism provides a corrective for new historicism's absolutist tendency; it counters deterministic ideology with the principle of indeterminacy. Conversely, new historicism provides a corrective for the epistemological nihilism that can grow from indeterminacy. I have tried to bring these two strong schools of contemporary theory into dialogue in a textual space that internally sanctions both approaches. In addition, I have tried to anchor this book in the bedrock of more traditional historicism and biographical criticism—not only as a check against irresponsibility but also as a demonstration of how old and new discourses can augment and enrich each other.

The dialogue between textuality and historicity influences the shape of critical argument. Poststructuralist maneuvers can produce something akin to what Jerome McGann has termed "the array": critical discourse characterized by lack of narrativized completion. McGann's examples are drawn from schematic forms such as bibliographical listings; although he may not agree, I think that these examples share with poststructuralist practice (or one potential of poststructuralist practice) a refusal to close significance by presenting to the reader an emplotted interpretation of meanings. In contrast, new-historicist methodology produces what McGann has called "the narrative": critical discourse characterized by an illusion of completion. McGann uses the word *illusion* deliberately because he believes that narrativized criticism duplicitously suggests that "completion is inherent to the historical [or textual] events rather than to the narrative of those events. No such moral illusion is either sought for or possible in a critical array."[7] McGann sets up dialectic as an alternate form of critical discourse, one that questions itself through digressions, contradictions, and revisions. According to McGann, much deconstructive work attempts the form of dialectic but fails because its revisionism is directed against something other than itself.

I do not think that any critical endeavor that includes interpretation can sustain the purity of arrayed discourse. Perhaps it should not; if I understand McGann correctly, he does not object to critical narrativization per se as much as to the denial of or blindness to such narrativization. Arguments themselves are plots, and we must acknowledge the subjective impositions they perform or be found guilty of moral illusionism. The advantage of combining competing theories in one critical discourse may be that it forces internal revisionism, that it sets in motion a mechanism for dialectically attracting and repulsing the power of a single narrativized argument.

Nonetheless, I found my work on Swift pulled increasingly in the direction of narrative, narrative that includes—in contrast to dominant modes of poststructuralism and new historicism—a clearly biographical element. If I am hostage to narrative desire, and if I must confront my own authorial subjectivity, should I not look for manifestations of parallel urges and needs in Swift's texts, albeit ones mediated by differences in history, culture, and personality? Cannot biography function as a received narrative that can partially disillusion the imposed narrative of critical argument? These questions prompted the use of psychological and biographical criticism throughout this book and particularly in chapter 4; my conclusions in turn prompted the more overt narrative of chapters 5 and 6.

As I was working on chapter 4, I went to the Republic of Ireland. This visit also influenced the narrative that was taking shape in my mind. In a last gesture toward critical dialectic before I have "done with all such visionary Schemes forever," I offer the following array of observations from that trip.

> Holyhead seems to be in the middle of nowhere, particularly at three o'clock in the morning.
>
> The air in Ireland is always clean because it is washed by sea winds (and there is neither much heavy industry nor heavy traffic).
>
> Irish citizens were extremely friendly, and most assumed that I was looking for my ancestral home.
>
> I got lost trying to find Laracor, Swift's first ecclesiastical post.
>
> Godwin Swift's manor house and the surrounding pastureland are beautiful.
>
> So is the nearby town of Kilkenny, where Swift spent much of his boyhood.
>
> At Kilkenny School, someone has donated a tennis court to commemorate Swift's student days.
>
> The man on the street (or the woman in the pub) knows who Swift is and thinks he was a great man, although many were surprised to find out that he was a writer.
>
> The Book of Kells, on display in the Trinity College Library, is a visual deconstructive pun.

> In Dublin, beggars and their children sit motionless on bridges spanning the Liffey.
> Near one bridge is a shop specializing in Irish woollens.
> Swift souvenirs are sold inside St. Patrick's Cathedral.
> Esther Johnson is buried next to Swift, and her grave marker on the floor is smaller than his.
> The most poignant section of *Gulliver's Travels* is the journey to Glubbdubdrib.
> Turfcutting still scars the Irish countryside.
> One sees many spectral shells of country estates burned during the uprisings of the early twentieth century.
> There are armed guards at border crossings to Northern Ireland.

Thus my trip. And thus the tragic narrative pattern, a subjective but I hope plausible fiction, that ends my critical discourse.

I feel compelled to give the last "last words" back to Swift, whose words are the subject of this book and have occasioned the observations in this postscript. By borrowing the prepublication awareness of the Tale-writer that he finally seems "to have done," I can let a purely textual creation speak for me, for himself, and perhaps for all authors—including Swift—who find that one can stop but one can never finish because the unruly nature of language will not allow it. Exposure and discovery are necessary concomitants of writing; we might grow as we master our own texts, but once texts are liberated from our control, the rate and direction of their independent growth become functions of their reception. At that point we can only hesitate, linger, plan resumption of our work, or cease altogether.

> But now, since by the Liberty and Encouragement of the Press, I am grown absolute Master of the Occasions and Opportunities, to expose the Talents I have acquired; I already discover, that the *Issues* of my *Observanda* begin to grow too large for the *Receipts*. Therefore, I shall here pause awhile. ["The Conclusion," *Tale*, 210]

NOTES

PREFACE

1. See Knapp and Michaels, "Against Theory," 732–42.
2. Barthes, *On Racine*, 162.
3. Hirsch, *Validity in Interpretation*, 4–6, 225–32.
4. Miller, "Stevens' Rock and Criticism as Cure, II," 345. Seeking or seeing the author through his texts—often at the expense of his text—is a recurring strain in studies of Swift. Nineteenth-century commentators presented a mythically demonic Swift whose loathsome creations were figures of his own incipient insanity (a useful overview can be found in Voigt, *Swift and the Twentieth Century*, 3–27). Twentieth-century attention to Swiftian personae is a profitable revisionist maneuver that nonetheless keeps central the question of Swift's authentic personality (see, for instance, Elliott, "Swift's 'I,'" 372–91). In fact, rarely is Swift's work treated without the issue of the "real" Swift being addressed, the shadowy and powerful director standing behind the scrim of words.
5. K. Williams, *Jonathan Swift*, 183.
6. Price, *Swift's Rhetorical Art*, 105.

CHAPTER I

1. S. Johnson, "Life of Swift," 52.
2. Alston, *Philosophy of Language*, 10–31.
3. Howell, "*Res et Verba*," 131–42.
4. For example, Bacon, *Advancement of Learning*, 29–30.
5. Hobbes, *Leviathan* 1.4.
6. Sprat, *History of the Royal Society*, 113.
7. Ann Cline Kelly ("After Eden," 33–54) offers a useful summary of seventeenth-century schemes for language reform with which Swift was probably familiar. One of the purposes of universal "real characters" was to increase the chances for global harmony through facilitating the interchange of goods and ideas. Swift mocks this linguistic utopian colonialism in a comment following his description of the new language of things: "[I]t would serve as an universal Language to be

understood in all civilized Nations . . . Embassadors would be qualified to treat with foreign Princes or Ministers of State" (*GT* 3.5.186).

8. Swift may have intended an additional devaluing materialism; he often referred to processes surrounding human evacuation as "business." See letter 5, Oct. 1710, *JS* 1:41: "[Mr. Harley] has appointed me an hour on Saturday at four, afternoon, when I will open my business to him; which expression I would not use if I were a woman. I know you smoakt it; but I did not till I writ it." The *Oxford English Dictionary* gives 1645 as the earliest date for "doing business" as a synonym for "easing one's bowels"; it also notes that as early as 1630, "business" was a euphemism for sexual intercourse, a double-entendre Swift may have also had in mind.
9. See Cohen, *Sensible Words*, 6–9.
10. Foucault, *The Order of Things*, 43.
11. This is one of the major themes treated by Ronald Paulson in his *Theme and Structure*. See also Andreasen, "Swift's Satire on the Occult," 410–21.
12. The phrase is from Stephen K. Land, *From Signs to Propositions*, 24.
13. Russell, *Principles of Mathematics*, 47 (italics added).
14. Wilkins, *An Essay Towards a Real Character*, 21. For a discussion of Swift's possible satire of Wilkins, see Probyn, "Swift and Linguistics," 425–32.
15. See Knight, *The Burning Oracle*, 117; Price, *Swift's Rhetorical Art*, 1–14. Price suggests that the new rhetoric practiced by Swift reacted against both Anglo-Catholic metaphysical style and convoluted Puritan exegesis.
16. One of Samuel Johnson's objections to Swift's style was that it could operate "by the mere weight of facts with very little assistance from the hand that produced them" ("Life of Swift," 48). Denis Donoghue sees this tendency not as a failing but as a virtue; Swift's "words are always ready to be tested in the light of facts, things, Nature. His style is not wordy, it is thingy" (*Jonathan Swift*, 142–43).
17. Two excellent discussions of Swift's verbal incarnationalism are Nokes, " 'Hack at Tom Poley's,' " 46–47, and Maresca, "Language and Body," 374–88.
18. Hugh Kenner believes Swift is the first author to exploit the possibilities of a book qua book (*The Stoic Comedians*, 39).
19. Locke, *Essay*, 3.2.1.
20. Smith, *Language and Reality*, 9–23.
21. Colie, "Gulliver," 58–62.
22. Keener, *The Chain of Becoming*, 89–126. Ronald Paulson maintains that Swift disagreed with the doctrine of *tabula rasa* but found the rest of Locke's philosophy of mind suited to the satiric mission of attacking unreasonable reason (*The Fictions of Satire*, 150).
23. Donoghue, *Jonathan Swift*, 101, 131.
24. Carnochan, *Lemuel Gulliver's Mirror for Man*, 116–65.
25. Dircks, "Gulliver's Tragic Rationalism," 134–49.
26. Aarsleff, *From Locke to Saussure*, 42–83.

27. In general, see Harth, *Swift and Anglican Rationalism*, and Carnochan, *Lemuel Gulliver's Mirror for Man*, 146–47.
28. Locke, *Essay*, 3.10.34 ("all the artificial and figurative application of words eloquence hath invented, are for nothing else but to insinuate wrong ideas, move the passions, and thereby mislead the judgment; and so indeed are perfect cheats").
29. Quintana, *Two Augustans*, 74.
30. Locke, *Essay*, 3.5.10.
31. Aristotle, *Rhetoric*, 1,2. Plato, *The Republic*, 10.595–609. *Criticism: The Major Texts*, edited by W. J. Bate, is the source for the following works: Horace, *Art of Poetry*, 56 (Horace also maintains that poems must "be affecting, and must lead to the heart of the hearer," 52); Longinus, *On the Sublime*, sect. 1–9.62–67; Sir Philip Sidney, *An Apology for Poetry*, 86–87 (poetry should "teach and delight . . . imitate the inconceivable excellencies of God . . . and lead and draw us to as high a perfection as our degenerate souls . . . can be capable of").
32. John Dryden, *Essays of John Dryden*, 2:71; Alexander Pope, *An Essay on Criticism*, 151–52 ("A perfect Judge will *read* each Work of Wit / With the same Spirit that its Author *writ*," lines 233–34; "In ev'ry Work regard the *Writer's End*" line 255); Joseph Addison, "The Pleasures of the Imagination," *The Spectator* #416, 558–61.
33. Bloomfield, *Language*, 139. For style as the vehicle by which meaning is transferred from authorial intent to readerly realization of its potential, see Riffaterre, "Criteria for Style Analysis," 135–55.
34. For an interesting discussion of this issue that relates Swift's activism to the Puritan *vita activa*, see Reilly, *Jonathan Swift*, 229–37.
35. Oliver W. Ferguson points out Swift's awareness and exploitation of this conventional satirist's dilemma ("Nature and Friendship," 24–25). In *A Short Character of the Earl of Wharton*, Swift's invective includes Wharton's insensitivity to shame and implies that satiric attack upon such a man is useless (*PW* 3:178). Swift, however, wrote with relish to Esther Johnson that Wharton did react to the piece, seeking out Swift at White's Chocolate House to ply him with false politeness (letter 36, Dec. 1711, *JS* 2:427).
36. Elaborations of these Heideggerian and Husserlian concepts can be found in Merleau-Ponty, *Signs*, 84–96.
37. Distinguishing between "real" and "verbal" truth has a long history. For instance, Aquinas differentiates between the truth of the thing and the truth of the intellect (the opinion or proposition expressed in words); the two truths can contradict each other yet remain true (*Summa Theologica*, 1.16.8).
38. Said, *The World*, 55.
39. Derrida, *Of Grammatology*, 29–37.
40. Sidney, *An Apology for Poetry*, 97.
41. Bakhtin, *Rabelais and His World*. He believes these "polyphonic" works are characterized by dialogism (symbolic discourse with the "other") and ambivalence

(crossing textual spaces and intersections with history). Bakhtin's analysis of the carnivalesque mode resembles in some respects Northrop Frye's analysis of the "anatomy" or Menippean Satire, the genre into which the *Tale* is placed. Frye also stresses "the free play of intellectual fancy" and the emphasis on dialogue (*Anatomy of Criticism*, 308–11).

42. Derrida, *Disseminations*, 63–171.
43. Seidel (*Satiric Inheritance*, 169) connects these satirically weakened familial lines of descent to the intellectual lineages of the ancients versus moderns controversy.
44. The Yale School of criticism treats literature and criticism as types of (weak and strong) misreading. See, for example, De Man, "Literature and Language," 184–88; Miller, "Deconstructing the Deconstructors," 24–31; Bloom, *A Map of Misreading*.
45. The reading process has been described by Paul De Man as a confrontation with textual unreadability; language is the locus of meaning but it continually subverts its promise of truth, and critical writing is necessarily an allegory of the reading experience (*Allegories of Reading*, ix, 113–16).
46. This is an example of what W. B. Carnochan ("The Consolations of Satire," 19–42) identifies as Swift's compensatory strategy—making denials that are generative as well as destructive (gaudy tulips rising from the dung).

CHAPTER 2

1. In general, see Saussure, *Course in General Linguistics*.
2. For a Heideggerian critique of literary spatiality, see Spanos, "Breaking the Circle," 104.
3. As a corrective for "negative" assessments of Swift, Pat Rogers ("Swift and the Idea of Authority," 25–37) characterizes Swift's writings as special affirmations of authoritarian values. Swift's authoritarianism is most marked during the years he lived in England; in Ireland, he increasingly questioned English governmental authority, although he did not lose faith in the authority of his church.
4. Barthes, *S/Z*, 104.
5. In an article examining the lexification of intercourse with the Divine, Richard Jacobson asserts that "[i]nsofar as resort to written codes [the Law and the Scriptures] expropriates these essentially present modes of Authority, the existence of the code itself points to absence—an authoritative absence . . . God is replaced by the Text, which then becomes the signifier both of God and the index of his silence" ("Absence, Authority, and the Text," 137–38, 146).
6. For a view that *A Tale of a Tub* presents harsh Hobbesian realities, see Fisher, "An End to the Renaissance," 1–22. For a view of Swift's satire of Hobbes, see Hopkins, "The Personation of Hobbism," 372–76.
7. Patrick Reilly (*Jonathan Swift*, 87–115) links Swift's acute sense of historical

and institutional decay with seventeenth-century beliefs (e.g., the Goodman-Hakewell debate) and with his religious conservatism.
8. See Hall, "'An Inverted Hypocrite,'" 64.
9. R. Frye, "Swift's Yahoos," 201–7.
10. Wyrick, "Life Interminable," 48–56.
11. Nigel Dennis suggests that Swift's opinions can be described in terms of nakedness and clothing but implies that he somehow values the naked truth of the body because clothes are vain and dishonest disguises (*Jonathan Swift*, 53–57).
12. The *locus classicus* may be the brief remarks by Ricardo Quintana that contrast the false but fair exterior with the true but disturbing interior (*Mind and Art*, 96). Martin Price also sees a dichotomy, and it leads him into contradiction: he believes that the "clothes religion is a worship of the outside of things, and dissolves the inside altogether" but that the only thing that has "permanence... is the body" (*To the Palace of Wisdom*, 210–11).
13. Swift uses the same technique in the *Vindication of Lord Carteret*; the false authorities to which he satirically appeals include such a-graphic sources as rumor, spies, curators of Bedlam, and majority opinion. See the discussion in Beaumont, *Swift's Classical Rhetoric*, 106.
14. Here Swift anticipates Jacques Derrida, (*Of Grammatology*, 44–65). Derrida's criticism of the false binarism of contemporary linguistics and semiotics perhaps stems from Gaston Bachelard, who takes issue with the concept of the aggressive dialectic of division that the terms "outside" and "inside" entail (*The Poetics of Space*, 211–12).
15. This is an interesting permutation of the much more commonplace assertion in *The Tatler* #230: an abuser of language is a coxcomb "who, because Words are the Cloathing of our Thoughts, cuts them out, and shapes them as he pleases, and changes them oftner than his Dress" (*PW* 2:176).
16. Hugh Sykes Davies discusses Swift's *Proposal* in the context of other seventeenth- and eighteenth-century writers' desires to restrict language in "Irony and the English Tongue," 129–38.
17. Davis and Landa, Introduction to *PW* 4:xii–xiv.
18. Watt, "The Ironic Tradition," 305–26.
19. S. Johnson, *The Plan of an English Dictionary*, 1–22.
20. S. Johnson, "Preface to the English Dictionary," 23–54. For an illuminating discussion of Johnson's struggle with the concepts of literary stability and verbal coherence, see Knoblauch, "Coherence Betrayed," 235–60.
21. Lionel Rubinoff (*The Pornography of Power*, 55–62) suggests that both the classical humanist and the Hobbesian conceptions of society can lead to degradation of human freedom.
22. Martin Price's discussion of Swift's view of institutions emphasizes Swift's devotion to the right (duty) rather than to the good (pleasure) and his belief that state and church institutions are essential to preserving societal order; however, Price

maintains that Swift is "little interested in the saving vision of Order" (*To the Palace of Wisdom*, 188) when Order is sought by system-building.

23. Edward Rosenheim, for instance, believes that the simplicity of the advice is colored by Swift's awareness of the simplicity of his audience (*Swift and the Satirist's Art*, 236); Martin Price warns against taking the words in too narrow a sense (*Swift's Rhetorical Art*, 15).

24. Davis and Landa, Introduction to *PW* 9:xxii–xxiv.

25. For the religious backgrounds of order and Orders, see Waterston, *Order and Counter-Order*, 2–14.

26. Rudolf Arnheim (*Entropy and Art*, 1–15) explains that in a harmoniously ordered construct, outer order (form) represents inner order (function). He believes that the world of order is posited upon the conservation of energy, that simplicity is rooted in the principle of least action.

27. Derrida, "Fors," 64–116.

28. See Miller, "The Critic as Host," 217–53, who presents citations as parasites upon the printed text, whereas Swift implies that the citor is the first-generation parasite.

29. Kelly, "Swift's *Polite Conversation*," 204–24.

30. Rawson (*Gulliver and the Gentle Reader*, 95–99) compares it to Ionesco's *The Bald Soprano* in which the Martins replace the Smiths and in another family all members are named Bobby Watson.

31. Pat Rogers thinks that Swift uses clichés not to encapsulate banality but to test and often to prove the accuracy of popular wisdom ("Swift and the Revival of Cliché," 203–26).

32. See Price, *Swift's Rhetorical Art*, and Milic, *A Quantitative Approach*. Milic argues against those who think each Swiftian persona has a separate style (e.g., Ewald, *The Masks of Jonathan Swift*, 184; Fussell, "Speaker and Style," 64).

33. For instance, Swift sarcastically penned "Admirable authority" in the margin next to this passage from Burnet's *History*: "He told it to a person, from who Tillotson had it, who told me" (*PW* 5:281).

34. Part of this control derives from generic choice. Satire draws authority from moral imperative; allegory relies on a pre-text as, in a different way, does parody. These issues are cogently treated by Everett Zimmerman (*Swift's Narrative Satires*, 17–35).

35. Irony also exposes the nature of linguistic power. As Shoshana Felman maintains, "irony precisely consists in dragging authority as such into a scene which it cannot master, of which it is *not aware* and which, for that very reason, is the scene of its own self-destruction ... literature, by virtue of its ironic force, fundamentally deconstructs the fantasy of authority [by telling] us that authority is a language effect" ("To Open the Question," 8).

36. Irvin Ehrenpreis (*Literary Meaning and Augustan Values*, 33–34), for example, sees ironic readings as another way to escape the insistent explicitness of Augustan

texts; he disputes such interpretations as Barry Slepian's ("The Ironic Intention," 249–56).
37. A. E. Dyson terms this shifting irony a technique of betrayal, heightened by a gentlemanly, polite style that lulls us into assent ("Swift: The Metamorphosis of Irony," 56) and that results in an essentially negative view of life and the possibilities for beneficial change. See also Leavis, "The Irony of Swift," 73–87.
38. Excellent discussions of Swift's sense of alienation and his sour opinion of Ireland can be found in Fabricant, *Swift's Landscape*, 210–19. Michael McKeon makes provocative comments about Swift's feelings of deprivation and exile, particularly as they are transferred to and transformed by Lemuel Gulliver (*The Origins of the English Novel*, 338–41).
39. See also Swift's *A Proposal for Giving Badges to Beggars*, PW 13:131–40. This tract exhibits a heightened vocabulary of coercion. The "profligate, vagabond Wretches [who] corrupted all the rest" and "infest every Part of the Town" ought to be whipped, expelled, and—if possible—"rooted out off the Face of the Earth" (p. 139); the badges of the "Original Poor" should be "always visible on Pain of being whipt and turned out of Town" (p. 132).
40. Wotton, "Observations," 316–17, 322.
41. See "The Apology," *Tale*, 9–10; "Thoughts on Various Subjects," *PW* 4:248; letter to Pope of 26 Nov. 1725, *Corr.* 3:118.
42. Footnotes by a second author imply some sort of variorum edition or an annotated edition postdating the original, usually published after the death of the primary author. Stanley Fish has called attention to the variorum's presupposition that meaning can be pinned down through scholarship ("Interpreting the *Variorum*," 147–73), a presupposition that Swift questions through his placement of Wotton in the *Tale*. Reversing the temporal sequence of second-author scholarly notes may be Swift's way of limiting intertextuality even as he seems to exploit it. See J. Levine ("Originality and Repetition," 113) for the precarious hierarchy invested in footnotes. Swift is not doing the same thing that Jacques Derrida does when he uses footnotes to create a countertext (e.g., his essay on Maurice Blanchot, "Living On," 117–56), but he does anticipate Derrida by challenging the "finished nature" of the *Tale* through adding apparatus as the book goes through successive editions, a Scriblerian device exploited even further by Pope in the *Dunciad Variorum*.
43. Shari Benstock believes that footnotes in fiction reinforce authorial authority by addressing the reader and involving him in the process of determining meaning: they refer to the inter- and the intratext. In the case of works like the *Tale* and *Tristram Shandy*, the notes undermine the texts' normal "authors" and enhance the "editors" and, ultimately, the actual authors ("At the Margin of Discourse," 204–25). See also Kenner (*The Stoic Comedians*, 39–40) who emphasizes the importance of notes' spatial organization as disruptions of temporal sequence.
44. The lures and snares Swift places in his texts are instances of what Robert W.

Uphaus (*The Impossible Observer*, 2) sees as a tendency of eighteenth-century writers to challenge readers to reflect on the nature of interpretation.
45. Swift owned a copy of Spenser's work according to the inventory in H. Williams's *Dean Swift's Library*, 76.
46. The classic work on Swift's sources is Eddy, *Gulliver's Travels: A Critical Study*. This work, like most subsequent source studies, relies mainly on internal evidence, not on any admissions of influences by Swift. As Jenny Mezciems ("Swift's Praise of Gulliver," 246) admits, "Swift acnowledges no direct debts." Mezciems suggests that the infrequency of references to the great Renaissance humanists stemmed from Swift's assumption that his readers were familiar with the works and did not need to have allusions specified.
47. Spenser, *The Faerie Queene*, 1.1.25.
48. John Traugott's identification of the Spider with Swift's idea of himself is based upon different premises—the Spider's radical individualism and demonic energy ("A Tale of a Tub," 94–95).
49. Gaston Bachelard calls a corner "[t]hat most sordid of havens." Nevertheless, he emphasizes the peace of immobility inherent in the corner, even as it provides negative space—space for withdrawal or for being "cornered" (*The Poetics of Space*, 137). One thinks of Swift's unsavory corners: the Bedlam kennels in "A Digression Concerning Madness," the fetid bedrooms of the scatological ladies, the hellish cells for the members of the Legion Club. Swift's textual "cornering" is obviously not a personal wish for incarcerating spatial contexts; fond of walking and riding, he valued exercise and fresh air, perhaps as methods of escape from corners.
50. The Spider's web of interlocked, convoluted passageways can be considered as a structure of tropes, of defensive turnings that are both rhetorical and psychic (see Bloom, *A Map of Misreading*, 88–89).

CHAPTER 3

1. The most extensive study of the language trifles is Mayhew, *Rage or Raillery*.
2. Vaughan (writing under his alchemical pseudonym, "Philalethes") lists the stages of the *opus magnum* as "distillation, sublimation, calcination, assation, reverberation, dissolution, descension, and coagulation" (quoted in Grillot de Givry, *Picture Museum*, 367). Guthkelch and Smith's essay, "Notes on Swift's Dark Authors," supplies more alchemical references for this passage from the *Tale*. They trace *via humida*, for instance, to Edward Kelly's 1676 work, "The Humid Path, or Discourse on the Vegetable Menstruum of Saturn" ("Dark Authors," *Tale*, 354–55).

Frederik N. Smith suggests that *Reincrudation* "may be an irreverent allusion to the Incarnation of Christ" (*Language and Reality*, 161). This seems to stretch Swift's satire unduly; a pun on *Incarnation* would be a criticism of alchemists'

religious errors, not a display of irreverence on Swift's part. Nevertheless, Smith's discussion and glossary of Swift's neologisms and odd usages are generally very helpful.
3. See, for example, Derrida, *Of Grammatology*, 27–44.
4. Swift uses this transparent trick in "The Account of the Court and Empire of Japan" (1728, but first printed in 1765); "Nena" is Queen Anne, "Regoge" is King George, and "Lelop-Aw" is Walpole.
5. Kristeva's paragrams are overtly political, antibourgeois saboteurs in a verbal class struggle (*Récherches*, 109–42). Swift's anagrams have an ideological role insofar as they represent liberal textocentric eruptions in a generally conservative textocentric program. It is not until the Irish political tracts, however, that Swift uses wordplay itself to challenge an existing political institution; otherwise, Swift's wordplay challenges ways of thinking and reading, including his own.
6. Bloom, *Kabbalah and Criticism*, 46.
7. See Starobinski, *Les mots sous les mots*, and Pierssens, *The Power of Babel*.
8. Swift, through parody, anticipates J. Hillis Miller's discussion of etymology: "The effect of etymological retracing is not to ground the word solidly but to render it unstable, equivocal, wavering, abysmal" ("Ariadne's Thread," 70).
9. The satire of "modern etymology" is explored by Kelly in "Swift's Satire Against Modern Etymologists," 21–36. Kelly also connects "A Discourse" with Sophocles' inventive and perhaps ironic etymologies recorded in Plato's *Cratylus*. Her argument that puns reinforce linguistic stability by recalling traditional linguistic expectations seems tenuous; in "A Discourse," Swift's puns not only satirize etymological methods but also expose the potential for dislocations and corruption inherent in all words.
10. Locke, *An Essay Concerning Human Understanding* 3.1.5.
11. Freud, *Jokes and Their Relation to the Unconscious*. Freud also points out that puns and jokes work through displacement (p. 151).
12. Psychoanalysis identifies the following triad: frustration, aggressivity, regression. Jacques Lacan locates frustration in discourse, in the necessary dispossession of being that is involved in having one's words received and reinterpreted by another. Resultant aggression is directed at the audience and, more deeply, at the alienated self; it takes the form of desire for death. Regression, then, actualizes in discourse a fantasy self that defends against the decomposition of ego structure (*Speech and Language in Psychoanalysis*, 10–14).
13. Arbuthnot et al., *Martinus Scriblerus*, 128.
14. Swift's more general aim to force readers into positions they will subsequently abandon is discussed in Sams, "Swift's Satire of the Second Person," 36–44.
15. See Barash, Introduction to Callois, *Man, Play, and Games*, vii-viii.
16. Callois, *Man, Play, and Games*, 23–24.
17. Robert C. Elliott ("Swift's Satire," 427) believes, however, that Swift stacks the satiric deck in order to put the author in a privileged position.

18. The seminal discussion appears in M. Quinlan, "Swift's Use of Literalization," 516–21.
19. Critical readings of the *Tale* tend to be of two types. Some, perhaps following Northrop Frye's definition of Menippean satire (Frye's nomination for the genre of the *Tale*) as an exuberant, encyclopaedic intellectual structure that causes "violent dislocations in the customary logic of narrative" (*Anatomy of Criticism*, 310), emphasize the chaotic nature of the text. See, for instance, Cary Nelson's characterization of the book as a pulsating mass of intestines with too many openings (*The Incarnate Word*, 105–25) or the mimetic thesis of John R. Clark in *Form and Frenzy*. Others valiantly try to reshape the *Tale* into some sort of symmetry. See Quintana, *Mind and Art*, 86–96; Paulson, *Theme and Structure*. Two compromises are C. J. Rawson's view that the *Tale*'s form is purposefully restless and disruptive (*Gulliver and the Gentle Reader*, 57), and Pat Rogers's idea that the book represents not formlessness but hypertrophic, useless form ("Form in *A Tale of a Tub*," 142–59).
20. Many readers believe instead that Pope and Swift use topsy-turvy inversions in the same manner. See, for example, Sutherland, *English Satire*, 59–64.
21. According to Gilbert Highet (*Anatomy of Satire*, 13–14), these are the main categories of satire, each one supposedly being distinct.
22. So do the reasons for his satire. There seem to be four basic motives for satire: personal revenge; punitive excoriation of vice and folly; remedial exposure of vice and folly; and aesthetic pleasure. Most satirists will admit freely to the second and third motives and will deny harboring the first or the fourth. Pope (and Dryden and Gay) appears to be deeply concerned with aesthetic excellence—not only the lack of it in other writers but also the exhibition of it in their own works. Although Swift was in no way a careless author, the first three motives seem to be more important to his satires than the last motive, particularly if he defined it as truth-clouding exhibitionism. He wished to disturb his readers more than he wished to impress them, and I suspect that he believed a too conscious artistry fed personal vanity to a dangerous degree.
23. This is the direction of Peter Steele's brief discussion of vertigo in his excellent chapter on games and Swift's writings (*Preacher and Jester*, 170–75).
24. For the standard discussion of Swift's health, see Wilson, "Swift's Deafness," 291–305.
25. More and Rabelais relied largely on Greek and Latin for their linguistic inventions, and Rabelais also exploited the cryptic punning potentials of his vernacular. Émile Pons suggests that More also used Persian ingredients in order to satisfy his intellectual fancy and to provide a broad and diverting linguistic spectacle for his readers ("Les Langues Imaginaires," 589–607). See also Seeber, "Ideal Languages," 586–97.
26. Such readerly expectations are one concern of Frank Kermode in *The Genesis of Secrecy*, 53.

27. Sturm, "Gulliver: The Benevolent Linguist," 46–48.
28. Kelling, "Some Significant Names," 776. Other interpretations have also been put forward. Roland Smith believes *Nardac* to be Gaelic for *nobleman* ("Swift's Little Language," 178–96), and Paul Odell Clark decodes the word into "*Mal-gat*, that is, *Ill (be)got*" (*Gulliver Dictionary*, 18).
29. Probyn, "Swift and the Human Predicament," 75.
30. Kelling, "Some Significant Names," 769. Marjorie W. Buckley ("Key to the Language of the Houyhnhnms," 272) suggests "who inhuman."
31. Clark, *Gulliver Dictionary*, 11, 20.
32. Kelling, "Some Significant Names," 764.
33. Steiner, *Language and Silence*, 50.
34. Lacan suggests that baby talk, the most extreme linguistic manifestation of regression, is based on absence of real, present contact (*Speech and Language in Psychoanalysis*, 14). Ernest Jones, identifying the exchange of linguo-palatals in pathological adult baby talk as an accurate representation of childhood speech, nevertheless suspects that these manifestations of regression are not actual but purposely simulated childlike behavior, often acted out to create linguistic barriers against adult communication ("Simulated Foolishness in Hysteria," 141–53).
35. Irvin Ehrenpreis ("Swift's 'Little Language,'" 80–88) analyzes the word-formative "rules" of Swiftian baby talk.
36. See Harold Williams's introduction to the *Journal to Stella* 1:lvi-lviii.
37. For instance, in *A Proposal for Correcting . . . the English Tongue*, Swift excoriates "that barbarous Custom of abbeviating Words . . . as to form such harsh unharmonious Sounds . . . They have joined the most obdurate Consonants, without one intervening Vowel, only to shorten a Syllable . . . most of the Books we see now-a-days, are full of those Manglings and Abbreviations" (*PW* 4:11).
38. Pons, "Du nouveau," 210–29.
39. This conclusion is based on my examination of the *Journal to Stella* manuscripts (British Museum Add. MSS 4804–6). Since abbreviations usually terminate a daily section, they function like signatures do in conventional letters, and signatures are normally written with a distinctiveness that sets them apart from the texts they close. The individual letters in Swift's abbreviations, however, are not appreciably larger than any other capital letter in the *Journal*.

The deletions are problematic. None seems to be written in ink perceptibly different from that used for the text of the *Journal* entries. Some strike-throughs are dark, thick, and heavy; these must have been meant to obliterate mistakes or (if added later) imprudent information. Most deletions, though, consist either of light linings-out or of looping overlays. Neither of these types leaves deeper impressions on the paper than do the penstrokes of the legible text, the original words can be read through them, and the loops often look tantalizingly like an enchained series of *l*'s and *e*'s. Another problem is that many intimate abbreviations are not lined out or disguised at all. I do not detect any systematic strike-through code, whether utilized during the writing or added during subsequent editing.

The apparent sameness of ink and pen pressure makes me think that Swift made most of the deletions as he was writing to Esther Johnson. Their transparency suggests that they may have been intended as guides for later editing, with the extra benefit of teasing the letters' recipient with a mock cancellation of declared affection. Their randomness indicates that any plans Swift may have had for future publication were at best hazy and, in fact, frequently forgotten.

40. The *Journal to Stella* shows most clearly the struggle between what Denis Donoghue (*Ferocious Alphabets*) has called "epireading" (searching for the speaking self: to recover meaning) and "graphireading" (analyzing the play of the written word: to discover meaning). Swift as author sets up this interpretive conflict by involving himself in dichotomies of "epiwriting" and "graphiwriting."
41. F. Smith, "Dramatic Elements," 332–52.
42. For example, H. Williams's introduction to the *Journal to Stella* 1:xxxvi–xxxviii; Quintana, *Mind and Art*, 26–28. For a brief review of theories about Swift's sexuality, see Quintana, *Two Augustans*, 90–95. James L. Clifford believes Swift's negation of sexuality to be part of a harsh, uncompromising idealism ("Gulliver's Fourth Voyage," 41).
43. See Ehrenpreis, *Swift* 2:66–73, 138, 657–61.
44. "[B]ut be assured that no one in the world has ever been more loved, honored, esteemed, and adored by your friend than you; if you understand everything sufficiently" (my translations).
45. These observations are based on my examinations of Swift's correspondence with Esther Vanhomrigh and others (British Museum Add. MSS 39839) as well as of the *Journal to Stella* manuscripts.
46. For Swift's early life, see Ehrenpreis, *Swift* 2:21–27. Also revelatory is the litany of woes Swift records in his autobiographical fragment (*PW* 5:192–93).
47. See Paulson, "Swift, Stella, and Permanence," 298–314.

CHAPTER 4

1. The general idea of having Martin undertake satirically educative travels was discussed among members of the club (see Arbuthnot et al., *Martinus Scriblerus*, 315–20). The actual planning and composition probably did not begin until the early 1720s; Swift's first specific reference to the *Travels* is in a letter to Charles Ford of 15 Apr. 1721 (*Corr.* 2:381).
2. Swift wanted fulsome praise. Marmaduke Cogwell reported that the inscription was to laud Swift "whom for his great zeal, unequalled abilities and distinguished munificence in asserting the rights, defending the liberties, and encouraging the manufactures of the kingdom, they justly esteemed the most eminent patriot and

greatest ornament of this his native city and country" (quoted in Ehrenpreis, *Swift* 3:651). For a full account of this event, see Ferguson, "Jonathan Swift, Freeman of Dublin," 405–9.
3. The social backgrounds of authorial disavowal are discussed in Davis, "A Social History of Fact and Fiction," 120–48. Davis links this practice to the wish to be considered part of the discourse of history or journalism rather than of fiction, and to the fuzzy boundaries between fiction and "news."
4. Murry, *Jonathan Swift*, 449.
5. And the traps continue to snap. Two recent articles conclude that *A Panegyric* was written not by Swift but by James Arbuckle (A. Williams, " 'A Vile Encomium,' " 178–99; Woolley, "Arbuckle's 'Panegyric,' " 191–209). If so, Swift, as well as subsequent readers, was caught by his own devices. The intricate mechanisms and surprising results of Swiftian anonymity are demonstrated just as well by Swift not having written the poem as by Swift having been the true author.
6. The seminal study is by William B. Ewald, *The Masks of Jonathan Swift*.
7. Benveniste, *Problems in General Linguistics*, 226.
8. Lacan, *Écrits*, 1–7.
9. Hartman, *Saving the Text*, 101, 125. Hartman extends his theory to include primal "scenes of nomination," personal annunciations that generate literature in a way similar to but more personal than Saussure's concept of the controlling name hidden in Latin poetry.
10. See notes on p. 87 of Arbuthnot et al., *Martinus Scriblerus*.
11. This is a reading first suggested by Jack Gilbert, "The Drapier's Initials," 217–18. See also Ehrenpreis, *Swift* 3:208.
12. Sheridan, *Life*, 472.
13. Rossi and Hone, *Swift, or the Egoist*, 311.
14. An excellent overview of this topos can be found in Abrams, *The Mirror and the Lamp*, 8–14, 30–35. Richard Rorty subjects the mirror analogy to extended questioning in his *Philosophy and the Mirror of Nature*; he asserts that Western philosophy is grounded on mistaken or at least misleading sublimation of the swerve of epistemology into metaphor.
15. Plato, *The Republic* 10.596.
16. Puttenham, *The Arte of English Poesie* [1589], 153–54; Dryden, *Essays of John Dryden*, 251–53. See also Locke's view of the mind of man as mirror in *An Essay Concerning Human Understanding*, 2.1.25. Milton's depiction of Eve's awakening into self-recognition by looking in a mirroring pond and learning that the reflection *indicates* selfhood but *is* neither self nor other accurately forecasts Lacan's analysis (*Paradise Lost*, 4:449–71).
17. In various private letters, Swift did refer to men as animals and, specifically, as Yahoos. But these comments are always qualified in some way, often by raillery or self-satire. The famous letter to Pope in which Swift asserts that he "hate[s] and detest[s] that animal called man" is softened not only by the possibility of loving

individuals but by the satiric close that tries to bully and bribe Pope into immediate acceptance of misanthropy (29 Sept. 1725, *Corr.* 3:103). The letter calling Stella and Bolingbroke's wife Yahoos is a railing reproach to Ford for having injudiciously talked about Swift's work-in-progress (19 Jan. 1723/24, *Corr.* 3:4). Swift's advice to Sheridan, "expect no more from man than such an animal is capable of, and you will every day find my description of Yahoos more resembling" (11 Sept. 1725, *Corr.* 3:94) comes from a letter consoling Sheridan for the loss of preferment and reminding him of the need for caution when dealing with men like the despised Sir Richard Tighe. Even in this letter, Swift emphasizes resemblance, not identity.

18. Braudy, "Penetration and Impenetrability," 181; Keener, *The Chain of Becoming*, 89–126.
19. In this sense, it participates in the satirist-satirized topos; see, for example, Elliott, *The Power of Satire*, 188–89.
20. Swift evidently performed similar categorical namings in real life. He bestowed mock-pastoral names upon female beggars in Dublin; the epithets were determined by their diseases and deformities (e.g., "Cancerina" and "Stumpa-Nympha"). See Ehrenpreis, *Swift* 3:812–13.
21. For the possible influence of travelers' accounts about great apes and primitive men, see Frantz, "Swift's Yahoos," 49–57; Montagu, "Tyson's *Orang-Outang*," 84–89; and the travel books owned by Swift as listed in H. Williams, *Dean Swift's Library*.
22. Hartman, *Saving the Text*, 126.
23. Ehrenpreis, *Swift* 1:68–70; see also 41–42.
24. Samuel Johnson states that Swift broadcast the "report" that he "was born in Leicester, the son of a clergyman, who was minister of a parish in Herefordshire." Johnson did not regret leaving the question of Swift's birthplace "in the obscurity in which he delighted to involve it"; he was obviously neither amused nor intrigued by the fact that Swift invented an English pedigree complete with a thoroughly respectable (and in the invention, apparently alive) father ("Life of Swift," 2).
25. Pilkington, *Memoirs*, 57–58.
26. Ehrenpreis, *Swift* 1:92, 142–49; Ehrenpreis emphasizes Swift's feelings of *mutual* benefit in the relationship. See also Murry, *Jonathan Swift*, 25–41. A. C. Elias, Jr. has designed his recent book (*Swift at Moor Park*) as a corrective to what he calls the "biographical clichés" (p. 128) about Swift as ultimately embittered hero-worshipper.
27. See, for example, Eagleton, *The Function of Criticism*.
28. For a discussion of this epitaph, see M. Johnson, "Greatest Epitaph in History," 814–27. The Latin epitaph reads: "Here lies the body of Jonathan Swift S.T.D., Dean of this Cathedral, where savage indignation can no longer tear his heart. Go, traveler, and imitate, if you can, one who struggled manfully for the vindication of liberty" (my translation).

29. This concept is explained by Hartman, *Beyond Formalism*, 311–36.
30. Said, *The World*, 66.
31. Pope, *The Dunciad Variorum* 2:129–31 (pp. 380–81).
32. Ibid., 1:18 (p. 351). Ehrenpreis (*Swift* 3:670–74) discusses Pope's influence on the Market Hill poems with a different emphasis.
33. Swift's mock-epic and mock-sublime practices are thoroughly and revealingly treated (often in contrast with those of Pope) by C. J. Rawson, "'I the Lofty Stile Decline,'" 79–115.
34. Weiskel, *The Romantic Sublime*, 43–44.
35. Carnochan, "The Consolations of Satire," 35–39.
36. Phyllis Greenacre (*Swift and Carroll*, 97) thinks that this defilement reeks of Oedipal crime; Swift had "killed" his father by his birth. She also detects a complicated father substitution: the temple is Sir William Temple, and Swift is somehow his son who committed suicide.
37. Samuel Johnson ("Life of Swift," 63) asks, "what depravity of intellect took delight in revolving ideas from which almost every other mind shrinks with disgust." William Makepeace Thackeray rants against Swift's filthy and obscene thoughts, words, and deeds ("Swift" [1853], 35–37). Aldous Huxley, misreading a word used in the eighteenth century to mean "inward seat of emotions," accused Swift of a "hatred of the bowels" (*Do What You Will*, 105). One of Greenacre's most ingenious theories is that Swift suffered from an anal fixation due to severe toilet training (*Swift and Carroll*, 94–95, 107; most psychoanalytic studies of Swift have grown from Sandor Ferenczi's "Gulliver Phantasies," 283–300). Norman O. Brown's influential work, "The Excremental Vision," appears in his *Life Against Death*, 179–201. C. J. Rawson discusses excremental squalor, particularly in relation to urban antipastoral, in "The Nightmares of Strephon," 57–99. Carole Fabricant outlines the unpleasant realities of Irish sanitary conditions in *Swift's Landscape*, 24–30; St. Patrick's stood (and stands) on very low ground and was subject to flooding of the polluted Liffey.
38. Greenacre, *Swift and Carroll*, 56.
39. Brown is surely right to point out the "damned-if-you-do, damned-if-you-don't" attitude of those who suspect that Swift's high standards of cleanliness mask a repressed love of filth (*Life Against Death*, 182–84).
40. Rifflet-Lemaire, *Jacques Lacan*, 219.
41. Swift's linguistic habits also resemble a child's subjectifying treatment of his own excrement. Lacan, for instance, describes how a child "registers as victories and defeats the heroic chronicle of the training of his sphincter, enjoying (jouissant) the imaginary sexualizations of his cloacal orifices, turning his excremental expulsions into aggressions, his retentions into seductions, and his movements of release into symbols" (*Écrits*, 53).
42. See Fineman, "The Structure of Allegorical Desire," 45.
43. See Derrida, *Disseminations*, 61–171. Swift touches on the same paradox in "Thoughts on Various Subjects" when he notes that Apollo (patron of poetry) was

"the God of Physick, and Sender of Diseases; Both were originally the same Trade, and still continue" (*PW* 4:247).

44. C. J. Jung (*Symbols of Transformation*, 190) explains this fantasy, not uncommon in male artists.
45. Arbuthnot et al., *Martinus Scriblerus*, 98.
46. See the discussion of this fear in Hartman, *The Fate of Reading*, 78–80.
47. The sexual rhythms of narrative are explored in Brooks, "Freud's Masterplot," 280–300. Brooks's attention to the way narrative beginnings can arouse intentions through invoking masturbation (p. 291) call to mind Gulliver's infamous Master Bates (since the word has a Latin cognate, the fact that the *Oxford English Dictionary* does not record its usage in English until after Swift's death may be inconsequential) and the "hasty conveyance by the post" jokes in *The Mechanical Operation of the Spirit*.
48. It may also have a fourth: Swift himself. Mist's *Weekly Journal* reports that on Swift's return to Dublin from England in 1726, the city's celebrations were so widespread "that there's scarce a street in town without a representation of him for a sign" (quoted in Ehrenpreis, *Swift* 3:496). If Swift had this demonstration in mind, it provides another case where his excremental allegory seeped onto his textual self.

CHAPTER 5

1. This satiric target is pointed out by Oliver W. Ferguson in *Jonathan Swift and Ireland*, 72–74.
2. See N. Frye's discussion of allegory in *Princeton Encyclopedia of Poetry and Poetics*, 12.
3. Quilligan, *The Language of Allegory*, 21–32.
4. See Derrida, *Of Grammatology*, 30–40.
5. Boethius, commenting on Aristotle, compared imposing meaning on words with impressing a ruler's face on a coin; money and words are not just objects but also exchange tokens which represent the value of another thing (*Commentarii in Librum Aristotelis*, 32–33). Sir William Temple compared deriving meaning from words to accepting money: "The best is to take words as they are most commonly spoken and meant, like coin as it most currently passes, without raising scruples upon the weight or the alloy, unless the cheat or the defect be gross and evident." He also compares poetic composition to mixing metal alloys for coins: "But the modern poets, to value this small coin [nonheroic poetic genres], and make it pass, though of so much a baser metal than the old, gave it a new mixture from two veins" (*Of Poetry* [1690], 17, 29). As Temple's secretary and literary executor, Swift was intimately acquainted with Temple's works.
6. For parallels between economic and linguistic systems, see Foucault, *The Order of Things*, 166–211.

7. Swift did not begin the written resistance to Wood's halfpence. In 1722, Archbishop King was writing letters against it, and soon afterwards James Maculla produced a vehemently worded pamphlet against the scheme. Swift entered the fray in February, 1724. See Ehrenpreis, *Swift* 3:189–207.
8. Ehrenpreis discusses reasons why the *History of England* is unfinished in "Swift's *History of England*," 177–85. Concerning this matter, Hayden White's analysis of the stages and modes of history writing may be helpful. Swift left his *History of England* at the "chronicle" stage, where events are simply "there" (and in Swift's project, "there" only in a previous chronicle text); he was unwilling or unable to make these events function in a plot, and therefore unable to give meaning to history via archetypal emplotment. The plot most congenial to Swift is obviously satire, which, according to White, views historical "hopes, possibilities, and truths Ironically, in the atmosphere generated by the apprehension of the ultimate inadequacy of consciousness to live in the world happily or comprehend it fully [and by] awareness of its own inadequacy as an image of reality" (*Metahistory*, 10). While prudential considerations were paramount, the inappropriateness of emplotting Queen Anne's reign in satiric shape may also explain why Swift never published *The Last Four Years*. History centered on Irish problems, however, was ripe for satiric treatment.
9. Lentricchia, *Criticism and Social Change*, 118. For conceptions of history as fiction, see Mink, "The Autonomy of Historical Understanding," 160–92.
10. Barthes, *Critical Essays*, 152. Barthes's systematic study of fashion writing appears in *Système de la mode*.
11. Barthes, *Système de la mode*, 265–67.
12. The effect of this layering is similar to what Samuel R. Levin describes as "coupling," the way in which the position of one syntagmatic unit to parallel another structurally establishes equivalence between the two (*Linguistic Structures in Poetry*, 30–41). Swift, however, counteracts mechanical equivalence by increasing the interpenetration of his discourses until they tumble together into the same chapter (section 11, for instance, concerns both Jack's devotional acts and a digression upon ears).
13. For example, the Tale-writer states: "[A]s I have often told the Reader, [the Will] consisted wholly in certain plain, easy Directions about the management and wearing of their Coats" (*Tale* 11.190). Dryden explains that "the Scriptures ... Are uncorrupt, sufficient, clear, intire, / In all things which our needful Faith require ... It speaks it Self," even though he acknowledges that human transmission has sometimes obscured the biblical message (*Religio Laici*, 112–13.297–300, 368).
14. See De Man, "The Rhetoric of Temporality," 173–209, cf. 190.
15. See J. A. Levine, "The Design of *A Tale of a Tub*," 198–227. G. Douglas Atkins, who believes the *Tale* centers on reading and interpretation, finds that while the text overtly insists on the writer's authority and the dangers when readers usurp that authority, its figurative language—in particular, the horseriding imagery—

shows that the author needs the reader in order to move along "the journey that is writing" (*Reading Deconstruction*, 105–117 [quoted passage on p. 114]). I would shift emphasis somewhat; Swift's divestitures in the *Tale* seem to indicate that readers are necessary for the text's journey into time, after it has left parental authorial custody.

16. Barthes, *Critical Essays*, 48–49.
17. See Wiemann, *Structure and Society in Literary History*, 195.
18. The self-interest of the prefaces was also economic; *On Poetry: A Rapsody* charges that they were "meerly writ at first for filling / To raise the Volume's Price, a Shilling" (*SPW*: 576.253–54).
19. I am thinking of investment in tradition in the sense that T. S. Eliot explains it in "Tradition and the Individual Talent" (pp. 525–29); "the great labour" that involves consciousness "not only of the pastness of the past, but of its presence" and that entails both being judged by the standards of the past and taking responsibility for altering the received tradition. My concept of struggling against the tradition, particularly as it is cast in terms of fathers and sons, is based on Bloom, *Anxiety of Influence*.
20. Biblical homily and Christian moralizations used dress to delineate vices and interest in clothing in general to indicate pride (e.g., "And somme putten hem to pride, apparailed hem þerafter / In contenaunce of cloþynge comen d[is]gised," William Langland, *Piers Plowman*: 228.23–24). The Gospel basis for the false pride/false garments analogy seems to be 1 Cor. 4, which reminds men that our bodies go naked back to God.

   For Shakespeare, see *Love's Labours Lost* 5.2.407–14 (Berowne's abandonment of "Taffeta phrases" for "russet yeas and honest kersey noes"). For Jonson, see *Timber*, 562–649 (e.g., wit is "good dressing," p. 573; well-joined words are "the skinne, and coat" of style, p. 626). For Butler, see *Hudibras*, 149–68 (e.g., Sir Hudibras's "*Babylonish* dialect" of "parti-colour'd dress," 1.1.93–95, p. 151). For Locke, see *An Essay Concerning Human Understanding* 3.9.23 (on the will of God being clothed in words). For Gay, see *The Guardian* #149, p. 461 ("There is another kind of Occasional Dress in Use among the Ladies, I mean the Riding Habit, which some have not injudiciously styled the Hermaphroditical, by Reason of its Masculine and Feminine Composition; but I shall rather chuse to call it the Pindaric . . . as it is a Mixture of the Sublimity of the Epic with the easie Softness of the Ode").
21. Hartman, *Beyond Formalism*, 337–38; see Aristotle, *Poetics* 16.
22. S. Johnson, "Life of Swift," 51.
23. Aristotle, *Poetics* 10, 11, 16.
24. Aristotle, *Rhetoric* 3.2; 3.10.
25. See Black, "Metaphor," 284–85.
26. Barthes, *Critical Essays*, 45.
27. This act, designed "for the better securing the Dependency of . . . Ireland," gave

additional force to the Woolen Act of 1699 that provided England with a monopoly in Irish raw wool. See Ferguson, *Jonathan Swift and Ireland*, 7–11, 45–46.
28. For example, Swift praises Esther Johnson's spare wardrobe ("On the Death of Mrs. Johnson [Stella]," *PW* 5:232–33) and suggests that the new wife of his friend John Rochfort dress modestly and inexpensively (*A Letter to a Young Lady, PW* 9:87–91).
29. Seventeenth- and eighteenth-century illustrated political tracts often highlighted physical abuse as a means of political suppression. An anti-Irish-Catholic pamphlet of 1647, for instance, depicts the atrocities suffered by Protestants during the Confederation of Kilkenny rebellion. One engraving has this caption: "Arthur Robinsons daughter 14 yeares old the Rebbels bound her armes a broad, deflowered her one after another, tell they spoyled her then pulled the haire from her head and cut out her tongue that she might not tell of their Cruelty but she declared it by writing." The tongue cutting is the subject of the picture; it is reproduced in John Ranelagh, *Ireland*, 103.
30. Here I am using the word *rape* to imply a violent act motivated by aggression and hostility, not necessarily by sexual lust. See Brownmiller, *Against Our Will*, 11–15.
31. Booth, "Metaphor as Rhetoric," 60–61.
32. Swift's ambivalence toward Pallas is questioned by the author of *A Defense of English Commodities*, a humorless response to the *Proposal for the Universal Use*. After expounding that "[b]y Arachne, according to the best Mythologists, is meant the Devil; and by Pallas, the Deity," the anonymous author continues: "But on which side does our wise Projector declare himself; for Pallas or Arachne?" (*PW* 9:273).
33. Pope, *An Essay on Criticism*, 153, line 297.
34. For example, see Greene, "On Swift's 'Scatological' Poems," 672–89.
35. Laura Brown suggests that Pope uses the language of "commodity fetishism" in Belinda's toilet scene to show how mercantile expansion "dresses nature to advantage" and "makes concrete the metaphor for the operations of 'True Wit' in the *Essay on Criticism*" (*Alexander Pope*, 9). According to this argument, Belinda possesses a sort of true beauty and artistry that reflects an underlying imperialist ideology to which Pope subscribes. Swift's anti-Belindas neither ratify nor criticize such an ideology. Their clothes and makeup are not described in terms of luxurious foreign trade; instead we see frowzy petticoats and homemade dogskin nightgloves (e.g., *The Lady's Dressing Room, SPW* 477.29–32, 48). The commodities most prized by Swift's nymphs are the products of their own body, the most sordid kind of domestic manufacture. Politico-economic criticism in these scatological poems, therefore, may be ironically directed at the idealism of Swift's own schemes, such as the *Proposal for the Universal Use*. However, if Brown is correct in assuming that Pope's catalogue technique, by jamming bibles and billet-doux indiscriminately in phonetically attractive lines, reveals the "moral irresponsibility" of material acquisition (pp. 10–12), then Swift's listing rhetoric reveals harsh

moral responsibility. All items are of the same unsavory order and the lines are made phonetically unattractive through plosives and end-stopped consonants (e.g., "Sweat, Dandruff, Powder, Lead, and Hair," *The Lady's Dressing Room*, *SPW* 477.24).
36. Ehrenpreis, *Swift* 3:103–7.
37. S. Johnson, "Life of Swift," 51, n. 3; quoted from Wharton.
38. This image places Wood in an iconographic tradition of displaying money-hungry people in coin-bedecked livery. For example, *The Castle of Perseverance* (272.700–745) describes the investiture of Mankind into the feoff of World as the donning of garments made of coins.
39. Pope, *Peri Bathous*, 18, 33–38.
40. Swift's method is the opposite of Marx's view of how characters appear in history: "Hegel remarks somewhere that all facts and personages of great importance occur, as it were, twice. He forgot to add, the first time as tragedy, the second as farce" (*The Eighteenth Brumaire*, 103). Marx's statement implies that the transformation of tragedy to farce is predicated upon increased wisdom; a populace or audience cognizant of its own collective power can demystify a threatening figure. Swift's progression from farce to tragedy seems to be predicated upon continual foolishness of the populace, their refusal or inability to learn from history and act in their own best interests. Swift's angry reaction to the Irish people's failure to follow his *Proposal for the Universal Use* is evidence of this conviction.
41. Making Gaelic speakers learn, write, and talk in English was one method by which England tried to control and in effect colonize Ireland. See K. Quinlan, "Their Language, So Familiar and So Foreign," 116. It is difficult to measure Swift's awareness of this type of linguistic colonialism. In the *Humble Address* and elsewhere he implies that Gaelic is an impediment to Ireland's national goals, yet his own use of Irish dialect and occasionally of Gaelic (e.g., "The Description of an Irish-Feast," *SPW*, 195–97; "A Pastoral Dialogue," *SPW*, 393–95; "The Grand Question debated," *SPW*, 396–401) suggests a growing consciousness of indigenous Irish culture and language, although most of his "Irishisms" serve comic purposes. My guess is that he viewed replacing Gaelic with standard English as a prerequisite for Irish equality, not as a capitulation to colonialist domination.
42. Swift repeats this wording in his sermon "Doing Good," delivered against Wood and the halfpence. After stating that Wood's project is "an open attempt . . . to make a great kingdom one large poor-house . . . to make the country a desart for wild beasts and robbers, to destroy. . . the very tillage of the ground," Swift asserts that he must "cry out" and "warn" his flock so all can stand together for the common good (*PW* 9:235–36).
43. Thomas Hobbes, *Leviathan* 2.29.
44. This conservative, land-based value system grounds Swift's complaints to Pope about setting up monied interests in opposition to landed ones (10 Jan. 1721, *Corr.* 2:372–73); it also explains the plutocratic bias of the King of Brobdingnag's

response to Gulliver's political projects (*GT* 2.7.135–36) and of the Drapier's closing paean to farmers (*PW* 10:141).
45. See Ferguson, *Jonathan Swift and Ireland*, 119–28.
46. Gramsci, *Prison Notebooks*, 5–14.
47. Burke, *Attitudes Toward History*, 328.
48. Foucault, *Language, Counter-Memory, Practice*, 154.
49. Some critics believe that the hidden agendum for all of the *Drapier's Letters* is to shake off all forms of Irish dependency. See, for example, Downie, *Jonathan Swift: Political Writer*, 231–47.
50. Louise K. Barnett (*Swift's Poetic Worlds*, 120–21) assigns this poem to a group she calls Swift's "verbal universe," works that remain in the world of language and do not lead back to the social world that has occasioned them.
51. Examinations of how Swift shapes the Letters into a contest between Wood and the Drapier, into one between Ireland and England, and into one between concealing and revealing the Drapier persona, can be found in Ehrenpreis, *Swift* 3:241–43, 290–94.
52. The poems' narrative voices are relentless and self-reflexive story tellers. For example, one narrator comments, "I told you one Tale, I will tell you another" (*A Serious Poem Upon William Wood*, *SPW* 272.70); another begins with a Virgilian litotes, "I Sing not of the *Draper's* Praise, nor yet of *William Wood*" (*An Excellent New Song*," *SPW* 275.1); another imitates a Horatian Ode, drawing attention to his resuscitation of the governing metaphor ("Horace, Book I, Ode XIV," *SPW* 282.5–8); another refers to the "*Grecian* Tale" upon which he constructs his conceit ("On Wood the Iron-monger," *SPW* 285.1). These maneuvers resemble the assertion in the first *Drapier's Letter*, that the writer is going to tell the reader "the plain Story of the Fact" (*PW* 10:4), and the promise at the end of the sixth letter, that language cannot be prohibited from telling the truth because it is impossible to destroy all past, present, and potential texts. Even rustling reeds will serve to carry the word (*PW* 10:115), as they served Midas's barber when common verbal recourse was interdicted, and as they served Pan, transvesting (in the legend of Syrinx) transient physical desire into enduring artistic instrument.
53. J. A. Downie notes that whereas Wood is depicted as tiny, Walpole is depicted as gigantic, perhaps to imply that Walpole is the prime mover behind Wood's project (*Jonathan Swift: Political Writer*, 251). William Empson has remarked that size shifts give Swift "a sort of scientific authority" for his judgments, small men being seen as "spiritually petty" and large men as "physically loathsome" (*Some Versions of Pastoral*, 267).
54. The Drapier also defines himself by his work, but the letters' treatment of the transvested textiles indicates that his proper work is writing. Furthermore, the Drapier's frequent apologies for his pamphleteering keep the persona ensconced in an appropriate perception of his place in society; his metaphorical use of his trade and the hints about his true identity (sufficient to convince most Dubliners

that the Drapier was Swift) suggest that his real position in the social hierarchy provides sufficient authorization for his writing project.
55. Here Swift seems to anticipate Georg Lukács's criticism of "reification," seeing all relations between people and between human institutions as commodity exchanges (*History and Class Consciousness*, 83–110).
56. Addison, *The Spectator* #61, 1:259–63.
57. An interesting short discussion of this relationship can be found in Nokes, "'Hack at Tom Poley's,'" 42–48.
58. The care with which Swift provided for the hospital, and the fate of these provisions and of the asylum, are examined in Moore, "Swift's Philanthropy," 137–56. Moore maintains that Swift "did not merely collect money, he planned in detail the constitution of the hospital, he took care who should govern it, where it should be situated and how it should be run" (p. 156).
59. Yeats, *Explorations*, 348.

CHAPTER 6

1. See Jauss, "Literary History," 10–16. Swift's views about reception are stated in a letter to the Abbé des Fontaines, the French translator of *Gulliver's Travels*: "l'auteur qui n'ecrit que pour une ville, une province, un Royaume, ou meme un siecle, merite si peu d'etre traduit qu'il ne merite pas d'etre lu" (the author who writes only for a city, a province, a kingdom, or even an era, has so little merit to be translated that he does not even merit to be read) (my translation), July 1727, *Corr.* 3:217.
2. For instance, soon before Esther Johnson's death, while he himself was feeling ill, Swift wrote to Sheridan: "The last act of life is always a tragedy at best" (2 Sept. 1727, *Corr.* 3:236). Irvin Ehrenpreis explores the deaths of Esther Johnson and Archbishop King, as well as Swift's declining health and advancing age, as causes of his unhappiness in the late 1720s (*Swift* 3:550–52, 620). Ehrenpreis also emphasizes that Swift spent his last years among friends, pursuing the entertainments he enjoyed. My comments about Swift's sense of tragedy are directed at the textual identities he creates more than at the biographical person.
3. These statements mirror Swift's early farewell to the writing of "serious" poetry ("Occasioned by Sir William Temple's Late Recovery and Illness," *SPW* 42.151–54) and Gulliver's cranky statement to Sympson, first published in the 1735 Dublin edition of the *Travels*: "I should never have attempted so absurd a Project as that of reforming the *Yahoo* . . . I have now done with all such visionary Schemes for ever" ("Letter to Sympson," *GT*, 8).
4. Other poems of the 1730s use the same topos and the same cursing rhetoric but direct them at other groups, e.g., at the clergy in "On the Irish Bishops" (1732), *SPW*, 532–34; at lawyers in *Helter Skelter* (1731), *SPW*, 513–14; at everybody in *The Place of the Damn'd* (1731), *SPW*, 515.

5. See Elliott, *The Power of Satire*, 18–48; Rawson, "'I the Lofty Style Decline,'" 105–8.
6. Steiner, *The Death of Tragedy*, 3–10.
7. For a reading of *A Modest Proposal* as anti-Irish as well as anti-English, see Ferguson, *Jonathan Swift and Ireland*, 170–76. Most subsequent commentators have agreed with Ferguson. An event in early 1985 reconfirmed the work's ability to outrage even a sophisticated audience that reveres Swift as a voice of Irish patriotism. Peter O'Toole was booed off the stage when he tried to read *A Modest Proposal* as part of the reopening ceremonies for Dublin's Abbey Theatre.
8. See Schakel, "Virgil and the Dean," 427–38.
9. Later gospels correct this unhappy ending by making the possessed man go to Jesus's ship of exile, where Jesus charges him with returning home to bear witness to God's power (Mark 5:18–20; Luke 8:37–40).
10. This is part of Carlyle's reading of Swift's vestmental metaphor; Teufelsdrockh explains, for instance, that "Society is founded upon Cloth." Carlyle is less concerned than Swift is with the writing-as-weaving basis of the trope, and instead extends its cultural and symbolic aspects. As Teufelsdrockh states, "Clothes, as despicable as we think them, are so unspeakably significant. Clothes, from the King's mantle downwards are Emblematic ... On the other hand, all Emblematic things are properly Clothes, thought-woven or hand-woven; must not the Imagination weave Garments, visible Bodies, wherein the else invisible creations and inspirations of our Reason are, like Spirits, revealed?" (*Sartor Resartus*, 159, 174). Everett Zimmerman (*Swift's Narrative Satires*, 132–34) also discusses the social implications of Gulliver's clothes; he emphasizes Gulliver's failure to recognize clothings' religious and judicial significance.
11. Their neglect extends to food and shelter. Gulliver bakes his own bread, and he catches his own meat in springes he makes from Yahoo hair. The Houyhnhnm master did order a "Place for [him] to lodge in ... six Yards from the House" (*GT* 4.2.233); this rude abode, however, was plastered, floored, and furnished by Gulliver himself. The somewhat helpless nonchalance of the Houyhnhnms vis-à-vis Gulliver's necessities of life constrasts sharply with the busy enterprise of Lilliput, the careful contrivances of Brobdingnag, and even the uncomplaining "tourguide-ism" of the peoples in book 3.
12. See Dennis, *Jonathan Swift*, 122–33.
13. Hearing the serpent speak, Eve asks the creature:

> What may this mean? Language of man, pronounced
> By tongue of brute, and human sense expressed?
> The first at least of these I thought denied
> To beasts, when God on their creation-day,
> Created mute to all articulate sound.
> [Milton, *Paradise Lost* 9.553–57]

14. This pride is, after all, quite understandable, since by the end of the book Gulliver

can converse in Lilliputian, Brobdingnagian, Laputian (sometimes called Balnibarbian), Luggnaggian (one supposes, since he dispensed with the services of his interpreter during his stay), and the Houyhnhnm language—as well as in English, Dutch, German, French, Italian, Portuguese, and various East and West Indian languages.

15. See Hernadi, *Beyond Genre*, 152–56. A polycentric genre differs from, for instance, Northrop Frye's category of Menippean Satire, or anatomy, (*Anatomy of Criticism*, 309–12) because it suggests the copresence of a multiplicity of genres, not a specified subtype of one genre. For a discussion of genre as an exploratory tool, see Jameson, "Magical Narratives," 150–60; for a view of how the insistence upon literal truth subverts fictional genres, see Seidel, *Satiric Inheritance*, 61.

16. Many readers perceive a substantial difference in book 4, usually in relation to a darkening of theme. Edward W. Rosenheim, Jr. (*Swift and the Satirist's Art*, 159–67), discusses the shift in terms of contending narrative structures (the single complex experience in Houyhnhnmland versus the episodic patterns of the earlier travels). Not many readers, however, consider book 4 in terms of tragedy. Richard J. Dircks suggests this approach ("Gulliver's Tragic Rationalism," 134–49) but concentrates on the context of irony that determines Gulliver's "tragic misanthropy."

17. Four years after the publication of *Gulliver's Travels*, Fielding wrote *The Life of Tom Thumb the Great, a Tragedy* (later retitled *The Tragedy of Tragedies*). This burlesque draws mocking attention to the tragic potentialities inherent in Swift's work, particularly in books 1 and 2. Fielding, for instance, replaces Gulliver's redemptive eagle with a voracious cow that eats Tom Thumb, a tragic death that drives all other characters into an insane frenzy of murderous grief, whereupon they all kill each other. The spirit of Fielding's "commentary" upon *Gulliver's Travels* has been preserved in the twentieth century by André Breton (*Anthologie de l'humeur noir*, 17, 25) and C. J. Rawson (*Gulliver and the Gentle Reader*, 34–35), who place Swift in the pattern of black humor in the drama of the absurd.

18. For the standard attributes of a tragic hero and the necessity of high aspiration, see N. Frye, *Anatomy of Criticism*, 206–18. Frye's description of the "pathetic" hero of low-mimetic tragedy, an obsessed individual on our own level excluded from a social group he is trying to join (pp. 38–41), also applies to Gulliver.

19. Odysseus as archetypal comic hero is treated by Robert M. Torrance in *The Comic Hero*, 12–36. Torrance, who emphasizes a comic hero's desire to return to the unheroic world of everyday reality, points out that a comic hero is no less heroic than a tragic hero; the former's heroism is manifested in a choice of life, often at great costs, rather than in the latter's choice of noble death. For an overview of Gulliver as comic hero, with comparisons to Odysseus and to Robinson Crusoe, see Mezciems, "Gulliver and Other Heroes," 189–208.

20. Girard, *Deceit, Desire, and the Novel*, 2–12.

21. For exportation as a device for making heroes in an unheroic age (à la Robinson Crusoe), see Hunter, "Fielding and the Disappearance of Heroes," 131.

22. Piaget, *Genetic Epistemology*, 16–17.
23. Robert M. Philmus ("Swift, Gulliver," 62–79) examines the confusions of fact, truth, and fiction in the linguistic domain of Houyhnhnmland.
24. For the patterns of language acquisition used throughout the *Travels*, see Kelly, "After Eden," 33–54.
25. Terry Castle makes this point in a Derridean discussion of Swift's stance toward the text ("Why the Houyhnhnms Don't Write," 31–44). Castle believes that the Houyhnhnms's lack of writing indicates their proximity to a sort of platonically ideal discourse, unmediated by the corruption that is writing, and that Swift is haunted by an anxious grammaphobia, a fear of the text, textuality, and textual indeterminacy.
26. That Swift was using Gulliver as a horse-stalking stalking horse is implied by Gulliver's blithe citation of Sinon's protestations of existential misery and verbal honesty (*GT* 4.12.292), as it was Sinon who induced the Trojans to accept the wooden horse.
27. Heidegger, *On the Way to Language*, 112.
28. Quoted in Heidegger, *On the Way to Language*, 136.

POSTSCRIPT

1. As my references and bibliography illustrate, deconstruction has appeared in Swift studies (see works by Atkins, Castle, and Rawson, among others); even so, such efforts are the exception rather than the rule. Other major figures of the period have received even less poststructuralist attention than has Swift.
2. For an excellent discussion that includes a thoughtful critique of the theory under investigation, see Howard, "The New Historicism in Renaissance Studies," 13–43.
3. Texts referred to are: McKeon, *Politics and Poetry in Restoration England*; Eagleton, *The Function of Criticism*, 9–43; Fabricant, *Swift's Landscape*; L. Brown, *Alexander Pope*; Kernan, *Printing Technology, Letters, and Samuel Johnson*. There have also been rewarding studies by new-historically inclined feminists, such as Felicity Nussbaum's *The Brink of All We Hate* and Ellen Pollak's *The Poetics of Sexual Myth*. In addition, new historicism is evident in recent studies of the eighteenth-century English novel, particularly those that deal with novels by women.
4. See Claus Uhlig's concept of textual stratification, discussed in "Literature as Textual Palingenesis."
5. Herbert Lindenberger ("New History," 16–23) uses these grounds to distinguish between old and new historicism.
6. M. Butler, "Against Tradition," 44.
7. McGann, "Some Forms of Critical Discourse," 399–417 (quoted material on p. 406).

SELECT BIBLIOGRAPHY

WORKS BY JONATHAN SWIFT

The Correspondence of Jonathan Swift. Edited by Harold Williams. 5 vols. Oxford: Clarendon, 1963–65.
Jonathan Swift Correspondence. British Museum Add. MSS 39839.
Journal to Stella. Edited by Harold Williams. 2 vols. Oxford: Clarendon, 1948.
Journal to Stella Manuscripts. British Museum Add. MSS 4804–6.
The Prose Works of Jonathan Swift. Edited by Herbert Davis. 14 vols. Oxford: Clarendon, 1937–68.
Swift's Poetical Works. Edited by Herbert Davis. London: Oxford University Press, 1967.
A Tale of a Tub. Edited by A. C. Guthkelch and D. Nichol Smith. 2d ed. Oxford: Clarendon, 1958.

OTHER WORKS

Aarsleff, Hans. *From Locke to Saussure: Essays on the Study of Language and Intellectual History.* Minneapolis: University of Minnesota Press, 1982.
Abrams, M. H. *The Mirror and the Lamp: Romantic Theory and the Critical Tradition.* London: Oxford University Press, 1953.
Adams, Joseph Quincy, ed. *The Castle of Perseverance.* In *Chief Pre-Shakespearean Dramas,* 265–87. Cambridge, Mass.: Houghton Mifflin/Riverside, 1924.
Addison, Joseph, and Richard Steele. *The Spectator.* Edited by Donald F. Bond. 5 vols. Oxford: Clarendon, 1965.
Alston, William P. *Philosophy of Language.* Englewood Cliffs, N.J.: Prentice-Hall, 1964.
Andreasen, N. J. C. "Swift's Satire on the Occult in *A Tale of a Tub.*" *Texas Studies in Literature and Language* 5 (1963): 410–21.
Aquinas, Thomas. *Summa Theologica.* Chicago: Encyclopedia Britannica, 1952.
Arbuthnot, John, Alexander Pope, Jonathan Swift, John Gay, Thomas Parnell, and Robert Harley. *Memoirs of the Extraordinary Life, Works, and Discoveries of Martinus*

Scriblerus. Edited by Charles Kerby-Miller. New Haven: Yale University Press, 1950.
Aristotle. *Poetics*. Chicago: Encyclopedia Britannica, 1952.
———. *Rhetoric*. Chicago: Encyclopedia Britannica, 1952.
Arnheim, Rudolf. *Entropy and Art: An Essay on Disorder and Order*. Berkeley: University of California Press, 1971.
Atkins, G. Douglas. *Reading Deconstruction/Deconstructive Reading*. Lexington, Ky.: University Press of Kentucky, 1983.
Bachelard, Gaston. *The Poetics of Space*. Translated by Maria Jolas. Boston: Beacon Press, 1970.
Bacon, Francis. *Advancement of Learning*. Edited by William Wright. Oxford: Oxford University Press, 1920.
Bakhtin, Mikhail. *Rabelais and His World*. Translated by Helene Iswolsky. Cambridge, Mass.: MIT Press, 1965.
Barnett, Louise K. *Swift's Poetic Worlds*. Newark, Del.: University of Delaware Press, 1981.
Barthes, Roland. *Critical Essays*. Translated by Richard Howard. Evanston, Ill.: Northwestern University Press, 1972.
———. *On Racine*. Translated by Richard Howard. New York: Hill & Wang, 1964.
———. *Système de la mode*. Paris: Seuil, 1967.
———. *S/Z: An Essay*. Translated by Richard Miller. New York: Hill & Wang, 1974.
Beaumont, Charles Allen. *Swift's Classical Rhetoric*. Athens, Ga.: University of Georgia Press, 1961.
Benstock, Shari. "At the Margin of Discourse: Footnotes in the Fictional Text." *PMLA* 98 (1983): 204–25.
Benveniste, Émile. *Problems in General Linguistics*. Translated by Mary E. Meek. Miami Linguistics Series, no. 8. Coral Gables, Fla.: University of Miami Press, 1971.
Black, Max. "Metaphor." *Proceedings of the Aristotelian Society* n.s. 55 (1955): 273–94.
Bloom, Harold. *The Anxiety of Influence: A Theory of Poetry*. New York: Oxford University Press, 1975.
———. *Kabbalah and Criticism*. New York: Continuum/Seabury, 1975.
———. *A Map of Misreading*. New York: Oxford University Press, 1975.
Bloomfield, Leonard. *Language*. London: George Allen & Unwin, 1935.
Boethius. *Commentarii in Librum Aristotelis Periermeneias*. Edited by Carolus Meiser. Vol. 1. Leipzig, 1887.
Booth, Wayne. "Metaphor as Rhetoric: The Problem of Evaluation." In *On Metaphor*, edited by Sheldon Sachs, 47–70. Chicago: University of Chicago Press, 1981.
Braudy, Leo. "Penetration and Impenetrability in *Clarissa*." In *New Approaches to*

Eighteenth-Century Literature: Selected Papers from the English Institute, edited by Philip Harth, 176–206. New York: Columbia University Press, 1974.
Breton, André. *Anthologie de l'humeur noir*. Paris: Pauvert, 1972.
Brooks, Peter. "Freud's Masterplot." In *Literature and Psychoanalysis/ The Question of Reading: Otherwise*, edited by Shoshana Felman, 280–300. Baltimore: Johns Hopkins University Press, 1982.
Brown, Laura. *Alexander Pope*. Oxford: Basil Blackwell, 1985.
Brown, Norman O. "The Excremental Vision." In *Life Against Death: The Psychoanalytical Meaning of History*, 179–201. London: Routledge & Kegan Paul, 1959.
Brownmiller, Susan. *Against Our Will: Men, Women, and Rape*. New York: Simon & Schuster, 1975.
Buckley, Marjorie W. "Key to the Language of the Houyhnhnms in *Gulliver's Travels*." In *Fair Liberty Was All His Cry*, edited by A. Norman Jeffares, pp. 270–78. London: Macmillan, 1967.
Burke, Kenneth. *Attitudes Toward History*. Boston: Beacon Press, 1961.
Butler, Marilyn. "Against Tradition: The Case for a Particularized Historical Method." In *Historical Studies and Literary Criticism*, edited by Jerome J. McGann, 25–47. Madison: University of Wisconsin Press, 1985.
Butler, Samuel. *Hudibras*. In *A Collection of English Poems 1660–1800*, edited by Ronald S. Crane, 149–68. New York: Harper & Row, 1932.
Callois, Roger. *Man, Play, and Games*. Edited by Meyer Barash. London: Dent, 1962.
Carlyle, Thomas. *Sartor Resartus*. In *A Carlyle Reader*, edited by G. B. Tennyson, 124–337. New York: Modern Library, 1969.
Carnochan, W. B. "The Consolations of Satire." In *The Art of Jonathan Swift*, edited by Clive T. Probyn, 19–42. New York: Barnes & Noble, 1978.
_____. *Lemuel Gulliver's Mirror for Man*. Berkeley: University of California Press, 1961.
Castle, Terry. "Why the Houyhnhnms Don't Write: Swift, Satire, and the Fear of the Text." *Essays in Literature*/Macomb 7 (1979): 31–44.
Clark, John R. *Form and Frenzy in Swift's "Tale of a Tub."* Ithaca, N.Y.: Cornell University Press, 1970.
Clark, Paul Odell. *A Gulliver Dictionary*. New York: Haskell House, 1972.
Clifford, James L. "Gulliver's Fourth Voyage: 'Hard' and 'Soft' Schools of Interpretation." In *Quick Springs of Sense: Studies in the Eighteenth Century*, edited by Larry S. Champion, 33–49. Athens, Ga.: University of Georgia Press, 1974.
Cohen, Murray. *Sensible Words: Linguistic Practice in England 1640–1785*. Baltimore: Johns Hopkins University Press, 1977.
Colie, Rosalie L. "Gulliver, the Locke-Stillingfleet Controversy, and the Nature of Man." *History of Ideas Newsletter* 2 (1956): 58–62.
Davies, Hugh Sykes. "Irony and the English Tongue." In *The World of Jonathan*

Swift, edited by Brian Vickers, 129–38. Cambridge, Mass.: Harvard University Press, 1968.

Davis, Lennard J. "A Social History of Fact and Fiction: Authorial Disavowal in the Early English Novel." In *Literature and Society: Selected Papers from the English Institute, 1978*, edited by Edward W. Said, 120–48. Baltimore: Johns Hopkins University Press, 1980.

De Man, Paul. *Allegories of Reading: Figural Language in Rousseau, Nietzsche, Rilke, and Proust*. New Haven: Yale University Press, 1979.

———. "Literature and Language: A Commentary." *New Literary History* 4 (1972): 181–92.

———. "The Rhetoric of Temporality." In *Interpretation: Theory and Practice*, edited by Charles S. Singleton, 173–209. Baltimore: Johns Hopkins University Press, 1969.

Dennis, Nigel. *Jonathan Swift: A Short Character*. New York: Macmillan, 1964.

Derrida, Jacques. *Disseminations*. Translated by Barbara Johnson. Chicago: University of Chicago Press, 1981.

———. "Fors." *Georgia Review* 31 (1977): 64–116.

———. "Living On: *Border Lines*." In *Deconstruction and Criticism*, edited by Harold Bloom and Geoffrey Hartman, 117–56. New York: Seabury, 1979.

———. *Of Grammatology*. Translated by Gayatri Chakravorty Spivak. Baltimore: Johns Hopkins University Press, 1982.

Dircks, Richard J. "Gulliver's Tragic Rationalism." *Criticism* 2 (1960): 134–49.

Donoghue, Denis. *Ferocious Alphabets*. Boston: Little, Brown, 1981.

———. *Jonathan Swift: A Critical Introduction*. Cambridge: Cambridge University Press, 1969.

Downie, J. A. *Jonathan Swift: Political Writer*. London: Routledge & Kegan Paul, 1984.

Dryden, John. *Essays of John Dryden*. Edited by W. P. Ker. Vol. 2. New York: Russell & Russell, 1961.

———. *Religio Laici*. In *A Collection of English Poems 1660–1800*, edited by Ronald S. Crane, 106–15. New York: Harper & Row, 1932.

Dyson, A. E. "Swift: The Metamorphosis of Irony." *Essays and Studies* 11 (1959): 53–67.

Eagleton, Terry. *The Function of Criticism: From the Spectator to Post-Structuralism*. London: Verso, 1984.

Eddy, W. A. *Gulliver's Travels: A Critical Study*. Princeton: Princeton University Press, 1923.

Ehrenpreis, Irvin. *Literary Meaning and Augustan Values*. Charlottesville: University Press of Virginia, 1974.

———. *Swift: The Man, His Works, and the Age*. 3 vols. Cambridge, Mass.: Harvard University Press, 1962–83.

---. "Swift's *History of England.*" *Journal of English and Germanic Philology* 51 (1952): 177–85.
---. "Swift's 'Little Language' in the *Journal to Stella.*" *Studies in Philology* 45 (1948): 80–88.
Elias, A. C., Jr. *Swift at Moor Park: Problems in Biography and Criticism.* Philadelphia: University of Pennsylvania Press, 1982.
Eliot, T. S. "Tradition and the Individual Talent." In *Criticism: The Major Texts*, edited by W. J. Bate, 525–29. New York: Harcourt Brace Jovanovich, 1970.
Elliott, Robert C. *The Power of Satire: Magic, Ritual, Art.* Princeton: Princeton University Press, 1960.
---. "Swift's 'I.'" *Yale Review* 62 (1973): 372–91.
---. "Swift's Satire: Rules of the Game." *ELH* 41 (1974): 413–28.
Elliott, Robert C., and Maximillian E. Novak. "Jonathan Swift: The Presentation of Self in Doggerel Rhyme." In *The Poetry of Jonathan Swift*, edited by Robert C. Elliott and Arthur H. Scouten, 1–23. Los Angeles: Clark Memorial Library/University of California Press, 1981.
Empson, William. *Some Versions of Pastoral.* London: Chatto & Windus, 1950.
Ewald, William B. *The Masks of Jonathan Swift.* Cambridge, Mass.: Harvard University Press, 1954.
Fabricant, Carole. *Swift's Landscape.* Baltimore: Johns Hopkins University Press, 1982.
Felman, Shoshana. "To Open the Question." In *Literature and Psychoanalysis/The Question of Reading: Otherwise*, 5–10. Baltimore: Johns Hopkins University Press, 1982.
Ferenczi, Sandor. "Gulliver Phantasies." *International Journal of Psychoanalysis* 9 (1928): 283–300.
Ferguson, Oliver W. *Jonathan Swift and Ireland.* Urbana: University of Illinois Press, 1962.
---. "Jonathan Swift, Freeman of Dublin." *Modern Language Notes* 71 (1956): 405–9.
---. "Nature and Friendship: The Personal Letters of Jonathan Swift." In *The Familiar Letter in the Eighteenth Century*, edited by Howard Anderson, Philip B. Daghlian, and Irvin Ehrenpreis, 14–33. Lawrence, Kans.: University Press of Kansas, 1966.
Fineman, Joel. "The Structure of Allegorical Desire." In *Allegory and Representation: Selected Papers from the English Institute, 1979–80*, edited by Stephen J. Greenblatt, 26–60. Baltimore: Johns Hopkins University Press, 1981.
Fish, Stanley. "Interpreting the *Variorum.*" In *Is There a Text in This Class?: The Authority of Interpretive Communities*, 147–73. Cambridge, Mass.: Harvard University Press, 1980.
Fisher, Alan S. "An End to the Renaissance: Erasmus, Hobbes, and *A Tale of a Tub.*"

Huntington Library Quarterly 38 (1974): 1–22.
Foucault, Michel. *Language, Counter-Memory, Practice*. Edited by Donald F. Bouchard. Translated by Donald F. Bouchard and Sherry Simon. Ithaca, N.Y.: Cornell University Press, 1977.
———. *The Order of Things: The Archaeology of the Human Sciences*. New York: Vintage, 1973.
Frantz, R. W. "Swift's Yahoos and the Voyagers." *Modern Philology* 29 (1931): 49–57.
Freud, Sigmund. *Jokes and Their Relation to the Unconscious*. Vol. 7 of *The Complete Psychological Works of Sigmund Freud*. Standard Edition, edited by James Strachey. London: Hogarth, 1960.
Frye, Northrop. "Allegory." In *The Princeton Encyclopedia of Poetry and Poetics*, edited by Alex Preminger, 12–15. Princeton: Princeton University Press, 1974.
———. *Anatomy of Criticism: Four Essays*. New York: Atheneum, 1967.
Frye, Roland M. "Swift's Yahoos and the Christian Symbols for Sin." *Journal of the History of Ideas* 15 (1954): 201–17.
Fussell, Paul. "Speaker and Style in *A Letter of Advice to a Young Poet* (1721) and the Problem of Attribution." *Review of English Studies* 10 (1959): 63–67.
Gay, John. *The Guardian* #149. In *John Gay: Poetry and Prose*, edited by Vinton A. Dearing, 459–64. Vol. 2. Oxford: Clarendon, 1974.
Gilbert, Jack. "The Drapier's Initials." *Notes & Queries* 208 (June 1963): 217–18.
Girard, René. *Deceit, Desire, and the Novel: Self and Other in Literary Structure*. Translated by Yvonne Freccero. Baltimore: Johns Hopkins University Press, 1980.
Gramsci, Antonio. *Selections from the Prison Notebooks*. Edited and translated by Quentin Hoare and Geoffrey Nowell Smith. New York: International, 1971.
Greenacre, Phyllis. *Swift and Carroll: A Psychoanalytic Study of Two Lives*. New York: International Universities Press, 1955.
Greene, Donald. "On Swift's 'Scatological' Poems." *Sewanee Review* 75 (1967): 672–89.
Grillot de Givry, Émile. *Picture Museum of Sorcery, Magic, and Alchemy*. New Hyde Park, N.Y.: University Books, 1963.
Hall, Basil. "'An Inverted Hypocrite': Swift the Churchman." In *The World of Jonathan Swift*, edited by Brian Vickers, pp. 38–68. Cambridge, Mass.: Harvard University Press, 1968.
Harth, Philip. *Swift and Anglican Rationalism: The Religious Background of "A Tale of a Tub."* Chicago: University of Chicago Press, 1961.
Hartman, Geoffrey. *Beyond Formalism: Literary Essays 1958–1970*. New Haven: Yale University Press, 1970.
———. *The Fate of Reading and Other Essays*. Chicago: University of Chicago Press, 1975.
———. *Saving the Text: Literature, Derrida, Philosophy*. Baltimore: Johns Hopkins University Press, 1981.
Heidegger, Martin. *On the Way to Language*. San Francisco: Harper & Row, 1982.

Hernadi, Paul. *Beyond Genre: New Directions in Literary Classification.* Ithaca, N.Y.: Cornell University Press, 1972.
Highet, Gilbert. *The Anatomy of Satire.* Princeton: Princeton University Press, 1962.
Hirsch, E. D., Jr. *Validity in Interpretation.* New Haven: Yale University Press, 1967.
Hobbes, Thomas. *Leviathan.* Chicago: Encyclopedia Britannica, 1952.
Hopkins, Robert H. "The Personation of Hobbism in Swift's *Tale of a Tub* and *Mechanical Operation of the Spirit*." *Philological Quarterly* 45 (1966): 372–76.
Horace. *Art of Poetry.* In *Criticism: The Major Texts,* edited by W. J. Bate, 51–58. New York: Harcourt Brace Jovanovich, 1970.
Howard, Jean E. "The New Historicism in Renaissance Studies." *English Literary Renaissance* 16 (1986): 13–43.
Howell, A. C. "*Res et Verba*: Words and Things." *ELH* 13 (1946): 131–42.
Hunter, J. Paul. "Fielding and the Disappearance of Heroes." In *The English Hero, 1660–1880,* edited by Robert Folkenflik, 116–42. Newark, Del.: University of Delaware Press, 1982.
Huxley, Aldous. "Swift." In *Do What You Will,* 97–112. London: Chatto & Windus, 1929.
Jacobson, Richard. "Absence, Authority, and the Text." *Glyph* 3 (1978): 137–47.
Jameson, Fredric. "Magical Narratives: Romance as Genre." *New Literary History* 7 (1975): 135–63.
Jauss, Hans Robert. "Literary History as a Challenge to Literary Theory." In *New Directions in Literary History,* edited by Ralph Cohen, 11–41. Baltimore: Johns Hopkins University Press, 1974.
Johnson, Maurice. "Swift and the Greatest Epitaph in History." *PMLA* 68 (1953): 814–27.
Johnson, Samuel. "Life of Swift." In *Lives of the English Poets,* edited by G. B. Hill, 1–66. Vol. 3. Oxford: Clarendon, 1905.
―――. *The Plan of an English Dictionary.* In *The Works of Samuel Johnson, LLD.,* 1–22. Vol. 6. Oxford, 1825. Reprint New York: AMS, 1970.
―――. "Preface to the English Dictionary." In *The Works of Samuel Johnson, LLD.,* 23–54. Vol. 6. Oxford, 1825. Reprint New York: AMS, 1970.
Jones, Ernest. "Simulated Foolishness in Hysteria." In *Papers on Psycho-Analysis,* 141–53. Toronto: Macmillan, 1913.
Jonson, Ben. *Timber: or, Discoveries.* In *Ben Jonson,* edited by C. H. Herford Percy and Evelyn Simpson, 562–649. Vol. 8. Oxford: Clarendon, 1954.
Jung, C. J. *Symbols of Transformation.* Vol. 5 of *Collected Works.* 2nd ed. Princeton: Princeton University Press, 1956.
Keener, Frederik M. *The Chain of Becoming/The Philosophical Tale, the Novel, and a Neglected Realism of the Enlightenment: Swift, Montesquieu, Voltaire, Johnson, and Austen.* New York: Columbia University Press, 1983.
Kelling, H. D. "Some Significant Names in *Gulliver's Travels.*" *Studies in Philology* 48 (1951): 761–78.

Kelly, Ann Cline. "After Eden: Gulliver's (Linguistic) Travels." *ELH* 45 (1978): 33–54.

———. "Swift's *Polite Conversation*: An Eschatological Vision." *Studies in Philology* 73 (1976): 204–24.

———. "Swift's Satire Against Modern Etymologists in *The Antiquity of the English Tongue*." *South Atlantic Review* 48 (1983): 21–36.

Kenner, Hugh. *Flaubert, Joyce and Beckett: The Stoic Comedians*. London: W. H. Allen, 1964.

Kermode, Frank. *The Genesis of Secrecy; On The Interpretation of Narrative*. Cambridge, Mass.: Harvard University Press, 1979.

Kernan, Alvin. *Printing Technology, Letters, and Samuel Johnson*. Princeton: Princeton University Press, 1987.

Knapp, Steven, and Walter Benn Michaels. "Against Theory." *Critical Inquiry* 8 (1982): 732–42.

Knight, G. Wilson. *The Burning Oracle*. London: Oxford University Press, 1959.

Knoblauch, C. H. "Coherence Betrayed: Samuel Johnson and the 'Prose of the World.'" *Boundary 2* 7 (1979): 235–60.

Kristeva, Julia. "Pour une semiologie des paragrams." In *Semiotike/ Récherches pour une sémanalyse*, 109–42. Paris: Tel Quel, 1969.

Lacan, Jacques. *Écrits: A Selection*. Translated by Alan Sheridan. New York: Norton, 1971.

———. *Speech and Language in Psychoanalysis*. Translated by Anthony Wilden. Baltimore: Johns Hopkins University Press, 1981.

Land, Stephen K. *From Signs to Propositions: The Concept of Form in Eighteenth-Century Semantic Theory*. New York: Columbia University Press, 1974.

Langland, William. *Piers Plowman: The B Version*. Edited by George Kane and E. Talbot Donaldson. London: Oxford University Press, 1975.

Leavis, F. R. "The Irony of Swift." *Scrutiny* 2 (1934): 364–78.

Lentricchia, Frank. *Criticism and Social Change*. Chicago: University of Chicago Press, 1983.

Levin, Samuel R. *Linguistic Structures in Poetry*. The Hague: Mouton, 1969.

Levine, Jay Arnold. "The Design of *A Tale of a Tub* (With a Digression on a Mad Modern Critic)." *ELH* 33 (1966): 198–227.

Levine, Jennifer Schiffler. "Originality and Repetition in *Finnegan's Wake* and *Ulysses*." *PMLA* 94 (1979): 106–20.

Lindenberger, Herbert. "Toward a New History in Literary Study." In *Profession '84*, 16–23. New York: MLA, 1984.

Locke, John. *An Essay Concerning Human Understanding*. Chicago: Encyclopedia Britannica, 1952.

Longinus. *On the Sublime*. In *Criticism: The Major Texts*, edited by W. J. Bate, 62–75. New York: Harcourt Brace Jovanovich, 1970.

Lukács, Georg. *History and Class Consciousness: Studies in Marxist Dialectics*. Trans-

lated by Rodney Livingstone. Cambridge, Mass.: MIT Press, 1971.
McGann, Jerome J. "Some Forms of Critical Discourse." *Critical Inquiry* 11 (1985): 399–417.
McKeon, Michael. *The Origins of the English Novel 1600–1740.* Baltimore: Johns Hopkins University Press, 1987.
———. *Politics and Poetry in Restoration England: The Case of Dryden's "Annus Mirabilis."* Cambridge, Mass.: Harvard University Press, 1975.
Maresca, Thomas E. "Language and Body in Augustan Poetic." *ELH* 37 (1970): 374–88.
Marx, Karl. *The Eighteenth Brumaire of Louis Napoleon.* Vol 9 of *Karl Marx and Frederick Engels: Collected Works.* New York: International, 1979.
Mayhew, George P. *Rage or Raillery: The Swift Manuscripts at the Huntington Library.* San Marino, Cal.: Huntington Library, 1967.
Merleau-Ponty, Maurice. *Signs.* Translated by Richard C. McCleary. Evanston, Ill.: Northwestern University Press, 1964.
Mezciems, Jenny. "Gulliver and Other Heroes." In *The Art of Jonathan Swift,* edited by Clive T. Probyn, 189–298. New York: Barnes & Noble, 1978.
———. "Swift's Praise of Gulliver: Some Renaissance Backgrounds to the *Travels.*" In *The Character of Swift's Satire,* edited by Claude Rawson, 245–81. Newark, Del.: University of Delaware Press, 1983.
Milic, Louis T. *A Quantitative Approach to the Style of Jonathan Swift.* The Hague: Mouton, 1967.
Miller, J. Hillis. "Ariadne's Thread: Repetition and the Narrative Line." *Critical Inquiry* 3 (1976): 57–77.
———. "The Critic as Host." In *Deconstruction and Criticism,* edited by Harold Bloom and Geoffrey Hartman, 217–53. New York: Seabury, 1979.
———. "Deconstructing the Deconstructors." *Diacritics* 5 (1975): 24–31.
———. "Stevens' Rock and Criticism as Cure, II." *Georgia Review* 30 (1976): 330–48.
Milton, John. *Paradise Lost.* Edited by Scott Elledge. New York: Norton, 1975.
Mink, Louis O. "The Autonomy of Historical Understanding." In *Philosophical Analysis and History,* edited by William H. Dray, 160–92. New York: Harper & Row, 1966.
Montagu, M. F. Ashley. "Tyson's *Orang-Outang, Sive Homo Sylvestris,* and Swift's *Gulliver's Travels.*" *PMLA* 59 (1944): 84–89.
Moore, J. N. P. "Swift's Philanthropy." In *Jonathan Swift 1667–1967: A Dublin Tercentenary Tribute,* edited by Roger McHugh and Philip Edwards, 137–56. Dublin: Dolmen, 1967.
Murry, John Middleton. *Jonathan Swift: A Critical Biography.* London: Jonathan Cape, 1954.
Nelson, Cary. *The Incarnate Word: Literature as Verbal Space.* Urbana, Ill.: University of Illinois Press, 1973.

Nokes, David. "'Hack at Tom Poley's': Swift's Use of Puns." In *The Art of Jonathan Swift*, edited by Clive T. Probyn, 42–48. New York: Barnes & Noble, 1978.

Nussbaum, Felicity. *The Brink of All We Hate: English Satires on Women, 1660–1750*. Lexington, Ky.: University Press of Kentucky, 1984.

Paulson, Ronald. *The Fictions of Satire*. Baltimore: Johns Hopkins University Press, 1967.

———. "Swift, Stella, And Permanence." *ELH* 27 (1969): 298–314.

———. *Theme and Structure in Swift's "A Tale of a Tub."* New Haven: Yale University Press, 1960.

Philmus, Robert H. "Swift, Gulliver, and 'The Thing Which Was Not.'" *ELH* 38 (1971): 62–79.

Piaget, Jean. *Genetic Epistemology*. Translated by E. Duckworth. New York: Columbia University Press, 1970.

Pierssens, Michel. *The Power of Babel: A Study of Logophilia*. Translated by Carl R. Lovitt. London: Routledge & Kegan Paul, 1980.

Pilkington, Laetitia. *Memoirs*. Edited by J. Isaacs. London: Routledge, 1928.

Plato. *The Republic*. Chicago: Encyclopedia Britannica, 1952.

Pollak, Ellen. *The Poetics of Sexual Myth: Gender and Ideology in the Verse of Swift and Pope*. Chicago: University of Chicago Press, 1985.

Pons, Émile. "Du nouveau sur le 'Journal à Stella.'" *Études Anglaises* 1 (1937): 210–29.

———. "Les Langues Imaginaires dans le Voyage Utopique, un Précurseur: Thomas Morus." *Révue de Littérature Comparée* 10 (1930): 589–607.

Pope, Alexander. *The Art of Sinking in Poetry: Martinus Scriblerus' Peri Bathous*. Edited by Edna Leake Steeves. New York: Russell & Russell, 1968.

———. *The Dunciad Variorum*. In *The Poems of Alexander Pope*, edited by John Butt, 317–459. New Haven: Yale University Press, 1970.

———. *An Essay on Criticism*. In *The Poems of Alexander Pope*, edited by John Butt, 143–68. New Haven: Yale University Press, 1970.

Price, Martin. *Swift's Rhetorical Art: A Study in Structure and Meaning*. Hamden, Conn.: Archon, 1963.

———. *To the Palace of Wisdom: Studies in Order and Energy from Dryden to Blake*. New York: Archon, 1965.

Probyn, Clive T. "Swift and Linguistics: The Context behind Lagado and around the Fourth Voyage." *Neophilologus* 58 (1974): 425–32.

———. "Swift and the Human Predicament." In *The Art of Jonathan Swift*, edited by Clive T. Probyn, 57–80. New York: Barnes & Noble, 1978.

Puttenham, George. *The Arte of English Poesie*. In *Elizabethan Critical Essays*, edited by G. Gregory Smith, 1–66. Vol. 2. London: Oxford University Press, 1904.

Quilligan, Maureen. *The Language of Allegory: Defining the Genre*. Ithaca, N.Y.: Cornell University Press, 1979.

Quinlan, Kieran. "Their Language, So Familiar and So Foreign: The English Tongue and Its Irish Voice." *Postscript* 2 (1985): 115–21.
Quinlan, Maurice J. "Swift's Use of Literalization as a Rhetorical Device." *PMLA* 82 (1967): 516–21.
Quintana, Ricardo. *The Mind and Art of Jonathan Swift*. Gloucester, Mass.: Peter Smith, 1965.
———. *Two Augustans: John Locke, Jonathan Swift*. Madison: University of Wisconsin Press, 1978.
Ranelagh, John. *Ireland: An Illustrated History*. New York: Oxford University Press, 1981.
Rawson, C. J. *Gulliver and the Gentle Reader: Studies in Swift and Our Time*. London: Routledge & Kegan Paul, 1973.
———. "'I the Lofty Style Decline': Self-apology and the 'Heroick Strain' in Some of Swift's Poems." In *The English Hero, 1660–1880*, edited by Robert Folkenflik, 79–115. Newark, Del.: University of Delaware Press, 1982.
———. "The Nightmares of Strephon: Nymphs of the City in the Poems of Swift, Baudelaire, Eliot." In *English Literature in the Age of Disguise*, edited by Maximillian E. Novak, 57–99. Berkeley: University of California Press, 1977.
Reilly, Patrick. *Jonathan Swift: the Brave Desponder*. Carbondale, Ill.: Southern Illinois University Press, 1982.
Riffaterre, Michael. "Criteria for Style Analysis." *Word* 15 (1959): 135–55.
Rifflet-Lemaire, Anika. *Jacques Lacan*. Brussels: Dessart, 1970.
Rogers, Pat. "Form in *A Tale of a Tub*." *ELH* 22 (1972): 142–59.
———. "Swift and the Idea of Authority." In *The World of Jonathan Swift*, edited by Brian Vickers, 25–37. Cambridge, Mass.: Harvard University Press, 1968.
———. "Swift and the Revival of Cliché." In *The Character of Swift's Satire*, edited by Claude Rawson, 203–26. Newark, Del.: University of Delaware Press, 1983.
Rorty, Richard. *Philosophy and the Mirror of Nature*. Oxford: Basil Blackwell, 1980.
Rosenheim, Edward W., Jr. *Swift and the Satirist's Art*. Chicago: University of Chicago Press, 1963.
Rossi, Mario, and Joseph Hone. *Swift, or the Egoist*. London: Victor Gollancz, 1934.
Rubinoff, Lionel. *The Pornography of Power*. Chicago: Quadrangle, 1968.
Russell, Bertrand. *Principles of Mathematics*. London: Cambridge University Press, 1903.
Said, Edward. *The World, the Text, and the Critic*. Cambridge, Mass.: Harvard University Press, 1983.
Sams, Henry W. "Swift's Satire of the Second Person." *ELH* 26 (1959): 36–44.
Saussure, Ferdinand de. *Course in General Linguistics*. Edited by Charles Bally and Albert Sechehaye. Translated by Wade Baskin. New York: Philosophical Library, 1959.
Schakel, Peter J. "Virgil and the Dean: Christian and Classical Allusion in *The Le-*

gion Club." *Studies in Philology* 70 (1973): 427–38.
Seeber, Edward D. "Ideal Languages in the French and English Imaginary Voyages." *PMLA* 60 (1945): 586–97.
Seidel, Michael. *Satiric Inheritance: Rabelais to Sterne*. Princeton: Princeton University Press, 1979.
Shakespeare, William. *Love's Labours Lost*. In *William Shakespeare: The Complete Works*, edited by Alfred Harbage, 179–210. Baltimore: Penquin, 1969.
Sheridan, Thomas. *The Life of the Reverend Dr. Jonathan Swift, Dean of St. Patrick's, Dublin*. London: Rivington, 1787.
Sidney, Sir Philip. *An Apology for Poetry*. In *Criticism: The Major Texts*, edited by W. J. Bate, 82–106. New York: Harcourt Brace Jovanovich, 1970.
Slepian, Barry. "The Ironic Intention of Swift's Verses on His Own Death." *Review of English Studies* 14 (1963): 249–56.
Smith, Frederik N. "Dramatic Elements in Swift's *Journal to Stella*." *Eighteenth-Century Studies* 1 (1968): 332–52.
―――. *Language and Reality in Swift's* A Tale of a Tub. Columbus: Ohio State University Press, 1979.
Smith, Roland. "Swift's Little Language and Nonsense Names." *Journal of English and Germanic Philology* 53 (1954): 178–96.
Spanos, William V. "Breaking the Circle: Hermeneutics as Dis-Closure." *Boundary 2* 5 (1977): 421–57.
Spenser, Edward. *The Faerie Queene*. Edited by Robert Kellogg and Oliver Steele. New York: Odyssey, 1965.
Sprat, Thomas. *History of the Royal Society*. Edited by Jackson I. Cope and Harold W. Jones. St. Louis: Washington University Press, 1958.
Starobinski, Jean. *Les Mots sous les mots*. Paris: Gallimard, 1971.
Steele, Peter. *Jonathan Swift: Preacher and Jester*. Oxford: Clarendon, 1978.
Steiner, George. *The Death of Tragedy*. London: Faber & Faber, 1961.
―――. *Language and Silence: Essays on Language, Literature, and the Inhuman*. New York: Atheneum, 1967.
Sturm, N. A. "Gulliver: The Benevolent Linguist." *University of Dayton Review* 4 (1967): 43–54.
Sutherland, James. *English Satire*. Cambridge: Cambridge University Press, 1958.
Temple, Sir William. *Of Poetry*. In *Eighteenth-Century Poetry and Prose*, 3d ed. edited by John M. Bullitt, 16–34. New York: Ronald, 1973.
Thackeray, William Makepeace. "Swift." In *English Humorists of the Eighteenth Century*, 13–45. London: Grey Walls, 1949.
Torrance, Robert M. *The Comic Hero*. Cambridge, Mass.: Harvard University Press, 1978.
Traugott, John. "A Tale of a Tub." In *The Character of Swift's Satire*, edited by Claude Rawson, 83–126. Newark, Del.: University of Delaware Press, 1983.

Uhlig, Claus. "Literature as Textual Palingenesis: On Some Principles of Literary History." *New Literary History* 16 (1985): 481–513.
Uphaus, Robert W. *The Impossible Observer: Reason and The Reader in Eighteenth-Century Prose*. Lexington, Ky.: University Press of Kentucky, 1979.
Voigt, Milton. *Swift and the Twentieth Century*. Detroit: Wayne State University Press, 1964.
Waterston, G. C. *Order and Counter-Order: Dualism in Western Culture*. New York: Philosophical Library, 1966.
Watt, Ian. "The Ironic Tradition in Augustan Prose from Swift to Johnson." In *The Character of Swift's Satire*, edited by Claude Rawson, 305–26. Newark, Del.: University of Delaware Press, 1983.
Weiskel, Thomas. *The Romantic Sublime: Studies in the Structure and Psychology of Transcendence*. Baltimore: Johns Hopkins University Press, 1976.
White, Hayden. *Metahistory: The Historical Imagination in Nineteenth-Century Europe*. Baltimore: Johns Hopkins University Press, 1983.
Wiemann, Robert. *Structure and Society in Literary History: Studies in the History and Theory of Historical Criticism*. Baltimore: Johns Hopkins University Press, 1984.
Wilkins, John. *An Essay Towards a Real Character, and a Philosophical Language*. Edited by R. C. Alston. London: Marston, 1968.
Williams, Aubrey L. " 'A Vile Encomium': That 'Panegyric on the Reverend D——n S——t.' " In *Contemporary Studies of Swift's Poetry*, edited by John I. Fischer and Donald C. Mell, Jr., 178–90. Newark, Del.: University of Delaware Press, 1980.
Williams, Harold. *Dean Swift's Library*. Cambridge: Cambridge University Press, 1932.
Williams, Kathleen. *Jonathan Swift and the Age of Compromise*. Lawrence, Kans.: University of Kansas Press, 1958.
Wilson, T. G. "Swift's Deafness and His Last Illness." *Annals of Medical History*, 3d ser., 2 (1940): 291–305.
Woolley, James. "Arbuckle's 'Panegyric' and Swift's Scrub Libel: The Documentary Evidence." In *Contemporary Studies of Swift's Poetry*, edited by John I. Fischer and Donald C. Mell, Jr., 191–209. Newark, Del.: University of Delaware Press, 1980.
Wotton, William. "Observations upon *The Tale of a Tub*." In *A Tale of a Tub*, edited by A. C. Guthkelch and D. Nicol Smith, 313–28. Oxford: Clarendon, 1958.
Wyrick, Deborah Baker. "Life Interminable: Swift's Struldbruggs and Capek's Elina Makropolis." *The Comparatist* 7 (1983): 48–56.
Yeats, William Butler. *Explorations*. London: Macmillan, 1962.
Zimmerman, Everett. *Swift's Narrative Satires: Author and Authority*. Ithaca, N.Y.: Cornell University Press, 1983.

INDEX

Gulliver's Travels, A Tale of a Tub, and the *Drapier's Letters* have separate entries; Swift's letters are listed under the names of their recipients. All other titles of Swift's works are listed under the author's name.

Abrams, M. H., 209 (n. 14)
Acheson, Lady Ann, 115
Addison, Joseph, 164, 192; *The Spectator* #416, 16
Aesop, 60, 76, 138, 139
Aggression, linguistic, 24, 63, 65, 71, 120, 205 (n. 12), 211 (n. 41)
Alchemy and occultism, 6, 64, 204 (n. 2)
Allen, Joshua, second Viscount, 94
Alston, William P., 2
Anagrams and acrostics, 22, 63, 65–69, 70, 83–84, 126, 205 (n. 5)
Ancients versus Moderns controversy, 25, 60, 67, 133, 137–39, 200 (n. 43)
Anne (queen of England), 46, 123, 205 (n. 4)
Anonymity/anonymous authorship, 22, 51–52, 54, 94, 96–97, 98, 99, 133, 209 (n. 5)
Apollo, 182, 211–12 (n. 43)
Apollos, 122
Apuleius, Lucius: *The Golden Ass*, 78
Arbuckle, James, 209 (n. 5)
Arbuthnot, John, 72, 100; *The Memoirs of Martinus Scriblerus*, 72, 124, 208 (n. 1)

Aristotle, 15, 24, 58, 59, 62, 140, 142, 212 (n. 5); *The Poetics*, 141
Arnheim, Rudolf, 202 (n. 26)
Artephius (*Dr. Faustus*), 64
Ashe, Tom, 66, 69–70
Atkins, G. Douglas, 213–14 (n. 15), 221 (n. 1)
Atterbury, Bishop Francis, 25, 127
Augustine, Saint, 36, 37
Authorial intent, xv–xvi, 14, 16, 19, 21, 23–24, 48, 49
Authority, verbal, 29, 30–31, 39–40, 51, 64, 200 (nn. 3, 5), 202 (nn. 33, 34, 35), 203 (n. 43); estrangement from, 34–35, 39; through academies, 37, 40–41; through form, 42–43; through memory, 44; through institutions, 46–47, 158–59; of "authorities," 50; of narrative voice, 51–53; subversion through irony, 53, 202 (n. 35); challenged by wordplay, 64; through interpretive custody, 122; given to reader, 134

Babel, xvii, 33, 42, 62, 67, 84
Bachelard, Gaston, 201 (n. 14), 204 (n. 49)
Bacon, Sir Francis, 139
Bakhtin, Mikhail, 22, 199–200 (n. 41)
Barnett, Louise K., 217 (n. 50)
Barthes, Roland, xv, 34, 132–33, 134–35, 142, 213 (n. 10)
Beaumont, Charles Allen, 201 (n. 13)
Benstock, Shari, 203 (n. 43)

Bentley, Richard, 55, 58, 62, 67, 81, 138–39
Benveniste, Émile, 97
Bickerstaff, Isaac, 14, 84, 99–100, 101
Bloom, Harold, 66, 204 (n. 50), 214 (n. 19)
Boethius, 131, 212 (n. 5)
Böhme, Jacob, 6
Bolingbroke, Henry St. John, first Viscount, 25, 93, 127; letter to Swift, 63; Swift's letter to, 93; his wife as Yahoo, 209–10 (n. 17)
Book of Common Prayer, 42
Booth, Wayne, 145
Boswell, James, 188
Boyle, Robert, 138–39
Breton, André, 220 (n. 17)
Brooks, Peter, 212 (n. 47)
Brown, Laura, 191, 215–16 (n. 35), 221 (n. 3)
Brown, Norman O., 119, 211 (nn. 37, 39)
Brutus, Marcus, 101
Buckley, Marjorie W., 207 (n. 30)
Burke, Edmund, 145
Burke, Kenneth, 159
Burnet, Gilbert, 49; *History of his own Times*, Swift's opinion of, 13
Burton, Richard: *The Anatomy of Melancholy*, 78
Butler, Samuel, 78, 140; *Hudibras*, 214 (n. 20)

Cadavre exquise, 66
Callois, Roger, 75, 78
Cambridge Platonists, 46
Carlyle, Thomas, 188; *Sartor Resartus*, 219 (n. 10)
Carnochan, W. B., 10, 200 (n. 46)
Castle, Terry, 221 (nn. 25, 1)
Castle of Perseverance, The [anon.], 216 (n. 38)

Castration, 17, 99, 122, 140
Censorship, 22, 30, 37, 41
Cephas, 122
Cervantes, Miguel de, 59, 78; *Don Quixote*, 162
Cibber, Colley, 114
Cicero, 3, 17
Citations, 50, 51, 59, 116, 202 (n. 28)
Clark, John R., 206 (n. 19)
Clark, Paul Odell, 83–84, 207 (n. 28)
Clifford, James L., 208 (n. 42)
Clio, muse of history, 117, 175
Clothes and clothing, xvi–xvii, 10, 20, 32–33, 38–40, 42, 55, 74, 178, 201 (nn. 11, 15), 214 (n. 20), 219 (n. 10). *See also* Divestitures; Drapier, M. B.; Gulliver, Lemuel: clothes of; Investitures; *Tale of a Tub, A*: clothes allegory in; Transvestitures
Codes/ciphers, 22, 25, 30, 73–74, 82–83, 85, 86, 126–27, 177
Cogwell, Marmaduke, 208–9 (n. 2)
Coke, Sir Edward, 158
Colie, Rosalie, 10
Concanen, Matthew, 115
Cowley, Abraham, 137; "Clad All in White," 128
Creichton (Creighton), Captain John, 52
Criticism, Goddess of (*The Battel of the Books*), 57–60, 61, 114, 138, 139
Crusoe, Robinson, 220 (nn. 19, 21)
Curll, Edmund, 114–15

Davies, Hugh Sykes, 201 (n. 16)
Davis, Lennard J., 209 (n. 3)
Declaratory Act, 143, 150, 214–15 (n. 27)
Decoding/deciphering. *See* Codes/ciphers
Deconstruction. *See* Poststructuralism and deconstruction

Defense of English Commodities, A [anon.], 215 (n. 32)
Defoe, Daniel: *Robinson Crusoe*, 177, 188
Deictics, 97–98
Deism/Deists, 12, 180
Delany, Patrick, Chancellor of St. Patrick's Cathedral, 97
De Man, Paul, 200 (n. 45)
Demosthenes, 17
Dennis, Nigel, 201 (n. 11)
Derrida, Jacques, 22, 23, 49, 99, 190, 201 (n. 14), 203 (n. 42)
Descartes, René, 62, 101
Des Fontaines, the Abbé: Swift's letter to, 218 (n. 1)
Dingley, Rebecca, 86, 87, 90, 110
Dircks, R. J., 10, 220 (n. 16)
Disease: of communication and language, 17, 65, 69, 70, 73, 127; of costume, 135–36, 138–39, 142–43, 149, 151, 169; of body politic, 147, 152, 154–155, 168
Divestitures, 62, 63–92 passim, 94, 112, 125, 130, 140, 168, 169, 178–79, 188, 213–14 (n. 15); definition of, 63–65; as undressing, 69; as emptying, 73; through naming, 96–97, 102. *See also* Wordplay
Donne, John, 190
Donoghue, Denis, 10, 198 (n. 16), 208 (n. 40)
Downie, J. A., 217 (nn. 49, 53)
Drapier, M. B., 14, 21, 52, 131–32, 145, 175, 187, 216–17 (n. 44); style of, 52; meaning of name, 101; at risk, 150; as David, 150–51, 162; as political activist, 152–53, 157–62; as doctor, 154–55; as rhetorical controller, 158, 161–64; as persona, 166–67, 217–18 (nn. 51, 54)
Drapier's Letters, 18, 21, 53, 93, 131–32, 144, 149–62, 165–68, 171–72, 174, 177, 184, 186, 190, 217 (nn. 49, 51); *To the Tradesmen, Shopkeepers, Farmers, and Country People in General* (first letter), 52, 131, 150–51, 158, 217 (n. 52); *Some Observations upon . . . the Report of the Privy Council* (third letter), 150–51, 158; *To the Whole People of Ireland* (fourth letter), 152–54, 158; *A Letter to . . . the Lord Viscount Molesworth* (fifth letter), 152–53; *To the Lord Chancellor Middleton* (sixth letter), 159, 217 (n. 52); *An Humble Address to Parliament* (seventh letter), 149, 150, 153–56, 216 (n. 41)
Dryden, John, 33, 62, 78, 105, 133, 135–37, 138, 139, 188, 190, 191, 206 (n. 22); *An Essay of Dramatic Poesy*, 16; *Religio Laici*, 133, 213 (n. 13)
Dublin, 52, 55, 82, 110, 112, 143, 195, 210 (n. 20), 212 (n. 48), 219 (n. 7); Freedom to, 94; polluted streets of, 125–26
Dyson, A. E., 203, n. 37

Eagleton, Terry, 191, 221 (n. 3)
Eddy, W. A., 204 (n. 46)
Ehrenpreis, Irvin, 202–3 (n. 36), 207 (n. 35), 208–9 (n. 2), 210 (nn. 20, 26), 211 (n. 32), 212 (n. 48), 213 (nn. 7, 8), 217 (n. 51), 218 (n. 2)
Elias, A. C., 210 (n. 26)
Eliot, T. S., 214 (n. 19)
Elliott, Robert C., 205 (n. 17), 210 (n. 19)
Empson, William, 217 (n. 53)
Enthusiasm/Enthusiasts, 5, 17, 45, 60, 79, 120
Epicureans, 12
Erasmus, Desiderius, 57, 59; *Moriae Encomium*, 22, 78
Etymologists/philologists, 67, 81, 100

Etymology/mock-etymology, 63, 67–69, 73, 83, 85, 205 (nn. 8, 9)
Ewald, William, 209 (n. 6)
Excremental concerns, 68, 69, 73, 198 (n. 8); and vertigo, 78–79; and texts, 95, 114–19, 127, 171, 186, 211 (nn. 37, 41), 212 (n. 48); allegories of reading and writing, 95, 119–21, 125–27, 148; excrementalized clothes, 128; excrementalized money, 129. *See also* Swift, Jonathan: and excremental strategies
Ezekiel, 5

Fabricant, Carole, 119, 191, 203 (n. 38), 211 (n. 37), 221 (n. 3)
Family romance, 98, 109–10
Felman, Shoshana, 202 (n. 35)
Feminist criticism, 193, 221 (n. 3)
Ferenczi, Sandor, 211 (n. 37)
Ferguson, Oliver W., 199 (n. 35), 208–9 (n. 2), 212 (n. 1), 214–15 (n. 27), 219 (n. 7)
Fielding, Henry, 100, 188; *The Life of Tom Thumb the Great, a Tragedy*, 220 (n. 17)
Filiation, textual, xvi, 23, 24, 27, 28, 30–31, 33–35, 39, 63, 120, 136–39
Fish, Stanley, 203 (n. 42)
Fisher, Alan S., 200 (n. 6)
Footnotes, 2, 56, 203 (nn. 42, 43)
Ford, Charles, Swift's letters to, 208 (n. 1), 209–10 (n. 17)
Foucault, Michel, 6, 159, 212 (n. 6)
Frantz, R. W., 210 (n. 21)
Free-Thinkers, 12
Freud, Sigmund, 70, 190, 205 (n. 11)
Frye, Northrop, 200 (n. 41), 206 (n. 19), 212 (n. 2), 220 (nn. 15, 18)

Game theory, 76–77
Gay, John, 72, 78, 100, 140, 206 (n. 22); Swift's letter to, 124–25; *The Guardian* #149, 214 (n. 20)
Gematria, 66
Genesis, xvi, 33, 35
Genet, Jean, 99
Genre/generic choice, 180–81, 202 (n. 34), 220 (n. 15)
George I (king of England), 205 (n. 4)
George II (king of England), 126
Gilbert, Jack, 209 (n. 11)
Girard, René, 181
Gramsci, Antonio, 159
Greenacre, Phyllis, 119, 211 (nn. 36, 37)
Gregory Misosarum, 100
Gresham's Law, 156
Gulliver, Lemuel, 10, 14–19, 24, 36, 44, 45, 58, 61, 76, 122, 126–27, 172, 212 (n. 47), 219 (n. 11); style of, 52; as linguist, 66, 80–83, 177, 180, 184, 219–20 (n. 14); meaning of name, 100–101, 179; image of self, 105–8, 169; succession of names, 106–7, 179; clothes of, 107, 135, 169, 177–79, 219 (n. 10); and excremental concerns, 117, 119, 120–21, 123; linguistic tragedy of, 176–86; as hero, 181–82, 220 (n. 19); as linguistic avenger, 184–86, 221 (n. 26)
Gulliver's Travels, 24–25, 36, 52, 63, 66, 76–77, 93, 98, 100, 106, 168–70, 184, 195, 208 (n. 1), 218 (n. 1), 219 (n. 11), 220 (n. 17); Lockean thought in, 10; Letter to Sympson, 18–19, 84, 218 (n. 3); languages in, 22, 80–85, 169, 180, 207 (n. 28), 221 (nn. 23, 24); pharmaceutical excrement in, 122–123; genre of, 180–181
—Book 1, 19, 80–81, 117, 119, 123, 177, 178, 181, 183
—Book 2, 16, 38, 61, 81, 106, 124, 177, 178, 181, 183, 216–17 (n. 44)

Index 241

—Book 3, 4, 25, 36, 44, 45, 46, 58, 66, 81, 101, 126–27, 135, 168, 181, 183, 197–98 (n. 7)
—Book 4, 10, 14–15, 17, 53, 83, 107, 117, 168, 176–85, 219 (n. 11), 220 (n. 16), 221 (nn. 23, 25, 26)
Guthkelch, A. C., 204 (n. 2)

Harding, John (printer), 159, 161
Hartman, Geoffrey, 99, 140, 209 (n. 9), 212 (n. 46)
Hegel, Georg W. F., 216 (n. 40)
Heidegger, Martin, 186
Heisenberg principle, 183
Hercules, 152, 153
Heroes, tragic and comic, 220 (nn. 18, 19, 21)
Hessy. *See* Vanhomrigh, Esther
Highet, Gilbert, 206 (n. 21)
Hirsch, E. D., xvi
Hobbes, Thomas, 4, 35, 46, 62, 106, 200 (n. 6), 201 (n. 21); *Leviathan*, 155
Hogarth, William, 172
Holyhead, 194
Homer, 58, 59, 67, 139, 140
Hopkins, Robert H., 200 (n. 6)
Horace, 15, 42, 45, 78, 116; *Art of Poetry*, 199 (n. 31)
Houyhnhnms, 10, 14–15, 36, 80, 105, 122; threats of, 16–17, 181–82; meaning of word, 83, 207 (n. 30); linguistic logic of, 178–79, 221 (n. 25); interpretations of, 180; textocentric consciousness of, 183–85
Howard, Jean E., 221 (n. 2)
Howell, A. C., 3
Hunter, J. Paul, 220 (21)
Huxley, Aldous, 119, 211 (n. 37)

Insides/outsides, 22, 25, 38, 40, 61, 121, 134, 142, 143, 152, 201 (nn. 12, 14)

Investitures, 19, 29, 30–62 passim, 103, 134, 140, 156, 168, 169, 171, 178, 183, 188; definition of, 30–33; in Anglican church, 32; as somatocentric trope, 37–38; as proper placement, 46–49; in textual territory, 54–62; contrast with divestiture, 63; through naming, 96, 102; hollow forms of, 104
Ionesco, Eugene: *The Bald Soprano*, 202 (n. 30)
Ireneus, 57
Irish Bank, 129, 155
Isaiah, 173

Jacobson, Richard, 200 (n. 5)
Jameson, Fredric, 220 (n. 15)
Johnson, Esther (Stella), xvi, 37, 86–91, 93, 101, 110, 146–47, 183, 195, 199 (n. 35), 207–8 (n. 39), 209–10 (n. 17), 215 (n. 28), 218 (n. 2)
Johnson, Maurice, 210 (n. 28)
Johnson, Samuel, 1, 43, 119, 140, 149, 188, 190, 191, 192, 198 (n. 16), 201 (n. 20); *The Plan of an English Dictionary*, 43; "Preface to the Dictionary," 43; "Life of Swift," 190, 210 (n. 24), 211 (n. 37)
John the Divine, Saint, 5, 9
Jokes, 30, 65, 68, 70, 72–73, 129, 205 (n. 11)
Jones, Ernest, 207 (n. 34)
Jonson, Ben, 140; *Timber*, 214 (n. 20)
Joyce, James, 83, 188
Jung, C. J., 212 (n. 44)

Keats, John, 190
Keener, Frederick, 10
Kelling, H. D., 83–84
Kells, Book of, 194
Kelly, Ann Cline, 197–98 (n. 7), 205 (n. 9), 221 (n. 24)

Kelly, Edward: "The Humid Path, or Discourse on the Vegetable Menstruum of Saturn," 204 (n. 2)
Kenner, Hugh, 198 (n. 18), 203 (n. 43)
Kermode, Frank, 206 (n. 26)
Kernan, Alvin, 192, 221 (n. 3)
Kilkenny (Ireland), 194
King, William, archbishop of Dublin, 213 (n. 7), 218 (n. 2); Swift's letter to, 41
Klein, Melanie, 120
Knoblauch, C. H., 201 (n. 20)
Kristeva, Julia, 66, 205 (n. 5)

Lacan, Jacques, 99, 102, 104, 190, 205 (n. 12), 207 (n. 34), 209 (n. 16), 211 (n. 41)
Lagado, Academy of, 4, 24, 44–45, 46, 51, 84, 126–27, 168
Langland, William, 36; *Piers Plowman*, 214 (n. 20)
Language, theories of: referential, 2, 3–9, 10, 16, 49, 99, 151; behavioral, 2, 5, 15–20, 22, 23, 48, 49, 167–68, 170, 175; ideational, 2, 9–15, 16, 22, 48, 49; textocentric, 2–3, 20–29. *See also* Textocentrism; Universal language schemes
Langue and *parole*, 30–31, 42, 45, 46, 47, 51, 97, 183
Laracor (Ireland), 194
Lemuel, King (Proverbs 31), 101
Lentricchia, Frank, 132
Levin, Samuel R., 213 (n. 12)
Levine, Jennifer Schiffler, 203 (n. 42)
Lindenberger, Herbert, 221 (n. 5)
Literalization, 4, 5, 8, 9, 22, 31, 32, 52, 54, 76, 105
"Little language" (*Journal to Stella*), 65, 85–92, 207 (n. 35)
Locke, John, xv, 5–6, 10–12, 14, 15, 33, 49, 64, 67, 74, 106, 140, 198 (n. 22); *An Essay Concerning Human Understanding*, 10, 11, 199 (n. 28), 209 (n. 16), 214 (n. 20)
Longinus, 15
Lukács, Georg, 218 (n. 55)

McGann, Jerome, 193
McKeon, Michael, 191, 203 (n. 38), 221 (n. 3)
Maculla, James, 213 (n. 7)
Mailer, Norman, 145
Malamud, Bernard, 188
Maresca, Thomas, 198 (n. 17)
Market Hill (country house of Sir Arthur Acheson), 211 (n. 32); erection of outhouses at, 115–16
Marx, Karl: *The Eighteenth Brumaire of Louis Napoleon*, 216 (n. 40)
Marxist criticism, 142, 192
Matthew, Saint, 176
Mayhew, George, 204 (n. 1)
Merleau-Ponty, Maurice, 199 (n. 36)
Mezciems, Jenny, 203 (n. 46), 220 (n. 19)
Milic, Louis T., 202 (n. 32)
Miller, J. Hillis, xvi, 202 (n. 28), 205 (n. 8)
Milton, John, 19, 35, 179–80, 190; *Paradise Lost*, 209 (n. 16), 219 (n. 13)
Mink, Louis O., 213 (n. 9)
Mist's *Weekly Journal*, 212 (n. 48)
Mock epic, 77, 211 (n. 33)
Mock-heroic mode, 77, 116, 139
Mock languages, 63, 65, 80–85
Mock Latin/Anglo-Latin trifles, 63, 71, 73–74
Mock-sublime, 116, 151, 211 (n. 33)
Montagu, M. F. Ashley, 210 (n. 21)
Moore, Edward, 114
Moore, Henry, 6
Moore, J. A. P., 218 (n. 58)
More, Sir Thomas, 59, 82, 206 (n. 25)

Index

Names and naming, 6, 7, 8, 11, 14, 122, 132; pet names, 89; as self-engenderment, 94; as prescription for history, 95; concealing proper name, 95, 98, 101; empty name, 98, 102; task-directing names, 99–100; finding proper name, 99–102; Gulliver's search for, 106–8; name-calling, 171–72; for beggars, 210 (n. 21). *See also* Specular name
Narcissus, 104
Nelson, Cary, 206 (n. 19)
Neologisms, 9, 30, 42, 43, 47, 64, 204–5 (n. 2)
Nessus, shirt of, 152–53, 178
New Historicism, xv, 191–94, 221 (nn. 2, 3, 4, 5)
Nietzsche, Friedrich, 35
Nokes, David, 198 (n. 17), 218 (n. 57)
Nussbaum, Felicity, 221 (n. 3)

Odysseus, 181, 220 (n. 19)
Oedipus, 154, 174
Oedipus complex, 109, 211 (n. 36)
Order, 32–33, 46, 48–49, 54, 62, 114, 201–2 (n. 22), 202 (nn. 25, 26)
Orrery, John Boyle, fifth Earl of Cork, 100; Swift's letter to, 102
Orwell, George, 188
Ovid, 140, 164
Oxford, Robert Harley, first Earl of, 41; Swift's letter to, 198 (n. 8)

Pallas, 169, Swift's identification with, 145–47, 149, 187, 215 (n. 32); as tutelar divinity for women, 146–47; as Biblical Gnosis, 187
Paracelsus, 6
Parnell, Thomas, 100
Part-object fixation, 120–21
Partridge, John, 6, 69, 99, 163
Pastoral/mock-pastoral, 116, 119, 147,
 210 (n. 20), 211 (n. 37)
Patrick, Saint, 169
Paul, Saint, 12, 36, 113, 121–22
Paulson, Ronald, 198 (nn. 11, 22), 206 (n. 19)
Penelope, 145
Philaris, 138
Philips, John: *The Splendid Shilling*, 156
Philmus, Robert M., 221 (n. 23)
Philomela, 140–41, 144–45, 149, 153
Piaget, Jean, 183
Pilkington, Laetitia, 109
Pindar, 136; Pindaric Odes, 137
Placement, systematics of, 31, 47, 51, 53–62. *See also* Propriety, verbal; Spatiality
Plato, 15, 62, 140; *Cratylus*, 205 (n. 9); *Phaedrus*, 23, 123; *Republic*, 104–5
Platonists, 12
Pollak, Ellen, 221 (n. 3)
Pons, Émile, 86, 205 (n. 25)
Pope, Alexander, 72, 100, 114–16, 147, 190, 191, 192, 211 (nn. 32, 33); Swift's letters to, 15, 18, 142, 203 (n. 41), 209–10 (n. 17), 216 (n. 44); nature of his satire, 77–78, 206 (nn. 20, 22), 215–16 (n. 35)
—works of: *Dunciad Variorum*, 77–78, 114–16, 203 (n. 42); *An Essay on Criticism*, 16, 147, 199 (n. 32), 215 (n. 35); *Peri Bathuos*, 151; *The Rape of the Lock*, 77, 116; *The Temple of Fame*, 116
Poststructuralism and deconstruction, xv, 21–22, 65, 188–91, 193–94, 221 (n. 1); Swift as deconstructive writer, xv, 65, 112, 120, 189–90, 201 (n. 14), 203 (n. 42), 211–12 (n. 43), 221 (n. 1)
Price, Martin, xvi, 198 (n. 15), 201 (n. 12), 201–2 (n. 22), 202 (n. 23)
Prior, Matthew, 91, 115
Probyn, Clive T., 83, 198 (n. 14)

Propriety, verbal, 31, 47–54. *See also* Placement, systematics of; Spatiality
Pseudonymity/pseudonyms, 22, 51–52, 54, 94, 97–101, 108, 111, 130
Puns, 9, 22, 30, 63, 65, 66, 69–70, 72, 82, 100, 108, 118, 126, 140, 149, 163–65, 205 (nn. 9, 11)
Purchas, Samuel, 101
Puritans/Puritanism, 33, 42, 198 (n. 15), 199 (n. 34)
Puttenham, George, 105

Quilligan, Maureen, 130
Quinlan, Kieran, 216 (n. 41)
Quinlan, Maurice J., 206 (n. 18)
Quintana, Ricardo, 14, 201 (n. 12), 206 (n. 19), 208 (n. 42)
Quintilian, 3

Rabelais, François, 59, 82, 206 (n. 25); *Gargantua and Pantagruel*, 22, 78
Ranelagh, John, 215 (n. 29)
Rape/sexual victimization, 215 (n. 30); of language, 24, 141, 149; of Philomela, 140; of Ireland, 144–45, 153–54; as political suppression, 215 (n. 29)
Rawson, C. J., 119, 202 (n. 30), 206 (n. 19), 211 (nn. 33, 37), 220 (n. 17), 221 (n. 1)
Regression, 65, 71, 88, 205 (n. 12), 207 (n. 34)
Reilly, Patrick, 199 (n. 34), 200–201 (n. 7)
Richardson, Samuel, 188
Riddles, 63, 72, 82
Riffaterre, Michael, 199 (n. 33)
Rochefort, Mrs. John, 215 (n. 28)
Rogers, Pat, 200 (n. 3), 202 (n. 31), 206 (n. 19)
Roman Catholicism, 40, 215 (n. 29)
Rorty, Richard, 209 (n. 14)

Rosenheim, Edward, 202 (n. 23), 220 (n. 16)
Royal Society, 7, 8
Rubinoff, Lionel, 201 (n. 21)
Russell, Bertrand, 7

Sacramental Test, 19, 37, 93, 144
Said, Edward W., 21, 114
St. Patrick's Cathedral, Dublin, 112, 143, 195, 211 (n. 37)
Sams, Henry W., 205 (n. 14)
Satire, 168, 184–85, 202 (n. 34), 206 (n. 21); in First Corinthians, 121–22; Menippean Satire or "anatomy," 199–200 (n. 41), 206 (n. 19), 220 (n. 15); motives for, 206 (n. 22). *See also* Swift, Jonathan: as satirist
Saussure, Ferdinand de, 30, 66, 209 (n. 9)
Scriblerian devices, 57, 77, 189, 203 (n. 42)
Scriblerians, 70, 72, 93, 100
Scriblerus, Martinus, 72, 100, 123–24, 208 (n. 1)
Seidel, Michael, 200 (n. 43), 220 (n. 15)
Self, textual, 93–127 passim; Swift's need to create, 93–94; through specular images and names, 102–4, 108–13; prescribing it for history, 113–19, 205 (n. 12); excrementalizing it, 119–27. *See also* Names and naming; Specular name; Swift, Jonathan: on fame and postmortem reputation
Shaftesbury, Anthony Ashley Cooper, first Earl of, 46
Shakespeare, William, 140, 191; *Love's Labours Lost*, 214 (n. 20)
Sheridan, Rev. Thomas, 94; Swift's language competitions with, 66, 71–72; Swift's letters to, 209–10 (n. 17), 218 (n. 2)
Sheridan, Thomas, the younger, 102

Sidney, Sir Philip, 22, 59; *An Apology for Poetry*, 199 (n. 31)
Simon (Magus; the Zealot; Peter), 100
Skelton, John, 36
Slepian, Barry, 202–3 (n. 36)
Smith, D. Nichol, 204 (n. 2)
Smith, Frederik N., 10, 204–5 (n. 2)
Smith, Roland, 207 (n. 28)
Socrates, 104–5
Sophocles, 140, 205 (n. 9); *Oedipus Tyrannos*, 182; *Tereus*, 140, 205 (n. 9)
South Sea Bubble, 155
Spanos, William V., 200 (n. 2)
Spatiality, xiii, 31, 53–56, 59–62, 200 (n. 2), 203 (n. 43), 204 (n. 49). *See also* Placement, systematics of; Propriety, verbal
Specular image, 94, 99, 102–3, 111, 113, 118, 120, 127
Specular name, 99–103, 120, 179, 209 (n. 9); Swift's search for, 108–13
Spellings/abbreviations, 39, 40–41, 43, 67, 74, 85–87, 89, 207 (n. 37)
Spenser, Edmund, 59, 139; Error (*The Faerie Queene*), 59
Spider, the (*The Battel of the Books*), 58, 76, 123–24, 144, 204 (nn. 48, 50); and the Bee, 60–62, 76, 139
Sprat, Thomas: *History of the Royal Society*, 4
Steele, Peter, 206 (n. 23)
Steele, Sir Richard, 100
Steiner, George, 84, 173
Stella. *See* Johnson, Esther
Sterne, Laurence, 188; *Tristram Shandy*, 77, 203 (n. 43)
Stopford, Rev. James: Swift's letter to, 61
Struldbruggs, 36, 44, 46, 168–69
Sturm, N. A., 83
Swift, Abigail, née Erick (Swift's mother), 109

Swift, Caveliero (early ancestor), 109
Swift, Godwin (Swift's uncle), 109, 194
Swift, Jonathan (Swift's father), 108
Swift, Jonathan: and prefaces, xiii, 214 (n. 18); style of, 1, 8, 52–53, 198 (nn. 15, 16); linguistic ideology, 3, 21, 41–42; dislike of "dark authors," 6, 26, 66; religious thought, 8–9, 11–12, 35–37, 84–85, 113, 121–22, 133–34, 200–201 (n. 7); and innate ideas, 11–12; on style, 12–13, 30, 47–52, 60; as satirist, 18, 77–78, 99, 105, 107, 120, 122, 124, 127, 136, 167, 168, 199 (n. 35); personae of, 21, 49, 50, 51–53, 78, 97, 197 (n. 4), 202 (n. 32); and institutions, 30, 43–44, 46–47, 158–59, 201–2 (n. 22); ideas of history, 35, 131–32, 136, 167, 169, 186, 200–201 (n. 7), 213 (n. 8), 216 (n. 40); on the human body, 36, 113–14, 119, 173, 201 (nn. 11–12); and sexuality, 36–37, 64, 88, 113, 117, 119, 130, 147–48, 198 (n. 8), 201 (nn. 11, 12), 208 (n. 42); on corruption, 36–37, 68, 81, 113, 119, 122, 129, 130, 135, 136, 141, 147, 157, 165, 173; attitudes toward women, 36–37, 87–90, 120, 143, 146–49, 172–73, 187; and excremental strategies, 36–37, 114–27, 147–49, 198 (n. 8), 204 (n. 49), 211 (nn. 37, 39, 41), 215–16 (n. 35); on economics, 37, 54, 130, 155–57, 216–17 (n. 44); authoritarianism, 37, 143; on fame and postmortem reputation, 43, 56, 95, 98, 111–21, 137, 139, 167, 183, 187–88; feelings of alienation and exile, 54, 94, 109–111, 203 (n. 38); on beggars and vagabonds, 54–55, 57, 60–61; on critics, 55–61; sources and influences, 59, 78, 137–40, 204 (n. 46), 214 (n. 19); and health, 78–

79, 120, 204 (n. 49); handwriting, 86, 90, 207–8 (n. 39); childhood, 91, 94, 109, 146, 174, 208, 210 (n. 24), 211 (nn. 36, 37, 41), 212 (n. 46); family, 94, 108–9; on heroism, 101, 210 (n. 26); last years, 102–3, 218 (n. 2); compensatory family, 110; estate of, 166, 176, 218 (n. 58); sense of failure, 167–76, 182–83, 185

—and England, 3, 7, 54, 89, 93, 200 (n. 3); attempts at English origin, 109, 210 (n. 24); opinion of oppressive policies, 127, 142, 143, 144, 150, 155, 159, 175, 216 (n. 41); England as Pallas, 144–45

—and Ireland, 3, 120, 200 (n. 3), 212 (n. 48); Irish patriotism, 21, 93, 94, 142–43, 145, 166; socio-political concerns, 43, 47, 127, 129, 167–76, 183, 217 (nn. 49, 51); opinion of, 54, 94, 203 (n. 38); feeling exiled in, 93, 110–11, 143; being spirited away from, 109–10; economics, 129, 131–32, 150–51, 153–57; clothing as political issue, 130–32, 142–45, 150–51, 153, 155; Ireland as Arachne, 144–45; Gaelic language in, 216 (n. 41). See also *Drapier's Letters*; Wood's halfpence scheme

—poetical works of: "An Answer to the Ballyspellin Ballad," 71–72; "Apollo: Or, A Problem Solved," 117; *A Beautiful Young Nymph Going to Bed*, 147–48; *Cadenus and Vanessa*, 90, 146; *Cassinus and Peter*, 147–48; *A Character, Panegyric, and Description of the Legion Club*, 117, 171–72, 175–76, 204 (n. 49); "Clad all in Brown," 128; *The Day of Judgement*, 97, 173; "Death and Daphne," 117; "The Description of an *Irish-Feast*," 216 (n. 41); "Desire and Possession," 79; *An Elegy on Mr.*

Patridge, 163; *An Epilogue*, 145–46; "An Excellent New Song," 217 (n. 52); "The Grand Question Debated," 216 (n. 41); "The Gulph of all human Possessions," 118–19, 129; *Helter Skelter*, 218 (n. 4); "Holyhead. Sept. 25, 1727," 54; "Horace, Book I, Ode XIV," 217 (n. 52); "Ireland," 54; *The Lady's Dressing Room*, 147, 148–49, 215–16 (n. 35); "A Letter," 72; *A Libel on Dr. Delany*, 94; "A Love Song in the Modern Taste," 140–41; "Occasioned by Sir William Temple's Late Recovery and Illness," xiv, 218 (n. 2); "Ode to the Athenian Society," 98, 113; "Ode to the King," 117; "Ode to William King," 165; "On his own deafness," 78; *On Poetry: A Rapsody*, 27–28, 79, 95–96, 122, 161, 173, 214 (n. 18); "On seeing Verses Written Upon Windows in Inns," 110–11; "On the Irish Bishops," 218 (n. 4); "On Wood the Iron-monger," 217 (n. 52); "A Panegyrick On the Dean in the Person of a Lady in the North," 115–17; *A Panegyric on the Reverend Dean Swift*, 97, 209 (n. 5); "A Pastoral Dialogue," 216 (n. 41); *The Place of the Damn'd*, 218 (n. 4); "Probatur Aletur," 72; "The Progress of Beauty," 125, 147; "The Progress of Marriage," 147; "Riddle" [on mirror], 103–5, 108; "Riddle" [on time], 186; "Riddle on the Posteriors," 129; "The Run upon the Bankers," 155; "St. Patrick's Well," 170, 188; *A Serious Poem Upon William Wood*, 164, 217 (n. 52); "A Simile on Our Want of Silver," 157; "Stella's Birth-day, 1721," 37; *Strephon and Chloe*, 147; "To Stella, Visiting me in my Sickness," 146–47; *Vanbrug's House*, 62; *Verses on*

the Death of Dr. Swift, 47, 53, 95, 97, 101, 113–15, 121, 132, 136, 166; "Verses to Vanessa," 147; "Whitshed's Motto on his Coach," 162; "Wood, an Insect," 165
—prose works of: *Abstract and Fragment of History of England,* 131, 213 (n. 8); "The Account of the Court and Empire of Japan," 205 (n. 4); *An Account of Wood's Execution,* 163–64, 165; *An Answer to a Paper called a Memorial,* 186–87; "Answer to Several Letters from Unknown Hands," 171, 172; "Answer to Several Letters from Unknown Persons," 170, 171, 172; *An Argument Against Abolishing Christianity,* 7–8, 10, 46; *The Battel of the Books,* 57, 58–62, 76, 105, 114, 123–24, 130, 135–39, 141, 143, 144, 159, 176; *The Bickerstaff Papers,* 6, 18, 69, 72, 99; "Causes of the Wretched Condition of Ireland," 54–55; *The Conduct of the Allies,* 18; "*A Consultation of* Four physicians *upon a* Lord that was dying," 73, 74–75, 80, 87; *Correspondence* (see names of individual correspondents); *Directions to Servants,* 160–61; "A Discourse to prove the Antiquity of the English Tongue," 67–69, 70, 71, 73, 100, 205 (n. 9); "Doing Good: A Sermon," 11, 32, 165, 216 (n. 42); "Epitaph," 112–13, 210 (n. 28); *An Examination of Certain Abuses, Corruptions, and Enormities, in the City of Dublin,* 125–27; *The Examiner,* 19, 75–76, 165; "Family of Swift," 108–9; "Further Thoughts on Religion," 35; *History of the Last Four Years of Queen Anne,* 131, 213 (n. 8); "Holyhead Journal," 174; *Journal to Stella,* xvi, 41, 65, 78–79, 83, 85–92, 199 (n. 35), 207–8 (n. 39), 208 (nn. 40, 42, 45); *A Letter Concerning the Sacramental Test,* 19; "A Letter on Maculla's Project About Halfpence," 156, 171, 174; *A Letter to a Young Gentleman, Lately enter'd into Holy Orders,* 17, 47–51, 85; *A Letter to a Young Lady,* 143, 215 (n. 28); "Letter to the Archbishop of Dublin, concerning the Weavers," 171, 172, 173; *The Mechanical Operation of the Spirit,* 17, 79, 212 (n. 47); *A Meditation upon a Broom-stick,* 46; "A Modest Defense of Punning," 164; *A Modest Proposal,* 18, 45, 53, 70, 96–97, 125, 144, 151, 169, 170, 171, 172, 173, 174–75, 219 (n. 7); "On False Witness," 11, 165; "On Mutual Subjection," 32, 165; "On the Death of Mrs. Johnson [Stella]," 215 (n. 28); "On the Poor Man's Contentment," 165; "On the Testimony of Conscience," 11; "On the Trinity," 9, 85; *Polite Conversation,* 44, 50–51, 52, 65, 72, 100, 161, 186; *Preface to the Bishop of Sarum's Introduction,* 100; *A Project for the Advancement of Religion, and the Reformation of Manners,* 8, 38; *A Proposal for Correcting . . . the English Tongue,* 1, 8, 39, 40–44, 46–47, 51, 67, 91, 98, 124, 143, 156–57, 159, 184, 201 (n. 16), 207 (n. 37); *A Proposal for Giving Badges to Beggars,* 203 (n. 39); *A Proposal for the Advancement of Christianity,* 46, 143; *A Proposal for the Universal Use of Irish Manufacture,* 142–45, 147, 149, 152, 161, 174, 215 (nn. 32, 35), 216 (n. 40); *Reasons . . . for Repealing the Sacramental Test,* 144; "Remarks upon Tindall's *Rights of the Christian Church,*" 11, 12–13, 19; *The Sentiments of a Church-of-England Man,* 32, 36, 41; "A Sermon upon the

Excellency of Christianity," 9, 12; *A Short Character of the Earl of Wharton*, 199 (n. 35); "Short Remarks on Bishop Burnet's History," 49; *A Short View of the State of Ireland*, 170; "Some Arguments Against Enlarging the Power of Bishops," 156; "Some Thoughts on Free-Thinking," 22–23; "The Story of an Injured Lady," 144, 145, 174; "The Substance of What was said by the Dean," 94–95; "Swift's Account of His Mother's Death," 109; *The Tatler*, 1, 8, 10, 39, 41–42, 47, 156, 201 (n. 15); "Thoughts on Religion," 37, 41; "Thoughts on Various Subjects," xiv, 20, 30, 105, 211–12 (n. 43); "To the Earl of Pembroke: the Dying Speech of Tom Ashe," 69–71, 72, 73; "A Tritical Essay Upon the Faculties of the Mind," 45, 51, 63; "Upon the Martyrdom of King Charles I," 33; *Vindication of Lord Carteret*, 201 (n. 13); *The Wonderful Wonder of Wonders*, 72, 129
Swift, Thomas (Swift's cousin), 96, 109

Tale of a Tub, A, xvi, xvii, 1, 15, 17, 21, 22, 28, 42, 47, 54, 63, 66, 68, 70, 79, 96, 98, 102, 105, 109, 117, 119, 123, 124, 125, 136, 137, 138, 168, 169, 172, 184, 189, 191, 195, 199–200 (n. 41), 200 (n. 6); spatiality and placement in, xiii, 55–58, 61, 204 (n. 49); language and meaning in, 1–2, 4–5, 6, 16, 20, 23–26, 37, 57, 64, 84, 133–34, 203 (nn. 42, 43), 213 (n. 13), 213–14 (n. 15); treatment of Locke in, 10, 14; clothes allegory in, 19–20, 24, 31–32, 33–35, 38–40, 128, 130, 132–35, 141, 143, 167; form of, 25, 44, 76–78, 133–34, 206 (n. 19), 213 (n. 12); fame in, 26–27
Temple, Sir William, 13, 109, 131, 137–39, 211 (n. 36); *Of Poetry*, 212 (n. 5)
Textocentrism, 26, 27, 28, 35, 48, 95, 115, 129, 133, 139, 160, 164, 167, 183; liberal impulses in, 21, 25, 30, 43, 63, 112, 155, 205 (n. 5); interpretive traps in, 21, 28, 73, 82, 92, 148, 180; conservative strategies of, 21, 39, 43, 57, 61, 62, 63, 111, 125, 130, 151, 156, 205 (n. 5); definition of, 21–22; as textual game, 25, 70. *See also* Language, theories of: textocentric
Thackeray, William Makepeace, 119, 211 (n. 37)
Theobald, Lewis, 114
Thomas Aquinas, Saint, 199 (n. 37)
Thompson, James, 190
Thyestes, 175
Tighe, Richard, 128, 209–10 (n. 17)
Tooke, Benjamin: Swift's letter to, 96
Torrance, Robert M., 220 (n. 19)
Tory, 19, 21, 41, 42, 89, 160
Tory anarchy, 21
Tragedy: of language, 166–68, 170–72, 174–76, 179–80, 183–88, 218 (n. 2); Irish writings as, 168, 173–76, 216 (n. 40); *Gulliver's Travels* as, 168–69, 177, 179–82, 184, 185, 220 (nn. 16, 17); time and history as, 169–70, 184; compared with justice, 173
Transvestitures, 127, 128–66 passim, 168; excrement as, 128–29; money as, 129, 130, 131, 132, 150–66, 167, 174; clothing as, 129, 130, 132–49, 167, 174, 177, 178; definition of, 129–31; of power, 166
Traugott, John, 204 (n. 48)
Trinity College, Dublin, 109, 194
Typography, significatory potential of, 9, 73, 102

Index

Uhlig, Claus, 221 (n. 4)
Universal language schemes, 4, 197–98 (n. 7)
Uphaus, Robert W., 203–4 (n. 44)

Vanessa. *See* Vanhomrigh, Esther
Vanhomrigh, Esther (Hessy, Vanessa), 88–90, 146; Swift's letters to, 89, 101, 208 (n. 45)
Vaughan, Thomas, 6, 57, 64, 204 (n. 2)
Venus, 146–47, 149
Verbal incarnationalism, 8–9, 19
Vertigo, principle of, 64, 74–80, 84, 206 (n. 23)
Virgil, 62, 78, 116, 135, 136; *Aeneid*, 176
Voigt, Milton, 197 (n. 4)
Von Humboldt, Wilhelm, 186

Wagstaff, Simon, 50–51, 52, 100, 101
Walpole, Sir Robert, 132, 154, 205 (n. 4), 217 (n. 53)
Waters, Edward (printer), 161
Waterston, G. C., 202 (n. 25)
Weiskel, Thomas, 116
Wharton, Joseph and Thomas, 190
Whig, 19, 21, 41, 75, 76, 97, 160
White, Hayden, 213 (n. 8)
Whiteway, Martha (Swift's cousin), 102
Whitshed, Chief Justice William, 161–62
Wilkins, John, 7, 198 (n. 14)
Williams, Harold, 204 (n. 45), 210 (n. 21)
Williams, Kathleen, xvi
Wilson, T. G., 206 (n. 24)
Withers, George, 62

Wood, William, 131, 154, 155, 157, 161; as Goliath, 150–51, 216 (n. 38); textualization of, 162–63; ridicule of, 163–64, 217 (n. 53); under rhetorical control, 164–65, 217 (n. 51)
Wood's halfpence scheme, 93, 131, 141, 150, 151, 153, 154, 155, 157, 158, 159, 167, 168, 213 (n. 7), 216 (n. 42)
Woolen Act, 150, 214–15 (n. 27)
Wordplay, 1, 63–65, 66, 67, 68, 69, 81, 83, 85, 92, 130, 205 (n. 5); as trap, 64, 65; repetitiousness of, 65, 71; violence in, 67–68, 73; morbidity of, 68, 69, 70, 73. *See also* Anagrams and acrostics; Divestitures; Etymology/mock-etymology; Jokes; "Little language"; Mock languages; Mock-Latin/Anglo-Latin trifles; Neologisms; Puns; Riddles; Spellings/abbreviations
Wordsworth, William: *The Prelude*, 55, 63, 95
Worrall, Rev. John: Swift's letter to, 158
Wotton, William, 55–58, 61, 133, 138, 139; "Observations upon the *Tale of a Tub*," 55

Yahoo, xvi, 17, 120, 122, 155, 178, 184, 218 (n. 3), 219 (n. 11); interpretations of, 36, 180; meaning of word, 80, 123, 180; and humans, 84, 105–7, 117, 170, 179, 185, 209–10 (n. 17)
Yeats, William Butler, 79, 166, 188

Zimmerman, Everett, 202 (n. 34), 219 (n. 10)

www.ingramcontent.com/pod-product-compliance
Lightning Source LLC
Chambersburg PA
CBHW021358290426
44108CB00010B/292